JOHN THE APOSTLE.

From a Panel by Albrecht Duerer.

John

Disciple

Evangelist

Apostle

Seven Colored Plates and One Hundred and Nine
Half-Tone Engravings

William Dallmann

Concordia Publishing House, St. Louis, Mo.

1932

ISBN: 978-0-7586-1802-3

From the Minutes of the Milwaukee English Conference,
        March 9, 1931: —

WHEREAS, There is on the market no work on John for the people; and

WHEREAS, We have profited from Dr. Dallmann's work; now, therefore, be it

Resolved, That we urge the publication of Dallmann's "John."   ERIC M. KELLER, *Secretary.*

ANALYSIS.

CONTENTS.

CONTENTS.

III. JOHN THE APOSTLE: HIS EPISTLES.

FIRST EPISTLE.

SECOND EPISTLE.

THIRD EPISTLE.

APPENDIX.

ILLUSTRATIONS.

* Indicates Colored Plates.

PAGE

[7]

ILLUSTRATIONS.

PART ONE.

JOHN THE DISCIPLE.

HIS LIFE.

CHAPTER 1.

JOHN'S YOUTH.

JOHN was the son of Zebedee and his wife Salome, who likely was a sister of the Virgin Mary, which would make him and his brother James cousins of Christ. Other cousins were Andrew and Simon, later known as Peter, sons of Uncle John. He was born on the shores of the most sacred sheet of water in all the world. It is 682 feet below sea level, its greatest depth 157 feet; it is thirteen miles long and about seven and a half miles wide. From the shape of a lute, *kinnor*, it was called Kinneret, or Kinnerot. From the plain to the northwest it was called Gennesar, or Gennesaret; later it was also called Tiberias. This Lake of Galilee rests a harplike opal in a goblet of gold, rimmed with emeralds. The beach is pearly white, in parts sandy, in parts pebbly. It was a burnished mirror set in a framework of rounded hills and rugged mountains, which rise and roll backward and upward to where hoary Hermon hangs the picture against the blue vault of heaven. It was "the very perfection of this style of beauty."

John was born at Beth Saida, Fishtown, toward the east of where the milklike Jordan rushes into the lake.

In 3 B. C., Herod Philip raised the village to a city and named it Julias, in honor of the fair and frail daughter of Caesar Augustus. The city was on the important highway from the East to the West. To the east was the fort of the tetrarch, where he died in 34 and was buried in the tomb built by himself. To the northwest, across the Jordan, was Chorazin, Matt. 11, 21. Further south, Capernaum, Kephar Nachum, on a hill of limestone, catching the breeze of the lake and the perfume of orange and pomegranate in the fertile plain of Ginnesar. It was on the great Way of the Sea from Damascus to the Mediterranean, a busy market for traders from many lands, a garrison for the troop of the Roman masters, a port for collecting custom from land and lake, where Levi Matthew sat at the receipt of custom. Here the centurion built the synagog of white limestone, 79×59 feet. The central chamber had a colonnade on the north, west, and south, with a row of smaller columns

[3]

SYNAGOG AT CAPERNAUM.

BASKET OF MANNA.
Carved capital of a pillar in the synagog
at Capernaum.

on the architrave; this second story for the women. The south façade had a triple doorway and was fronted with marble monoliths three feet thick and ten high, with elaborate Corinthian capitals. This façade and the architrave and frieze had rich ornaments of leaves and geometrical figures. It is now being reconstructed.

ARK OF THE COVENANT, CARVED IN STONE
AT CAPERNAUM.
The first ever found in Palestine.

To the south were the Seven Springs. Below was Magdala, Magdal Nunaija, Tower of Fish, the Greek Taricheae, where the fourteen kinds of fish were dried, salted, and shipped. Its 40,000 people had 230 or 330 smacks on the lake. In our day one party took five tons of fish in one day. A curious fish is the Chromis Simonis, Peter's Fish, whose male

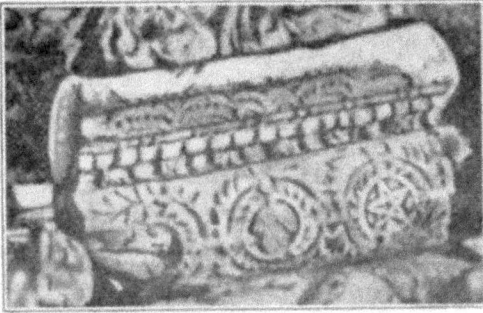

CARVED CAPITAL OF A COLUMN OF THE SYNAGOG AT CAPERNAUM.

carries the eggs and the young about in its mouth; another gives out a sound. There were ten villages on the short road to Nazareth.

About 22 Herod Antipas moved his capital from Sepphoris, a little north of Nazareth, to the new city he built and named in honor of Tiberius, from which the lake then was also called Tiberias.

Quite a change in climate — Nazareth is 350 meters above sea-level, Tiberias 208 below.

The hot springs of 143 degrees are very much like Carlsbad and good for rheumatism and skin diseases. Pliny wrote of their healing powers, and many astonishing cures have been recorded. The British Governor Plumer is replacing the Turkish shacks with modern buildings.

Josephus, the commander-in-chief of Galilee, fortified the city, but it willingly surrendered to Vespasian. After the destruction of Jerusalem, Tiberias became the chief seat of the Jews. The Sanhedrin was brought here from Sepphoris and the school of the Talmud from Jamnia. About 200 Rabbi Jehuda ha-Nasi published the Mishna, the ancient traditional law. Before 350 the Palestinian Gemara, forming, with the Mishna, the Jerusalem Talmud, came into being and between the sixth and seventh centuries the Western, or Tiberian, vocalization of the Old Testament, now generally accepted. Here Jerome learned Hebrew from a Rabbi. In the battle of Hattin, on July 3 and 4, 1187, Saladin will crush the power of the Franks, and the next day the Countess of Tripoli will surrender Tiberias.

John's home was in Galilee, from Galil, Circle, Circle of the

THE ONLY SCULPTURE OF THE GOLDEN CANDLESTICK OF THE TEMPLE AT JERUSALEM EVER FOUND IN PALESTINE.
One of the ornaments in the synagog at Capernaum.

TIBERIAS.

Gentiles, circled by Phenicia, Decapolis, and Samaria. It was about fifty miles from north to south, and about thirty from east to west, a bit larger than Rhode Island. The moisture from Mount Hermon made the rich soil very fertile, Palestine's garden spot, "a land flowing with milk and honey." "That unparalleled garden of God" Josephus calls the Plain of Gennesareth. Little Galilee was so fertile that it supported a teeming population, 204 cities and villages, the smallest with over 15,000 people. The Hon. Selah Merril, our consul at Jerusalem, says the population has been reckoned as about three million. In the Jewish War, Josephus in a few days levied 100,000 patriot recruits. "They were warriors from infancy, and

FISH FOUND IN THE SEA OF GALILEE.

cowardice never had hold of them," says the governor Josephus. He pictures them as fond of changes and seditions. From these volcanic people came the chief zealots and wildest fanatics. The country was crossed with highways, and the people were influenced by Roman civilization; it has been said every peasant could talk Greek. The country was divided.

"PETER'S FISH." SEA OF GALILEE.

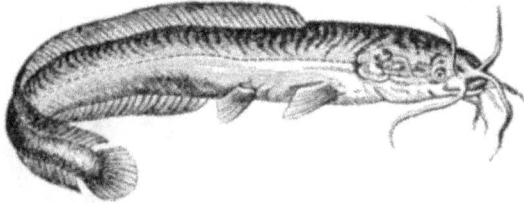

FISH FOUND IN THE SEA OF GALILEE.

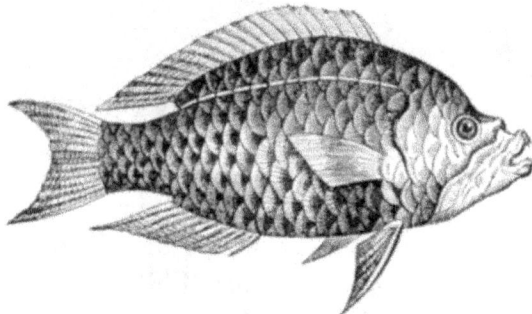

FISH FOUND IN THE SEA OF GALILEE.

Upper Galilee was the "Galilee of the Gentiles," the whole mountain range between the upper Jordan and Phenicia, wooded and varied by fertile upland plains, green forest glades, and wild, picturesque glens, breaking down to the east and the west. Lower Galilee included the great and famous Plain of Jezreel, or Esdraelon, which ran down to the Jordan and Lake Galilee, one of the richest and most beautiful parts of Palestine. Outside of a few rocky summits around Nazareth the hills are wooded and sink down in graceful slopes to broad, winding vales of richest green.

John was born in the world's greatest age, the times of Jesus Christ, John the Baptist, and Paul. It was the age of Caesar Augustus, when Vergil and Horace and Ovid were writing in Rome. About eight years after Julius Caesar, with a hundred ships, spent three weeks in Britain, the same Roman legions, under Pompey, marched from Damascus to the Hill of Evil Counsel on the south of Jerusalem and conquered Palestine,

MOUNT HERMON.   LAKE GALILEE.

in 63 B. C. Under the Roman governor of Syria, Herod the Great was king of the Jews. He willed his eldest son, Archelaus, Judea, with an income of $600,000 a year; Philip was given Batanaea, with $100,000; Antipas got Galilee, with $200,000. When, in 6 A. D., the taxing spoken of in Acts 5, 37 took place, Quirinius was the prefect of Syria and Coponius procurator of Judea. Judas the Gaulonite said, "We have no lord and master but God," and by his fiery eloquence stirred the Galileans into revolt against the foreign tyrants. They fought for four years; then Judas was killed, and his men were crushed.

"Only the vilest of men does not teach his child religion," said a Jewish proverb, and children were required to be able to read the Scriptures at the age of five. So we may be sure Zebedee and Salome did their duty by their children, just as Lois and Eunice had Timothy from a child know the Scriptures. When about six, John was sent to the House of the Book, where the Book of the Law was taught, in the school connected with the synagog, where a teacher was required for every twenty-five children. The Talmud says, "A town without a school must perish." "The world is preserved by the breath of the children in the schools."

JULIUS CAESAR. AUGUSTUS.

Simon ben Shetah, B. C. 80, introduced high schools in every large provincial town and ordered all the youth from the age of sixteen to attend them. Here were taught theology, philosophy, jurisprudence, astronomy, astrology, medicine, botany, arithmetic, geography, architecture. "The Talmud, which has preserved the topics discussed in the colleges, is an encyclopedia of all the sciences of that time and shows that in many departments of science these Jewish teachers have anticipated modern discoveries."

Every Jew had to teach his son some honest craft, or he was as if he taught him robbery; even the Rabbis had their handicrafts. As Jesus of Nazareth was taught carpentering and Saul of Tarsus tent-making, so John fishing. He would fish with hook and line, with a throw-net, and with a drag-net. He would fish at night, mend the nets in the morning, then cure and market the catch.

TO JERUSALEM FOR THE PASSOVER.

At about twelve or thirteen John would go to Jerusalem to celebrate the Passover and become a "Son of the Law," a full member of the Church. With a host of pilgrims he would go from Bethsaida down the western

MOUNT TABOR.

shore, see Mount Tabor on the west and then Mount Gilboa. "Ye mountains of Gilboa! . . . How are the mighty fallen and the weapons of war perished!" lamented David when Jonathan and Saul met death in the disastrous battle with the Philistines.

Near the battle-field is Jezreel, whither Ahab fled to his palace. And here is Naboth's vineyard, and here Jehu had Jezebel thrown out of the window, and dogs devoured her flesh and fulfilled the prophecy of Elijah.

In the Plain of Jezreel, or Esdraelon, or Megiddo, Barak and Deborah defeated the Canaanites, and Pharaoh Necho slew Josiah. The Crusaders will cross it, near it Napoleon will fight a battle, and Roosevelt will say, "We stand at Armageddon, and we battle for the Lord." Here Solomon's

PLAIN OF ESDRAELON. RUINS OF MEGIDDO.

THE JORDAN.

THE MAZZEBAH, OR SACRED CONICAL
STONE.

Emblem of the god Mekal in the great temple uncovered at Beth-Shan, or Beisan, or Scythopolis,
ninety miles north of Jerusalem.

stables will be uncovered, and here Allenby will defeat the Turks and bring Palestine under Christian rule.

In order to avoid the hostile Samaritans, John would cross the Jordan between Beth-shan, or Scythopolis, and Jabez Gilead and thus enter the wilderness of the Jordan valley, seventy miles from Lake Galilee to the Salt Sea. To the east Pella, whither the Christians will flee from Jerusalem during the Jewish War. Between the river and the mountains of Gilead, Laban overtook Jacob, and thence Jacob went to Mahanaim, on both sides of the river Jabbok. At the

MOUNT NEBO.

Damieh ford, where the Jabbok joins the Jordan, Jacob with his family, flocks, and herds crossed the Jordan, as perhaps Abraham before him. Here, too, the Gileadites killed 42,000 Ephraimites when they could not say Shibboleth, but said Sibboleth. Here the sons of Saul found refuge, and here David found shelter from his rebellious Absalom, and here was the home of Elijah the Tishbite, "the grandest and most romantic character that Israel ever produced." Then the famous Gerasa and Ramoth-Gilead and Gadara and Rabbath-Ammon, taken by Joab, 2 Sam. 12, 16—31, which Ptolemy II of Egypt surnamed Philadelphia. Also Heshbon, the city of King Sihon of the Amorites, given to Reuben, Num. 21, 25. Here Herod the Great had built a fort to which to retreat from the fury of Jerusalem, which he had aroused by his many crimes.

MOSES ON NEBO.

In the Pisgah range is Mount Nebo, 2,645 feet, from which Moses viewed the Promised Land, and where he was buried.

> And no man knows his sepulcher,
>   And no man saw it e'er;
> For the angels of God upturned the sod
>   And laid the dead man there. Deut. 34, 1—4.
>
> O lonely tomb in Moab's land!
>   O dark Beth-peor's hill!
> Speak to these curious hearts of ours
>   And bid them to be still.
>
> God hath His mysteries of grace,
>   Ways that we cannot tell;
> He hides them deep like the secret sleep
>   Of him He loved so well.

There Jeremiah is said to have hidden the Ark and other Temple furnishings. In the plain below, Elisha cried, "My father, my father, the chariots of Israel and the horsemen thereof!" when Elijah left him.

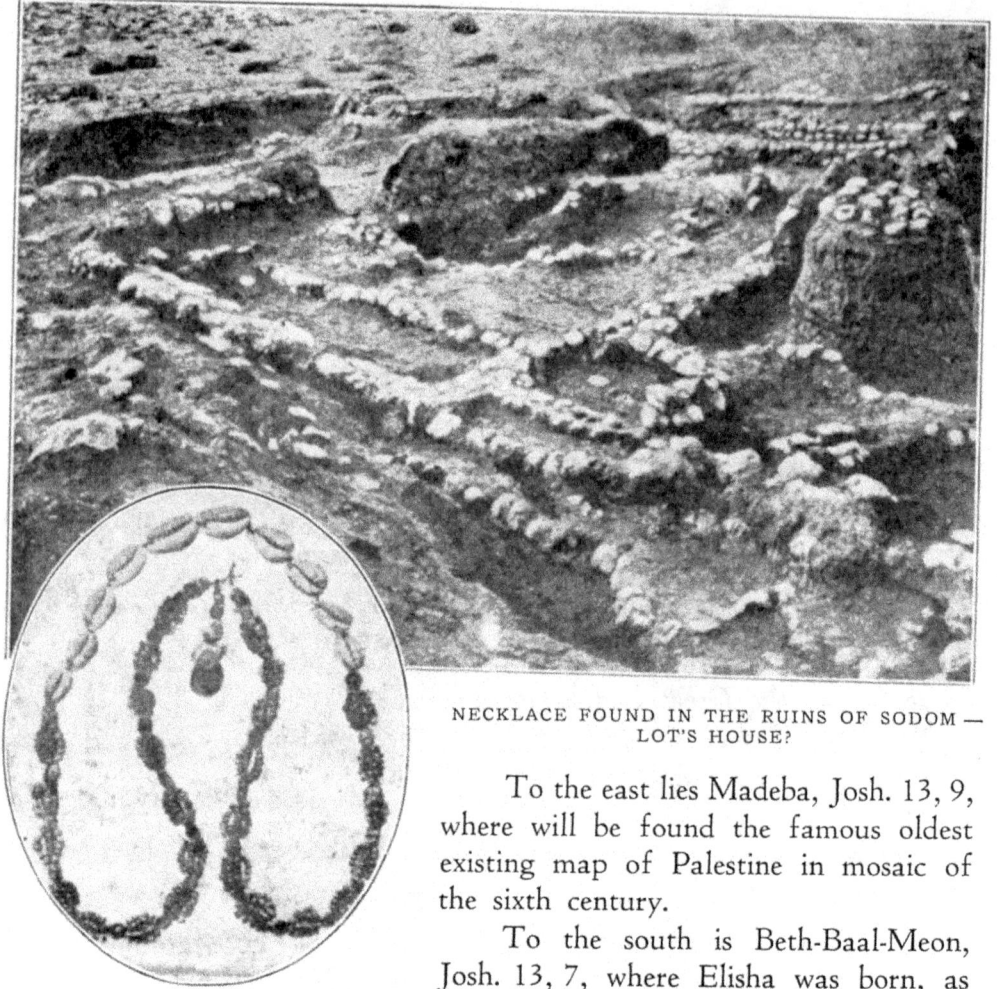

NECKLACE FOUND IN THE RUINS OF SODOM —
LOT'S HOUSE?

To the east lies Madeba, Josh. 13, 9, where will be found the famous oldest existing map of Palestine in mosaic of the sixth century.

To the south is Beth-Baal-Meon, Josh. 13, 7, where Elisha was born, as Eusebius tells us. The hot springs of Calirrhoe, where Herod hoped to cure his dread disease. Machaerus, 3,705 feet above the Dead Sea, destroyed by Gabinius, rebuilt by Herod the Great, called by Pliny "the second fortress of Judea after Jerusalem." Here John the Baptist will be beheaded. Dibon of Gad, Num. 32, 34, where the famous Moabite Stone of King Mesha will be found in 1868. Kir of Moab, Is. 15, 1; 16, 7. 11; 2 Kings 3, 25; Judg. 3, 12. Saul fought against Moab, and David, whose great-grandmother was a Moabitess, forced them to pay tribute. There is Tell Shagur, perhaps the Zoar to which Lot fled, Gen. 19, 20. The Vale of Siddim with the slime-pits, Gen. 14, 10. There was Sodom and Gomorrah. In December, 1929,

Father Mallon stumbled on the site, and René Neuville, chancellor of the French consulate at Jerusalem, helped dig up the place. Outside was found a strange, pillarlike formation — Lot's wife turned into a pillar of salt? Inside and near the main gate ruins of a fine, large house and a spacious courtyard with pond and fountain — Lot's house? Stone, flint, and bone tools and weapons, glass, mortars, grinding stones, pottery, ornamented plates and dishes, beautiful and artistic bracelets and necklaces, one of forty small white, polished pearls, skeletons of men and women, jars with little children, six jars in one house, along the walls under the floor, bricks

JERICHO.

cracked and reddened by great heat, and ashes, ashes, ashes. "The Lord rained upon Sodom and Gomorrah brimstone and fire," Gen. 19, 24.

A little beyond, the Jordan empties into Bar Lut, the Lake of Lot, the Dead Sea, 1,310 feet deep, 47 miles long, and 10 miles wide, about the size of the Swiss Lake Geneva and as salty as Salt Lake in Utah. It is the lowest spot on earth, 1,290 feet below sea-level, 700 feet deeper than our Death Valley.

On this trip John would hear the shriek of the hyena and the yell of the jackal and see bears and leopards prowling about. Huge birds of prey, with the formidable lammergeier at their head, would hover above, ready to swoop down with lightning speed on the faint of the flock or even to fight a desperate battle with the shepherd himself, who needed his "rod," which was a club about two feet long, with a huge rounded head, studded with heavy iron nails.

John would cross the Jordan where Joshua crossed it to possess the Promised Land and where Elijah divided the waters, 2 Kings 2, 8. He comes to Gilgal, where Joshua set up twelve stones, Josh. 4, 19; 1 Sam. 7, 16; 11, 14. Here was Jericho, taken in wondrous wise by Joshua, where

THE APOSTLES' WELL.

Elisha healed the waters with salt, 2 Kings 2, 19. Here is the castle of Docus, or Doc, where Simon Maccabaeus was assassinated by his son-in-law. Here Pompey destroyed the castles of Thrax and Tauros, which Herod replaced with Fort Kypros to guard the pass. Here are the fragrant groves that gave the balm of Gilead, so famous for perfume and medicine. Mark Antony gave them to Cleopatra, who sold them to Herod, who thought of killing that notorious queen. Here Herod built a pool and his castle for a winter resort, and here he died, which was announced to the soldiers and people in the amphitheater. He was buried in his castle of Herodium, near the Tekoa of Amos, south of Jerusalem. His Jericho castle was dug up by Professor Sellin of Berlin in 1909, and on April 8, 1931, Prof. John Garstang discovered the royal palace razed by Joshua. Here they will show the sycamore and house of Zacchaeus, Luke 19, 1—10. Here blind Bartimaeus will cry, "Thou Son of David, have mercy on me." Here Christian church councils will meet. Ahead is Mount Quarantana, which will be pointed out as the place where Jesus was tempted. On the left of the road is the Wadi el-kelt, which was shown as the Valley of Achor, or the Brook Cherith, where ravens fed Elijah the Tishbite.

MOUNT OF OLIVES. BETHANY.

"The City of Palms" lies 820 feet below the sea and Jerusalem more than 2,500 feet above; so there is a weary climb of three quarters of a mile in less than twenty miles, dreary rocky mountains with frightful ravines, gorges, and defiles on either side; it is the going up to Adummim, Josh. 15, 7; 18, 17, the "Ascent of Blood," where the Good Samaritan did his fine work, Luke 10, 30—37. At this point, half-way up, Sir Francis Henneker was treated like the man in the parable. The only water on the road is called the Apostles' Spring; but they must have been mighty thirsty to drink, for the water is not good. Bethany, the home of Mary and Martha and Lazarus; Bethphage. As the pilgrims mount up, they sing the "Songs of Up-going," the Psalms of Degrees, 120—135.

PLAN OF
JERUSALEM
IN THE
Time of Christ
Scale
0   500   1000   1500 feet

SEEING THE SIGHTS OF JERUSALEM.

Jerusalem! A jeweled crown on mountains towering 3,800 feet above Jordan. The City of God! "Mark ye well her bulwarks, tell the towers thereof," Ps. 48, 12. 13. "Beautiful for situation is Mount Zion," etc. The Temple area is enclosed by a double colonnade on the west, north, and east. This last is called Solomon's Portico, 400 ells high with halls 30 ells deep and 25 high; here the Rabbis taught their classes. To the

HEROD'S TEMPLE. SCHICK.

1. Tower of Antonia, named to flatter Mark Antony. 2. Holy of Holies. 3. Nicanor Gate. 4. Court of Women and Treasury. 5. The Gate Beautiful, where Peter and John healed the lame beggar and where Paul was arrested and taken to the Tower of Antonia, where the Roman soldiers were lodged. 6. The Porch of Solomon. 7. Court of the Israelites. 8. Court of the Gentiles. Jesus drove the sellers from 7 to 8. Between 7 and 8 was the Middle Wall of Partition, Eph. 2, 14, with tablets warning the Gentiles not to cross from 8 to 7. 9. Porch of Herod. 10. Wall built to form a plateau of Mount Moriah. 11. King's Palace. 12. Valley of the Brook Kedron. 13. Valley of Hinnom.

south, Solomon raised a terrace 400 cubits above the Kidron Valley; on it Herod built the royal portico, a triple colonnade, a forest of 162 columns, so large it took three men to embrace the shafts; the Corinthian capitals were of the finest workmanship; the ceilings were adorned with wood-carvings in relief and of varied designs. The whole work was so wonder-fully polished that those who had not seen it could not credit such magnificence, and those who beheld it were struck with admiration. Here, on the site of Solomon's palace, Herod built a fine basilica, which will be displaced by Justinian's church, which will be replaced by the Aksa Mosque, standing to-day.

West of Solomon's Portico, across the Court of the Gentiles, is the Beautiful Gate of Corinthian bronze, seventy-five feet high and adorned

MOUNT MORIAH, WHERE ABRAHAM WOULD HAVE SACRIFICED ISAAC.
Site of the Temple of Solomon, Zerubbabel, Herod, and Dome of the Rock.

with plates of silver and gold opening to the Court of the Women, with the treasury, thirteen trumpet-shaped collection boxes, each for a separate purpose; here the yearly half-shekel was paid. Here were the money-changers, ready to change foreign money for the required Jewish coin. Half-round stairs led to the large Nicanor Gate, opening to the Court of Holies.

Here, on Mount Moriah, is the rock on which Abraham would have sacrificed his only son Isaac, the rock which was the threshing-floor of Ornan, or Araunah, the Jebusite, which David bought for 600 shekels of gold and on which he reared an altar and brought sacrifice to stay the plague brought on by his counting the people. Here Solomon built his splendid Temple, rebuilt by Herod. Some of the stones in this superb structure were more than sixty feet long, eight high, and nine broad and of the whitest marble, so that, as Josephus writes, from a distance the Temple looked like a mountain of snow. Some parts were richly plated with gold, which reflected the sunbeams with such splendor as to dazzle

TABLET WARNING GENTILES AGAINST CROSSING THE WALL OF PARTITION.
M. Claremont Ganneau of the Palestine Exploration Society discovered it in the Via Dolorosa.

the beholder. On the northwest of the Temple, Herod the Great had built a great citadel and called it *Turris Antonia*, in honor of Mark Antony. The sheer sides of the hill were faced with polished marble so as to defy all attempts to scale the walls. At each angle of the castle there shot up a tower; the one to the south side was conspicuous by a turret, which gave the Roman garrison a clear view of the interior of the Temple, to the great annoyance of the priests. To make this marble camp an abode suitable for the Roman governor in times of danger, Herod had built, on a lower platform hewn out of the living rock, a sumptuous residence, combining Greek taste and oriental luxury. The castle was approached on its western side through an open court, or forum, leading to a noble Roman archway, flanked by two smaller ones. This triple archway opened into an area paved with red flagstones, called by the Greeks Lithostrotos and by the Jews Gabbatha. Beyond it sprang a grand staircase, sloping up to the balcony, or loggia, sweeping to the right and to the left of the hall. Here the Roman soldiers were lodged, who kept the peace during the feast. Some think Pilate used this Castle of Antonia for his praetorium.

To the west of the Temple is the Tyropoeon Valley, spanned by

HEROD'S PALACE. THE CITADEL.

a bridge leading to the court-house of the Sanhedrin, the Supreme Court, Luke 22, 66; Acts 4, 5; 6, 12; 22, 30. Close by is the Xystus, gymnasium, south of it the stadium, or hippodrome, and the beautiful amphitheater. In order to make the Romans feel at home, Herod had great games played every five years in honor of Augustus. And over the main gate of the Holy Place stood the golden eagle of Rome and of Jupiter, a double insult to religion and to liberty.

Farther south are the kings' graves, where David was the first to be buried and Ahaz the last. Neh. 3, 16; 1 Kings 2, 10; 2 Kings 16, 20. Peter will say: "David's sepulcher is with us unto this day," Acts 2, 29.

To the southeast Weill, in 1914, found a Greek tablet. "Theodotus, son of Vettenos, priest and ruler of synagog, son of ruler of synagog, grandson of ruler of synagog, built the synagog for the reading of the Law and instruction in the commandments and the hospice and the rooms

THE CITADEL.
Breach in the western wall through which Kaiser William II and General Allenby entered the city.

and the water-containers to shelter the strangers needing it, which [synagog] his fathers and the elders and Simonides had founded." This may have been the synagog of the Libertini, Acts 6, 9, enemies of St. Stephen.

Farther north stood the palace of the high priest. The Hasmoneans built a palace from whose roof the Temple could be observed; here lived King Herod Antipas when in town, Luke 23, 7.

The whole city was walled, and each quarter was defended by a wall with towers of solid masonry, over seventy of them.

At the Jaffa Gate, in the west wall, stood Herod's palace, large enough to hold a small army and so magnificent as to baffle description, says Josephus. It had three towers like the Pharos of Alexandria. The Tower of Hippicus, on the northwest, was about forty feet square and about a hundred and fifty feet high, with battlements and pinnacles. Next to it stood Phasael, David's Tower, a solid square of seventy feet and nearly a hundred feet high, of solid white marble. On the northeast stood the Tower of Mariamne. The palace had two wings, and the whole front was supported by massive columns, forming broad, shady colonnades. Around all was a park with walks, trees, and ponds, where fountains threw their sparkling jets high into the sunshine and flocks of doves plumed their feathers at the water's edge. In the front of the main building stretched a broad pavement with a raised platform, topped by a *bema,* or judgment-seat. Here lived Governor Gessius Florus when in Jerusalem to keep order among the millions gathered for the Passover; and Pontius Pilate may have lived here and judged and condemned Christ. Through this Jaffa Gate, Kaiser William II, dressed like a Crusader, will ride on a milk-white steed and Allenby will walk and put Jerusalem under Christian rule.

From the 256,500 lambs slain in the Temple the high priest reckoned the worshipers at 2,700,000 for the Procurator Cestius Gallus, 63—6 A. D.

John walked among these colorful millions from all parts of the world and with them kept the feast and then went back home to his fishing.

CHAPTER II.

JOHN COMES TO JESUS.

Luke 3, 1—23; John 1, 19—42.

Thine, Baptist, was the cry,
In ages long gone by,
Heard in the clear accents by the prophet's ear,
As if 'twere thine to wait
And with imperial state
Herald some Eastern monarch's proud career,
Who thus might march his host in full array
And speed through trackless wilds his unresisted way.

But other tasks hadst thou
Than lofty hills to bow,
Make straight the crooked, the rough places plain.
Thine was the harder part
To smooth the human heart,
The wilderness where sin had fixed his reign;
To make deceit his mazy wiles forego,
Bring down high, vaulting pride, and lay ambition low.

Such, Baptist, was thy care
That no objection there
Might check the progress of the King of kings,
But that a clear highway
Might welcome the array
Of heavenly graces which His Presence brings;
And where Repentance had prepared the road,
There Faith might enter in and Love to man and God. — *Richard Mant.*

IN the fifteenth year of the reign of Tiberius Caesar, Pontius Pilate being governor of Judea and Herod being tetrarch of Galilee, Annas and Caiaphas being the high priests, the word of God came to John, the son of Zacharias, in the wilderness. And he came and preached and baptized in all the country about Jordan. And he baptized Jesus when He was about thirty years of age. Straightway the Spirit driveth Jesus forth into the wilderness, where He was forty days tempted of Satan.

The Baptist said, "I am not the Christ. I am the voice of one crying in the wilderness, 'Make straight the way of the Lord,' as said Isaiah, the prophet. In the midst of you standeth One whom ye know not, even He that cometh after me, the latchet of whose shoes I am not worthy to unloose."

John humbled himself, wherefore Christ has greatly exalted him and given him a name that is great indeed — "Verily, I say unto you, Among them that are born of women there hath not risen a greater than John the Baptist," Matt. 11, 11; Luke 7, 28.

The missionary Alexander Duff visited the dying missionary William Carey, who said, "When I am gone, say nothing of Dr. Carey — speak only about Dr. Carey's Savior."

COSMOS PICTURES CO., NEW YORK.   LEONARDO DA VINCI.

HEAD OF CHRIST.

John seeth Jesus coming unto him and saith, "Behold the Lamb of God, which taketh away the sin of the world. . . . This is the Son of God."

A lamb is innocent and mild
        And merry on the soft green sod;
And Jesus Christ, the Undefiled,
        Is the Lamb of God:
Only spotless He
Upon His mother's knee;
White and ruddy, soon to be
Sacrificed for you and me.

Nay, lamb is not so sweet a word,
        Nor lily half so pure a name;
Another name our hearts hath stirred,
        Kindling them to flame:
"Jesus" certainly
Music is and melody;
Heart with heart in harmony
Carol we and worship we.·

                        C. G. Rossetti.

Two of the Baptist's disciples heard him, understood him — and followed Jesus. What a simple sentence! What a big sentence! Big with untold results. We are in the birth chamber of the Christian Church and see how she is coming into the world. That moment is a momentous moment in history. That spot in the wilderness is historic ground and holy ground. With our own eyes we see the passing of the Old Testament and the coming of the New Testament and a new civilization.

The Baptist preaches the Gospel; his disciples hear the Gospel, believe the Gospel, obey the Gospel — follow Jesus. The Baptist preaches Christ at a sacrifice, he loses followers. That is the purpose and power of preaching, to lead men to Christ, though it be at a personal sacrifice. As the candle burns itself to the socket to give light, and as the coal burns itself to ashes to give warmth, so we are to consume ourselves to bring men to Christ.

Hannah More says Dr. Samuel Johnson in his last sickness sent for a minister. Pastor Winstanley sent this text, "Behold the Lamb of God, which taketh away the sin of the world." The great scholar humbled himself and accepted Christ as his Savior.

"What seek ye?" asked Jesus of the two disciples that followed Him. The first words we have of Jesus in His public ministry. This question Jesus puts to all, and all must answer it, "What seek ye?"

> Seek ye Jesus and His light;
> Nothing else can serve you right.

The two disciples answered, "Rabbi, where art Thou staying?"

We say with Henry Vaughan in his

THE DWELLING PLACE.

> What happy secret fountain,
> Fair shade, or mountain,
> Whose undiscovered virgin glory
> Boasts it this day, though not in story,
> Was then Thy dwelling? Did some cloud,
> Fixed to a tent, descend and shroud
> My distressed Lord, or did a star,
> Beckoned by Thee, though very far,
> In sparkling smiles haste gladly down
> To lodge light and increase her own?
> My dear, dear God! I do not know
> What lodged Thee then, nor where nor how.
> But I am sure Thou dost now come
> Oft to a narrow, homely room,
> Where Thou, too, hast but the least part, —
> My God, I mean my sinful heart.

"Come, and ye shall see" — the second word of Jesus.

They came and saw where He dwelt and abode with Him that day; for it was about the tenth hour. One of these two disciples was John, and he was so impressed that he remembered the hour when in his old age he wrote his gospel. That hour was the great turning-point in his life. Old things had passed away, all things were made new. Bertel Thorwald-sen, the great Danish sculptor, did not know when he was born — "But

I arrived at Rome on March 8, 1797." That was his birthday as an artist, his real birthday. No doubt John felt what Philip Doddridge felt: —

> O happy day that fixed my choice
> On Thee, my Savior and my God!
> Well may this glowing heart rejoice
> And tell its raptures all abroad.

Jesus says to all, "Come and see." "Taste and see that the Lord is good," Ps. 34, 8.

> Oh, that the world may taste and see
> The riches of His grace!
> The arms of love that compass me
> Would all mankind embrace.

CHAPTER III.

JOHN CALLED TO BE A FISHER OF MEN.

Matt. 4, 12—22; Mark 1, 14—20; Luke 5, 1—11.

WHEN Herod the king put John the Baptist into the prison of Machaerus, beyond Jordan, Jesus departed into Galilee, Galilee of the Gentiles, to fulfil the words of Is. 9, 1. 2: "The people which sat in darkness saw a great light, and to them which sat in the region and shadow of death light is sprung up." From that time Jesus began to preach, "Repent, for the Kingdom is at hand."

Jesus walked by the Lake of Galilee, of which Mark Twain says: "In the starlight Galilee has no boundaries but the broad compass of the heavens and is a theater meet for great events, meet for the birth of a religion to save the world, and meet for the stately Figure appointed to stand upon its stage and proclaim its high decrees." (*Excursion to Europe and the Holy Land in the Steamer "Quaker City,"* pp. 512. 513.)

So eagerly did the people hang upon Jesus' lips to catch every word that they pressed upon Him, crowded Him to the water's edge. To-day some seek the seats farthest away from the preacher. Why?

In order to escape the crush, Jesus stepped into a boat and used that for a pulpit and taught the people — the Sermon on the Sea.

Peter and Andrew, James and John, were mending their nets. They were laboring people, laboring hard to make an honest living; they were getting ready for the next night's work; and yet they laid off needed work to hear the sermon. To-day some say they have no time for church, they must work for a living. They will have to tell that to the Judge.

After the sermon, Jesus said, "Launch out into the deep and let down your nets for a draught." Simon answered, "Master, we have toiled all the night and have taken nothing; nevertheless, at Thy word I will let down the net." Why do you work? Because without it you would starve? Then you are indeed a wage-slave. The Christian says, "At Thy word I will let down the net," and the work is turned into worship. He works that he may have to give to him that needeth, and the cursed

[29]

GEBHARD FUGEL.

JESUS PREACHING TO THE MULTITUDE, SEATED IN SIMON'S SHIP.

THE CALLING OF THE FISHERMEN.   BIDA.

slavery is turned into blessed philanthropy, and he becomes a partner with God Himself.

When they had let down the net, they enclosed a great multitude of fishes; and their net began to tear. They beckoned to their partners, which were in the other ship, that they should come and help. They came and filled both the ships, so that they began to sink.

Peter and Andrew, James and John, were astonished at this most unusual thing. How did the act of Christ react on the men? Simon fell down at Jesus' knees — "Depart from me; for I am a sinful man, O Lord." Like lightning it flashed upon him that this was the act of Almighty God. It was a gracious gift, unearned, undeserved. He was ashamed of his utter unworthiness.

How do you act when successful? Do you take credit for your ability, diligence, experience? Very well; but who gave you the keen intellect, the nimble wit, the ready tongue, the deft finger, the strong arm, the fleet foot? Who giveth thee power to get wealth? Jacob said, "I am not worthy of the least of all the mercies and of all the truth which Thou hast showed unto Thy servant," Gen. 32, 10. What do you say?

"Come ye after Me, and I will make you to become fishers of men." They forsook all and followed Jesus. John and James left their father Zebedee in the boat with the hired servants and followed Jesus.

What authority! What instant obedience to Christ! Well, why not? The call to leave all was a call to receive vastly more. By their sacrifice they were promoted. The fishers of fish became fishers of men. Is there anything in this world greater than men? Says J. H. Newman: —

> Two brothers freely cast their lot
> With David's royal Son,
> The cost of conquest counting not:
> They deem the battle won.

That call comes to all. How do you respond? Must you sell your business, quit your job, leave your family, and hurry to India or China? By no means. But you must learn that you and your business belong to Christ and that you must give to Christ His proper share. It means that you will make your boy or your neighbor's boys ministers or missionaries. Will you follow Christ? Will you follow, not half-heartedly, but wholeheartedly?

Marcus Dods says John —

Left all for God,
Self and the world and wealth,
    At God's own word,
Without question, without reserve,
    Without delay,
To be forever in the Church
The doctor, the prophet, and the patron,
    The comfort and the justification,
Of those who follow heavenly calls in the world's despite
    And who give themselves in love
As He gave Himself, without limit or condition,
    As creatures to their Creator. — *Christ and Man.*

CHAPTER IV.

JOHN SPENDS A SABBATH WITH JESUS.

Mark 1, 21—34.

OHN and James with Simon and Andrew followed Jesus into Capernaum, and on the Sabbath Jesus went into the synagog and taught. The people were astonished at His doctrine, for He taught them as one having authority and not as the scribes. The scribes taught with authorities, quoting one Rabbi after another; Christ preached with authority, His own authority, "I say unto you." We, too, do not preach like the scribes, quoting authorities — Popes, professors, presidents, commentators, councils, conferences, synods. We, too, preach with authority, the authority of Christ — "Thus saith the Lord." "If any man speak, let him speak as the oracles of God," 1 Pet. 4, 11.

After the sermon Jesus healed a man with an unclean spirit, and the people were all amazed. "What thing is this? What new doctrine is this? For with authority commandeth He even the unclean spirits, and they do obey Him."

After the service John went with the rest into the house of cousins Peter and Andrew, where he saw another miracle. Simon's mother-in-law lay sick of a fever. Jesus took her by the hand and lifted her up; and at once the fever left her. And she ministered unto them, got dinner for them. "The laborer is worthy of his food." Has the Lord healed you of the fever of sin? Do you minister unto Him in your duplex envelope?

At even, when the sun did set, the people brought many sick, and Jesus healed many. With our churches and schools and hospitals and asylums and orphanages and homes for the aged we still heal people and cast out the devils of idolatry and superstition, and polygamy and slavery, and child marriage and child murder, and adultery and gambling, and drunkenness. Pray and pay to keep the Lord's work going and growing.

Oliver Wendell Holmes tells us he had in his heart a little plant of reverence that needed watering once a week. Do you go to church regularly to water your plant of reverence?

JESUS TEACHING IN THE SYNAGOG.   BIDA.

GEBHARD FUGEL.

JESUS HEALING MANY THAT WERE SICK OF DIVERS DISEASES.
After Healing Peter's Mother-in-Law.

CHAPTER V.

JOHN IN THE HOUSE OF JAIRUS.

Matt. 9, 18—26; Mark 5, 21—43; Luke 8, 40—56.

The boat that bore the Master had crossed the silver sea,
And all along the mountain paths of rugged Galilee
Were sounds of voices eager-pitched, was throng of hurrying feet;
For then as now were weary hearts, and Jesus' words were sweet.

GIRL of twelve, a lovely bud of womanhood, an only daughter, was at the point of death. The doctors could do no more. Who could? The father was Jairus, a ruler of the synagog. Would it do for him to appeal to Jesus? What would his fellow-officers say? The officer pocketed his official pride and went to the unofficial traveling preacher from Nazareth. Seeing Jesus, Jairus falleth at His feet and beseecheth Him much, "My little daughter is at the point of death; I pray Thee that Thou come and lay Thy hands upon her that she may be made whole and live." True humility of the ruler, touching faith of the father.

While the ruler yet spake, a servant came and reported, "Thy

RAISING THE DAUGHTER OF JAIRUS.

[37]

daughter is dead; why troublest thou the Master any further?" How human! Dead — that ends all. Death is king; nothing is of use any more. Now everything is love's labor lost. That is human; is it divine?

Not heeding the word spoken, Jesus turned to the ruler, "Fear not; only believe, and she shall be made whole." What sublime and sovereign sentence!

Going into the house, Jesus took with Him Peter, James, and John. There they saw the professional mourners, the flute-players, and the crowd making a tumult, weeping and wailing greatly, crying their shrill, ear-piercing *olooleh.*

"Why make ye a tumult and weep? The damsel is not dead, but sleepeth." And they laughed Him to scorn. How human! Do not professional mourners know a corpse when they see one? A fine prophet, that Jesus!

Jesus put the mourners out of the room, took the girl by the hand, and said, "*Talitha, cumi* — Maiden, arise." She heard her Shepherd's voice and at once rose up and walked. Jesus commanded that something should be given her to eat. They were amazed straightway with a great amazement.

What did John learn in the house of Jairus? He learned that God is a God of the living and not of the dead. He learned it is not death to die, but to sleep and to awake again and rise again. A cemetery is a sleeping-place; if a sleeping-place, then also a rising-place. There comes out a new phrase in the language of the Christians — to die is to "fall asleep in Jesus," and back of that sleep is the dawn of that resurrection morn.

> Asleep in Jesus! Oh, for me
> May such a blissful refuge be!
> Securely shall my ashes lie
> And wait the summons from on high.

CHAPTER VI.

JOHN PRACTISES PREACHING.

Matt. 9, 36—11, 1; Mark 3, 13—19; 6, 7—13; Luke 6, 12—19; 9, 1—6; 10, 1—24.

> Thou who the night in prayer didst spend
> And then didst Thy apostles send
> And bidd'st us pray the harvest's Lord
> To send forth sowers of Thy Word, —
> Hear and Thy chosen servants bless
> With sevenfold gifts of holiness.

"THE harvest, truly, is plenteous, but the laborers are few; pray ye therefore the Lord of the harvest that He will send forth laborers into His harvest." The Savior practised what He preached. He went out into the mountain to pray, and He continued all night in prayer to God. And when it was day, He called His disciples, and He chose from them twelve that they might be with Him and that He might send them forth to preach. These He also named apostles: Simon, whom He also surnamed Peter, and Andrew, his brother; and James, the son of Zebedee, and John, the brother of James; and them He surnamed Boanerges, which is, Sons of Thunder; and Philip, and Bartholomew, and Matthew, and Thomas, and James, the son of Alphaeus, and Thaddaeus, and Simon, the Canaanean or Zealot, and Judas Iscariot, who also betrayed Him. He sent them out two by two. The command is:

1) "Preach, The kingdom of God is at hand." We preach Law and Gospel and thus prepare people for the Kingdom of Grace and for the Kingdom of Glory.

2) "Heal the sick." We do that in our hospitals, asylums, and medical missions in China and India.

3) "Ye have received it as a gift, give it away as a gift." We do that; we are always collecting money, money, always money. What for? In order to give it away. Every year we give away several hundred ministers and teachers, yes, give away, give to all parts of the world.

4) The commissary department — there is none. The army is to forage for itself, live off the country. When do we eat? When the hearers eat. What do we eat? What the hearers eat — "For the workman is worthy of his food." Christ classes the preacher as a workman — worth remembering. Even to-day and in a Christian country the preachers do

[39]

not grow rich in this world's goods.   "Poor, yet making many rich,"
2 Cor. 6, 10.

5) The method is this: "As ye enter into the house, salute it.   And
if the house be worthy, let your peace come upon it.   Whosoever shall not
receive you nor hear your words, shake off the dust of your feet."   If they
wish to be rid of you, do not force yourselves upon them.   They'll be rid
of you, but not of the Lord.   "Verily, verily, I say unto you, It shall be
more tolerable for the land of Sodom and Gomorrah in the Day of
Judgment than for that city."   Awful words!   What a dreadful thing
to reject God's ministers!   "He that despiseth you despiseth Me."

6) There will be worse than mere passive resistance.   "Behold, I send
you forth as sheep in the midst of wolves."   That is frank, if not refreshing.
They will not go into a fool's paradise.   Christ gives them the naked truth
in hard words, and they go out with eyes wide open.   How are they to
act in the circumstances?   "Be ye wise as serpents and harmless as doves."
Will that result in peace?   "I came not to send peace, but a sword. . . .
And a man's foes shall be they of his own household."   Be warned.   "He
that taketh not his cross and followeth after Me is not worthy of Me."

Garibaldi said to his dispirited men: "Soldiers, what I have to offer
you is fatigue, danger, struggle, and death, the chill of the cold night in
the open air, and heat under the burning sun; no lodgings, no munitions,
no provisions, but forced marches, dangerous watch-posts, and the con-
tinual struggles with the bayonet against batteries.   Those who love freedom and their country follow me."   And they followed him and freed
their beloved Italia.   Mussolini said: "You must be ready and willing to
fight to-morrow if necessary."   To whom was he talking?   To 10,000
wounded war veterans.   Did they retort they had done their share?   They
replied with a cheer they were ready and willing.

When Jesus had made an end of commanding His twelve disciples,
He departed thence to teach and preach in their cities.

Did the disciples on sober second thought change their minds and
refuse to set out on such a dangerous expedition?   They departed and
went throughout the villages and preached that men should repent.   They
had the sentiment of Mary Brown: —

> I'll go where you want me to go, dear Lord,
>   O'er mountain and valley and sea;
> I'll say what you want me to say, dear Lord;
>   I'll be what you want me to be.

THE TRANSFIGURATION
St. Matt. 17:3; St. Mark 9:4; St. Luke 9:30

How did their first campaign turn out? They came back flushed with victory. "And they cast out many devils," Mark 6, 13. "And the apostles gathered themselves together unto Jesus and told Him all things, both what they had done and what they had taught," Mark 6, 30.

Here was something new under the sun. Here was the beginning of the world revolution which is now going on and will not end till the kingdoms of this world have become the kingdom of God. Christ is the Mission Director, who prepares Himself by prayer and then selects His first missionaries and sends them out to practise preaching. A young carpenter from Nazareth sends a number of Galilean fishermen out into the world with nothing but the Gospel, and in a few years the enemies will complain, "The world is gone after Him." "They have turned the world upside down." John 12, 29; Acts 17, 6; Rom. 15, 18. 19. Where in all the world was there ever anything like this enterprise? This historical fact even infidels cannot deny. And this fact is a standing miracle, a standing proof of the truth of the Gospel. Even Shelley said: —

> The moon of Mahomet
> Arose, and it shall set
> While blazoned as on heaven's eternal noon
> The Cross leads generations on.

The Rev. W. Bright gives the explanation: —

> And the secret of their conquest
>   Let Thy kingdom's record tell;
> 'Twas the old faith once delivered,
>   Scorned so oft and proved so well.
> They adored Thee, God Incarnate;
>   They believed in heaven and hell.

And what about us?

> Lord, when we pray, "Thy kingdom come,"
>   Then fold our hands without a care
> For souls whom Thou hast died to save,
>   We do but mock Thee with our prayer.
>
> Thou couldst have sent an angel band
>   To call Thine erring children home,
> And thus through heavenly ministries
>   On earth Thy kingdom might have come.
>
> But since to human hands like ours
>   Thou hast committed work divine,
> Shall not our eager hearts make haste
>   To join their feeble powers with Thine?
>
> To word and work shall not our hands
>   Obedient move nor lips be dumb
> Lest through our sinful love of ease
>   Thy kingdom should delay to come?

CHAPTER VII.

JOHN WITNESSES THE GLORY OF JESUS.

Matt. 17, 1—13; Mark 9, 2—13; Luke 9, 28—36.

HEN the disciples confessed their faith in Christ as the Son of the living God, He for the first time plainly told them of His suffering, death, and resurrection. After six days He took Peter, James, and John apart upon a high mountain, certainly into a mysterious, supernatural, heavenly atmosphere. While Jesus was praying, the disciples were heavy with sleep. When they were fully awake, they had a vision, they saw His glory. He was transfigured before them, the fashion of His countenance was altered, His face did shine as the sun, and His garments became glistening, exceeding white and dazzling as the light, so as no fuller on earth can whiten them. And, behold, there appeared unto them Moses, the mighty man of the Law, and Elijah, the powerful prophet. They appeared in glory and talked with Jesus. What were they talking about? They spake of His decease, or departure, which He was about to accomplish at Jerusalem.

Do you ever talk about the most important thing?

While they were talking of the death of Jesus, Peter said, "Master, it is good for us to be here; and let us make three tabernacles, one for Thee and one for Moses and one for Elijah." "Not knowing what he said," dryly adds Luke. While Peter was yet speaking, behold, a bright cloud overshadowed them. And, behold, a voice out of the cloud, which said, "This is My beloved Son, in whom I am well pleased; hear ye Him." When the disciples heard it, they fell on their face and were sore afraid.

Jesus came and touched them and said, "Arise and be not afraid." Lifting up their eyes, they saw no one save Jesus only.

Leonardo da Vinci showed his famous Last Supper to a friend. "Exquisite! That wine-cup seems to stand out from the table like solid, glittering silver." The artist quietly brushed out the cup. "I meant the figure of Christ should be the foremost object to the observer." So we preach no one save Jesus only.

As they came down from the mountain, Jesus told His disciples again

MOUNT HERMON.

THE TRANSFIGURATION.

how it is written of the Son of Man that He should suffer many things and be set at naught.

Among the many wonders of the wonderful life of the Savior this most mysterious event on the mount certainly is unique, a solitary peak, standing in lonely splendor; there is nothing by which it can even be remotely approached. How did it impress John? "They feared. They fell on their face and were sore afraid." Jesus had to touch them and say, "Be not afraid." What did it teach John? There is a life after this life; Moses and Elijah bring the living proof. The suffering of the Savior was not a sad accident, it was the glorious plan of God and even written of the prophets, most plainly by Isaiah, chapter 53.

The infidel Sadducees, the ruling high priests Annas and Caiaphas, may crucify Christ, but Moses and Elijah worshiped Him. The suffering of the Savior was not to take the heart out of John; the transfiguration was to strengthen his faith in the final victory and glory of Christ.

On that day John received an authentic testimony — "This is My beloved Son, in whom I am well pleased." And he received an authoritative message — "Hear ye Him."

Faith and obedience belong together; faith begets obedience. Will you learn and do as John learned and did?

CHAPTER VIII.

JOHN GETS A LESSON IN TOLERANCE.

Luke 9, 49. 50; Mark 9, 38—50.

JESUS cast out a devil, and the dumb spake. Some sneered He cast out the devil by Beelzebub, the chief of devils. Others would be neutral and tempted Him by asking a sign from heaven. Think of it, asking a sign from heaven when they just now had seen a sign from heaven! They should have sided with Christ against the Pharisees; but they shirked their plain duty by trying to appear neutral, neither for Christ nor against Christ.

There are no neutrals, says Christ to these moral cowards, by strongly calling out to them the rousing words, "He that is not with Me is against Me, and he that gathereth not with Me scattereth."

He would bring them to a decision, to stand up, stand up for Jesus. "He that is not against us is for us ," says Jesus in our text. That does not disagree with the other text, spoken to different people in different circumstances; for circumstances alter cases.

I.

JOHN.

"Master, we saw one casting out devils in Thy name, and he followeth not us; and we forbade him because he followeth not us." On John's own showing the man did his work in the name of Christ, and from the words of Christ it seems the man was a believer in Christ. And the man was casting out devils, doing real and great good to his helpless neighbors. Faith worketh by love.

And yet John forbade him. Why? Simply "because he followeth not us." The disciples had confessed their failure to cast out a devil; this man succeeded in casting out devils, — was John a bit jealous of the man as well as zealous for Christ? Who told John to padlock the man? Was John himself following Christ in the spirit of Christ?

One Paul was casting out devils in the name of Christ, and the Judaizing Christians forbade him "because he followeth not us." He is not an apostle because not one of the original apostles.

[46]

One John Hus was casting out devils in the name of Christ, and the "Vicar of Christ" forbade him, burned him for a heretic. Martin Luther said, "It is against the Holy Ghost to burn heretics," and the "Vicar of Christ" forbade him and damned him, gave him over to the devil by excommunicating him. We are casting out devils in the name of Christ, yet we are "forbidden" by the "Successors of the Apostles" because not ordained by a bishop, one of the "Successors of the Apostles." They deny our children are confirmed because not confirmed by a bishop. Others would "forbid" us because not immersed by them. Others would "forbid" us for ignoring their man-made "blue-laws."

Men were forbidden to cast out devils in the name of Christ because they did it in English, not in German, Norwegian, or Dutch. President Roosevelt said his Church had lost many of the young because they were not given the Gospel in English; and he hoped the Lutherans would not make the same grievous mistake.

II.

JESUS.

Jesus said, "Forbid them not; for there is no man which shall do a miracle in My name that can lightly speak evil of Me. For he that is not against us is on our part. For whosoever shall give you a cup of water to drink in My name, because ye belong to Christ, verily I say unto you, he shall not lose his reward."

The other Protestant denominations follow not us Lutherans, but they do not revile Christ, and in His name they cast out many devils in many heathen lands. As long as people preach Christ Crucified, we respect them and their work; we do not try to steal their sheep, and we do not try to "forbid" them by force or by law.

When the Lutheran Salzburgers were persecuted by the Romanists, the English Episcopalians gave them a cup of cold water to drink in Christ's name because they were Christians and helped them find a home and religious liberty in Georgia. When the Saxons came to St. Louis, the Episcopalians gave them a cup of cold water to drink in Christ's name because they were Christians and opened their church for Lutheran services. And even at this day we thank them heartily.

Had John "offended" that man? It seems his action called forth this impressive warning, —

"Whosoever shall offend one of these little ones that believe in Me, it is better for him that a millstone were hanged about his neck and he were cast into the sea." Causing the weak to stumble is more than a capital crime. Death is by no means the worst; death is "better" than that man's punishment. These stern words of the loving Savior make us stand in silent awe.

"And if thy hand offend thee, cut it off; it is better for thee to enter into life maimed than, having two hands, to go into hell, into the fire that never shall be quenched, where their worm dieth not and the fire is not quenched. And if thy foot offend thee, cut it off; it is better for thee to enter halt into life than, having two feet, to be cast into hell, into the fire that never shall be quenched, where their worm dieth not and the fire is not quenched. And if thine eye offend thee, pluck it out; it is better for thee to enter into the kingdom of God with one eye than, having two eyes, to be cast into hell-fire, where their worm dieth not and the fire is not quenched." Christ is serious; do you take Christ seriously?

"Every one shall be salted with fire, and every sacrifice shall be salted with salt. Salt is good; but if the salt have lost his saltness, wherewith will ye season it? Have salt in yourselves and have peace one with another."

Our heart is as firm as granite and will not tolerate a single false doctrine. Our heart is burning with love wide as the world; it will try to turn a neighbor from the error of his way, but not forbid him by force.

CHAPTER IX.

JOHN IS REBUKED.

Luke 9, 51—56.

THE whole life of Christ was a journey to death. Here was the last stretch of the road to the cross. He set His face like flint, and with unflinching eye and unfaltering step He strode straight from Galilee to Jerusalem. He rejected a crown; He accepted the cross. He sent messengers before His face, who went and entered into a village of the Samaritans to make ready for Him a supper and lodgings.

The most sacred duty in all the East is hospitality; yet so deadly was their hatred of the Jews that "the Samaritans did not receive Him because His face was as though He would go to Jerusalem." There is race hatred for you! The spirit of these Samaritans stalks through all the world and curses it. In their intense hate men are so intolerant that they refuse the sacred duties of common humanity. Think back a few years to the World War. Even after the armistice the Allies kept up the blockade in order to starve women and children. Clemenceau said there were too many Germans by twenty millions; no wonder he is called "the Tiger." Thumbs down! Let them die! Have you the spirit of these Samaritans?

The disciples of Christ are still sent out to prepare a lodging in the heart with the Gospel, and most people will not receive Him. He came unto His own, and His own received Him not. True two thousand years ago, true to-day. When James and John saw the undeserved injury and stinging insult offered their Master, the rich red blood in these he-men boiled within them. They were angry through and through and all over. That was natural, human, and proper; Christians are not clams. When Christ was struck in the face, He resented the outrage. When Christ is insulted, do you rise to resent the outrage?

John was angry, that was right; but his anger was not all right. "Be ye angry and sin not," Eph. 4, 26. John was angry and sinned. They hotly said, with flashing eyes, "Lord, wilt Thou that we command fire to come down from heaven and consume them, even as Elias did?" 2 Kings 1, 10—12. No wonder the Lord called these two fiery Galileans "Boanerges," Sons of Thunder, Mark 3, 17.

The Lord turned and rebuked them — "Ye know not what spirit ye are of." We, too, are somewhat shocked by the spirit of these two brothers after they had been in the school of Christ for three years. Their anger was of the flesh, not of the spirit; it was an unholy anger of the earth and not a holy anger of heaven. The unholy revenge would not have cured the Samaritans; it would not have wiped out the insult to Christ; it would have brutalized the disciples.

This spirit of fierce persecution did not die out with these disciples. When Constantine the Great turned Christian, the persecuted Christians promptly persecuted the pagans. Charles the Great and other Christians in their zeal without knowledge "converted" the heathen Germans and Scandinavians with fire and sword. The Crusaders in their fiery fanaticism slaughtered Saracen prisoners in the Holy War for Jerusalem. Bohemond roasted Moslem spies on spits. On July 15, 1099, "in Solomon's Porch and in the Temple our men rode in the vile blood of the Saracens up to the knees of their horses." After killing 70,000 Moslems, these Christians prayed in the Church of the Holy Sepulcher!!!

At Constantinople Greek Christians tortured thousands of Latin Christians and sold four thousand into slavery and chanted thanksgiving when a cardinal's head was fastened to a dog's tail and dragged through the streets. Many is the time that Christians slaughtered Jewish men, women, and children. Without asking leave of Christ, the "Vicar of Christ" slaughtered the Christian Waldenses and Albigenses. The Inquisition tortured and burned thousands and thousands for the crime of being Lutherans.

In Brussels I was in the market where the first two young Lutherans, Heinrich Voes and Johann von Esch, were burned on July 1, 1523. In St. Ansgar's Church in Bremen I saw the picture of Heinrich von Zuetphen, who was brutally done to death in that region. In London I stood at St. Paul's Cross, where Luther's works and Tyndale's New Testament were publicly burned, and at Smithfield, where men were burned for being Lutherans. I was in Paris, where the Catholics massacred the Protestant Huguenots at St. Bartholomew's. At Geneva, Calvin burned Servetus, and Melanchthon applauded the burning. In America, Christians persecuted Christians and burned "witches." We have put into the chain-gang Christians who worshiped God on Saturday and peaceably worked on Sunday. Only recently a lady turned Hindu, and American Methodists promptly demanded a law against such a thing. Have you the spirit of these disciples?

On this text the Episcopal Bishop Lee of Delaware vigorously denounces "the atrocities perpetrated for a thousand years by that apostate dynasty which enthroned itself in the temple of God, showing itself as God, and which, when it has power, is always a persecutor."

Would you believe it? The Spaniard Paramo actually used this text as the charter of the Inquisition and claims our Lord Himself as "the Head of the present Inquisition." "Here is the punishment of heretics, namely, fire; for the Samaritans were the heretics of that age." (Bishop M. Creighton in Speaker's Bible, Luke, Vol. II, p. 90.)

Jesus turned and rebuked them — "Ye know not what manner of spirit ye are of. For the Son of Man is not come to destroy men's lives, but to save them." He came to save life at the cost of His own life; even on the cross He prayed for His enemies.

"I am come to send fire on the earth; and what will I if it be already kindled?" Luke 12, 49. With the Gospel fire He would set the whole world afire. On Pentecost He sent fire from heaven, the Holy Ghost in the form of fiery tongues. He fired the hearts of the disciples so that they preached the Gospel. The spirit of Jesus entered Philip, and he went down to Samaria, and many Samaritans now received Jesus as their Savior. Yes, and this very same fiery Son of Thunder became St. John and went down to Samaria and strengthened the Samaritans. That is the way to take revenge, take fiery coals. Paul went out to destroy Christians' lives; the spirit of Jesus entered into him; he went out to save men's lives by spending his own life for them. The Chinese chased our missionaries out of the country. Are we going to lie down and take a licking? Not we! We are going to command fiery coals from heaven upon the heads of these Chinese by sending still more missionaries, building more chapels, giving them more catechisms and hymnals. That revenge will be sweet.

By fleshly lusts Circe changed men into brutes; by heavenly love Christ changed brutes into saints. Said an African to a missionary, "There was a lion in my heart, but it has been cast out by your words." By fire and pressure, lumps of carbon have been turned into diamonds fit for the crown of a king; by fire and pressure, sinners are turned into jewels fit for the crown of the King of kings.

This love is heroic love. Jesus knew He was going to His cross, yet

He steadfastly set His face to go to Jerusalem; nothing could swerve Him. Paul was told what awaited him in Jerusalem, but he went resolutely; nothing could swerve him; Luther had the fate of Huss and Savonarola before him, yet went on to Worms; nothing could swerve him. Bunyan saw the jail of Bedford or death before him, yet he preached at Samsell; nothing could swerve him. "This day last year Livingstone died, a Scotchman and a Christian, loving God and his neighbor, in the heart of Africa. 'Go thou and do likewise.' " (*Mackay's Diary,* Berlin, May 4, 1847.)

In later years Lawrence Oliphant became a Christian and on his deathbed always had on his tongue the sacred name of Jesus. He told his nurse he was "unspeakably happy. Christ has touched me. He has held me in His arms. I am changed — He has changed me. His power has cleansed me — I am a new man."

CHAPTER X.

JOHN GETS A LESSON IN AMBITION.

Matt. 20, 20—28; Mark 10, 35—45.

I.

A BEAUTIFUL PICTURE.

ZEBEDEE'S wife, Salome, came with her strapping sons, James and John, and kneeled before Jesus. What a gripping picture! Boys and girls are kneeling before Jesus here in church this morning; where are the fathers and mothers? Fathers and mothers are kneeling before Jesus in church here this morning; where are their grown sons and daughters? God give us more Salomes who can bring their little boys and also their grown sons and daughters to kneel with them at the feet of the Savior!

II.

AN AMBITIOUS PRAYER.

"What wilt thou"? "Grant that these my two sons may sit, the one on Thy right hand and the other on the left, in Thy kingdom." What a sublime faith in Christ and His kingdom! A faith simple and strong despite all appearances. Have we such faith? "Lord, increase our faith." A touching prayer of a fond mother and her fine boys. Did they ask for worldly wealth and wisdom, for political place and power in the kingdom of this world? They prayed for high places in the kingdom of Christ. What is the secret wish deep down in your heart? Is it to be great in the kingdom of this world or in the kingdom of Christ? Alas! the best of Christians are far from perfect. In the New Man ever and anon crops out the yellow streak of the Old Adam. Our repentance needs to be repented of, our tears need washing, our prayers need purging. In order to push themselves forward, they would take a mean advantage of their companions. They had an eye to the main chance. They would be fore-handed, take time by the forelook, be hustlers and go-getters, unfairly beat the others to it.

Some hold Salome a sister of the Virgin and so an aunt of Jesus and her sons His cousins. Also Salome was one of the women that ministered

[53]

unto Him, contributed to his support, Mark 15, 40. 41. Did they think kinship and donations gave them a claim on Him? George Macdonald asks: —

> She would have had them lifted high
> Above their fellow-men,
> Sharing their pride with mother eye —
> Had been blest mother then.
> But would she praise for granted quest,
> Counting her prayer well heard,
> If of the three on Calvary's crest
> They shared the first and third?

III.

A SEARCHING QUESTION.

"Can ye drink of the cup that I drink of and be baptized with the baptism that I am baptized with?"

IV.

A CONFIDENT ANSWER.

"We can." What assurance! How glib and confident! And yet, when Jesus was in agony in Gethsemane and needed their sympathy, — they slept. When Jesus was arrested, they fell into a panic and took to their heels in cowardly flight. "We can." Easy — till you try it!

V.

A DIVINE REVELATION.

"Ye know not what ye ask." How often that is true of us! "Ye shall drink indeed of My cup and be baptized with the baptism that I am baptized with." The prophecy became history. James was the first of the apostles to become a martyr; Herod beheaded him. And John bore the cross for many a dangerous day. Jesus admits there will be degrees of nearness to His throne. They that sow sparingly shall reap sparingly, and they that sow bountifully shall reap bountifully. We shall differ as one star differs from another in glory. Jesus will place us as we earn the place. He will place at His right and left those "for whom it is prepared of My Father." The Father's rule is, "The way of the cross is the way of the crown." Heaven itself is strictly by grace; the place in heaven is strictly by merit. Paul says, "Faithful is the saying, If we died with Him, we shall also live with Him; if we endure, we shall also reign with Him."

After Paul had fought the good fight, finished the course, kept the faith, there was laid up for him the crown of righteousness, 2 Tim. 2, 11; 4, 8. He that overcometh, I will give to him to sit down with Me in My throne, as I also overcame and sat down with My Father in His throne, Rev. 3, 21. Likest Christ, nearest Christ.

> Then, welcome each rebuff
> That turns earth's smoothness rough,
>   Each sting that bids nor sit nor stand, but go.
> Be our joys three parts pain,
> Strive and hold cheap the strain;
>   Learn nor account the pang; dare, never grudge the throe.

Did they turn on their heels in anger and punish Him by "leaving the Church"? How many church-members do just that when they cannot have their way! This group did not. They remained loyal, and Salome went to embalm the body of Jesus early Easter morning, Mark 16, 1.

VI.

AN UNHOLY INDIGNATION.

When the ten other disciples heard of this sharp practise, they were moved with indignation against the two brothers. Naturally, didn't they have vanity and ambition of their own? Yes. We read a number of times that the disciples quarreled among themselves as to which of them was the greatest. Very instructive. Very plainly they did not know Peter was their Pope. Peter even did not know he was the Pope. Christ Himself did not know Peter was Pope, or He would once for all have stopped the rank wrangle about rank by simply pointing to Peter. He did no such thing. He did something else.

VII.

A SERMON ON SERVICE.

"Ye know that the princes of the Gentiles exercise dominion over them, and they that are great exercise authority upon them. But it shall not be so among you; but whosoever will be great among you, let him be your minister; and whosoever will be chief among you, let him be your servant." How radical! How revolutionary! Yes; but the Preacher was a good preacher; He practised what He preached. People like illustrations in sermons; Jesus gave an illustration in His sermon, a living, telling, convincing illustration.

VIII.

A WONDERFUL ILLUSTRATION.

"Even as the Son of Man came not to be ministered unto, but to minister." Serve, yes; but how much?

"To give His life."

What for?

"A ransom."

What is a ransom? A payment to redeem, to set the captive free. Christ gave His life to free the captives and slaves. He made a vicarious atonement, He is our Substitute.

For whom? "For many," the many, for all. Glory be! A universal atonement! Christ gave His life a ransom for all — that is the Gospel to be preached to all. Christ gave His life a ransom for all; the Christian gives his life to preach this Gospel to all. "Even as" — the Christian "even as" Christ. Who said so? Christ said so.

Would you like to be near Christ? You can be. Do like Christ. Likest Christ, nearest Christ.

Nearer, my God, to Thee,
 Nearer to Thee!
E'en though it be a cross
 That raiseth me,
Still all my song shall be,
Nearer, my God, to Thee,
 Nearer, my God, to Thee,
 Nearer to Thee!

Nearer, my Lord, to Thee,
 Nearer to Thee!
Who to Thy cross didst come
 Dying for me.
Strengthen my willing feet,
Hold me in service sweet
 Nearer, O Christ, to Thee,
 Nearer to Thee!

I ask no heaven till earth be Thine,
No glory crown while work of mine
Remaineth here. When earth shall shine
 Among the stars,
Her sins wiped out, her captives free,
Her voice a music unto Thee,
For crown, new work give Thou to me.
 Lord, here am I.

CHAPTER XI.

JOHN LEARNS OF THE FUTURE.

Mark 13; Matt. 24; Luke 21.

"MASTER, see what manner of stones and buildings are here!" So cried an enthusiastic and patriotic disciple as Jesus went out of the Temple. "Beautiful for situation, the joy of the whole earth, is Mount Zion, the city of the great King." Was this simply a patriotic boast of the Jews? Pliny, the Roman, says Herod made Jerusalem the most magnificent city of the East. No wonder the Jews cried, "Master, see what manner of stones and buildings are here!" "Seest thou these great buildings? There shall not be left one stone upon another that shall not be thrown down." That staggering statement certainly damped the enthusiasm of Jesus' disciples. It was a most improbable prophecy; yet it was literally fulfilled.

As He sat over against the Temple upon the Mount of Olives, seven hundred feet high and a mile long, John and others asked Him, "Tell us, when shall these things be, and what shall be the sign when all these things shall be fulfilled?" Jesus foretold the destruction of Jerusalem and merged with it the destruction of the world. In less than forty years, in 70, Titus destroyed Jerusalem, and in due time the other prophecy will also be fulfilled. At that time the Jews defiantly scoffed, "His blood be upon us and our children." It was, very much. In our day some scoff, "Where is the end of the world?" It will come.

The answer of Christ is most remarkable in that He says very little about the destruction of Jerusalem and the world. Yet it is a long answer. What does He stress?

"Take heed that no man lead you astray. For many shall come in My name, saying, 'I am Christ,' and shall lead many astray." Thus it was then, thus it is to-day. The religious condition of the world to-day is a standing proof of the truth of Christ's word. The world is full of false Christs, and many are led astray. People reject Christ and embrace the Christless lodge, and spirits, and Mrs. Eddy, and the monkey.

If they cannot seduce you, they will persecute you. "Take heed to yourselves; for they shall deliver you up to councils; and in synagogs shall

[57]

ye be beaten; and before governors and kings shall ye stand for My sake, for a testimony unto them. They shall kill you." They did it to Stephen, and James, and Peter, and John, and Paul, and Silas. They did it to the martyrs in the pagan persecutions, and they did it to the faithful in the papal persecutions. To-day they persecute us as far as they can. They abuse us as narrow-minded, hide-bound, bigoted, mossbacks, old fogies, back numbers, and what not.

"Watch and pray. Be ye also ready, for in an hour that ye think not the Son of Man cometh. He that endureth to the end, the same shall be saved."

> Rise, my soul, to watch and pray,
>   From thy sleep awake thee,
> Lest at last the evil day
>   Suddenly o'ertake thee;
>   For the Foe,
>   Well we know,
> Oft his harvest reapeth
> While the Christian sleepeth.

CHAPTER XII.

JOHN AT THE PASSOVER.

Luke 22, 7—30; Mark 14, 12—26; Matt. 26, 17—30; John 13, 21—30; 21, 20.

I.

JOHN PREPARES THE PASSOVER.

"O and prepare us the passover that we may eat it," said Jesus to Peter and John. "Where wilt Thou that we make ready?" "Behold, when ye are entered into the city, there shall meet you a man bearing a pitcher of water; follow him into the house wherein he goeth. And ye shall say unto the goodman of the house, The Master saith unto thee, Where is the guest-chamber where I shall eat the passover with My disciples? And he will show you a large upper room, furnished; there make ready."

They went and found as He had said unto them; and they made ready the passover.

When Jesus needed a boat for a pulpit, the owner lent it to Him. When Jesus needed a donkey to ride into Jerusalem, the owner lent it to Him. When Jesus needed a room for the passover, the owner lent it to Him. When Jesus needed embalming, Nicodemus brought a hundred pounds of a mixture of myrrh and aloes, and the women bought spices to anoint His body. When Jesus needed a shroud, Joseph brought Him one. When Jesus needed a grave, the owner gave his new-hewn rock tomb. When Jesus needs anything we have for His missions, we give it to Him. *Do you? Do you?*

When it was evening, Jesus came and sat down with the twelve apostles and said to them, "With desire have I desired to eat this passover with you before I suffer; for I say unto you, I will not any more eat thereof until it be fulfilled in the kingdom of God."

He received a cup, and when He had given thanks, He said, "Take this and divide it among yourselves; for I say unto you, I will not drink henceforth of the fruit of the vine until the kingdom of God shall come."

[59]

II.

JOHN AT THE LORD'S SUPPER.

After the Passover, the Sacrament of the Old Testament, or Covenant, Jesus instituted the Lord's Supper, the Sacrament of the New Testament, or Covenant. Here was the last of the Old and the first of the New; the last of the type, the first of the antitype; the last of the shadow, the first of the substance; the last to remind them of their freedom from the slavery of Egypt, the first to remind us of our freedom from the slavery of sin and Satan and to give us joy in the promised inheritance of the children of God.

Jesus took bread, blessed it, brake it, saying, "This is My body, which is given for you; this do in remembrance of Me." And He took the cup, gave thanks, and gave it to them, saying, "Drink ye all of it; this cup is the new testament in My blood, which is shed for many for the remission of sins."

Here we have a real presence of the bread and wine, not a real absence, as the Pope's Transubstantiation makes it. Here we have a real presence of the body and blood, not a real absence, as the Reformed Representation makes it. Here we have a Holy Communion of the bread and wine with the body and blood, not a Consubstantiation, or Impanation, as ignorant men charge us. Here we have a real means of grace, — "shed for the remission of sins," — not an empty rite or ceremony. It is for you, a sinner; for you for the remission of sins.

Here we have a powerful motive for holiness. When temptation comes near, "remember Jesus Christ." Remember what it cost to save you; remember what I have done for you; remember what I have given you. When you remember that, you will get strength to fight off temptation. When you remember that, you will have strength to grow more Christlike.

III.

JOHN LEANS ON JESUS' BREAST.

At the supper, Jesus was troubled in the spirit and testified, "Verily, verily, I say unto you that one of you shall betray Me." That startling statement came as a bolt out of the blue, and the disciples looked one on another, wondering of whom He spake. And every one asked, "Is it I?"

Really remarkable, this question. It shows each disciple thought him-

THE LORD'S SUPPER.

"MASTER, IS IT I?"

self capable of doing this dreadful and dastardly sin. To what deep depths even a disciple may fall! Are you aware of your weakness? "Security is mortal's chiefest enemy."

It seems Jesus did not answer at once, and so Peter motioned to John, leaning on Jesus' bosom, whom Jesus loved, to ask Him whom He meant.

> Oh, that I could with favored John
> Recline my weary head upon
>   My great Redeemer's breast!
> From care and sin and sorrow free,
> Give me, O Lord, to find in Thee
>   My everlasting rest.

It is worthy of note that in this tense moment Peter with all his boldness had not enough boldness to ask the Lord this question; he turned that question over to the disciple whom Jesus loved, and the bosom friend of Jesus made bold to ask the question, and the disciple leaning on Jesus' breast received the answer. He then, lying on Jesus' breast, asked, "Lord, who is it?" Jesus answered, "He it is to whom I shall give a sop when I have dipped it." And when He had dipped the sop, He gave it to Judas Iscariot.

CHAPTER XIII.

JOHN IN GETHSEMANE.

I.

THE SLEEPER.

Matt. 26, 36—46; Mark 14, 32—42; Luke 22, 39—46.

JESUS ended the Supper by singing the Great Hallelujah — singing on the way to His cross! They crossed the Kidron to go to the Garden of Gethsemane, on the Mount of Olives. On the way Jesus said, "All ye shall be offended because of Me this night; for it is written, 'I will smite the Shepherd, and the sheep shall be scattered,'" Zech. 13, 7. Upon this serious and solemn statement of the Savior the disciples all eagerly vowed they would rather die than deny.

When they came to Gethsemane, Jesus took Peter and James and John and said to them, "My soul is exceeding sorrowful, even unto death; tarry ye here and watch with Me." How human, this Son of Man! He needed sympathy, and He looked for it. A friend in need is a friend indeed.

He went a little farther and fell on His face and prayed, "O My Father, if it be possible, let this cup pass from Me; nevertheless, not as I will, but as Thou wilt." And there appeared unto Him an angel from heaven, strengthening Him. And being in agony, He prayed more earnestly, and His sweat became as it were great drops of blood falling down upon the ground.

In these bottomless depths of divine mysteries there is one thing that is quite plain, "The Lord hath laid on Him the iniquity of us all. Behold the Lamb of God, which taketh away the sin of the world," — and the sins of John, the disciple whom Jesus loved, His bosom friend, who leaned on Jesus' breast.

Lydia Sigourney says: —

> Thou who hast power to look
> Thus at Gethsemane, be still, be still!
> What are thine insect woes compared with His
> Who agonizeth there? Count thy brief pains
> As the dust atom on life's chariot wheels,
> And in thy Savior's grief forget them all.

[63]

JESUS IN GETHSEMANE.
Peter, James, and John Sleeping.

C. NOACK.

When Jesus rose up from His prayer, He came to the disciples and found them sleeping. Yes, even John, the disciple whom Jesus loved. And He said, "What, could ye not watch with Me one hour? Watch and pray that ye enter not into temptation; the spirit indeed is willing, but the flesh is weak." This is not a sleeping-tablet; this is a trumpet-blast for action.

When Jesus was suffering, His friend was asleep. When Jesus was suffering for His friend, His bosom friend was asleep.

John S. B. Monsell says: —

In Thine hour of sore affliction	Yet the eye that never slumbers
None their faithful watches kept;	Lights my darkness, cheers me on,
Even friends of Thine election	And the voice that never wearies
Through Thy deepest sorrows slept.	Pleads in me, "Thy will be done."

A second time Jesus went and prayed and returned, and a second time He found them asleep — also John. A third time He went and prayed and returned, and a third time He found them asleep — also John.

Certainly a serious case of sleeping sickness. Are we asleep when the Savior wants us to pray with Him and for Him? Do we pray earnestly against temptation?

And He said, "Behold, the hour is at hand, and the Son of Man is betrayed into the hands of sinners. Arise, let us be going; behold, he is at hand that betrayeth Me." The blackest name in ancient history is that of Ephialtes. Bribed with gold, he led the Persian hordes to massacre the handful of heroic Spartans under Leonidas at Thermopylae. The blackest name in American history is that of Benedict Arnold, who betrayed his country to the British. The blackest name in all history is that of Judas Iscariot, who took a bribe to betray his Master with a kiss of friendship.

II.

THE DESERTER.

Matt. 26, 47—56; Mark 14, 43—52; Luke 22, 47—53; John 18, 1—16.

While Jesus yet spake, lo, Judas cometh, and with him a great multitude with lanterns, and torches, and swords, and staves, and he goeth straightway to Jesus and saith, Master, Master, and kissed Him. Jesus saith unto him, Friend, wherefore art thou come? Judas, betrayest thou the Son of Man with a kiss?

We shut our eyes on the sickening sight. The heart-breaking accents still ring in our ears. Yes, but have I ever been a Judas to Christ?

Then Jesus asked the armed band, "Whom are ye seeking?" "Jesus the Nazarene." "I am He."

Then they — fell upon Him? No; they fell backward to the ground — the armed band hurled to the ground by one unarmed man. Was there a flash of His divinity through the flesh of His humanity? The sublime moral grandeur of the Man awed them, and they slunk back abashed.

Again He asked, "Whom are ye seeking?" Again they answered, "Jesus the Nazarene." Now He really had to urge them to do what they had come to do. "I told you that I am He; if therefore ye are seeking Me, let these go their way," that the word might be fulfilled which He spake, "Of those whom Thou hast given Me I lost not one," John 17, 12.

And Jesus asked the chief priests and captains of the Temple and elders, "Are ye come out as against a robber with swords and staves? When I was daily with you in the Temple, ye stretched not forth your hands against Me. But this is your hour and the power of darkness."

Then they seized Jesus and bound Him; and the disciples left Him and fled. One was in such hot haste as to leave his linen cloth in the clutches of the soldiers and to flee naked.

One hour ago they vowed to die rather than deny; now they would fly rather than die. All of them, even John, the disciple whom Jesus loved, John, who leaned on Jesus' breast, fled from his bosom Friend. Robert Browning has John say: —

> The torchlight and the noise,
> The sudden Roman faces, violent hands,
> And fear of what the Jews might do. Just that.
> And it is written, 'I forsook and fled';
> That was my trial, and it ended thus.

Whither did John run? Peter checked himself in his mad flight and followed Jesus afar off, and so did another disciple. Now, that disciple was known to the high priest and entered in with Jesus in the court of the high priest. Peter was standing at the door without. So the other disciple, who was known to the high priest, went out and spake unto her who kept the door and brought in Peter. The friendly service was a tragic disservice, for it opened the way to Peter's base denial of his Lord.

CHAPTER XIV.

JOHN'S ACTIVITIES TILL PENTECOST.

I.

JOHN RECEIVES INSTRUCTIONS.

Acts 1, 1—8.

ESUS showed Himself alive after His Passion to John and the other apostles by many infallible proofs, being seen of them forty days and speaking of the things pertaining to the kingdom of God.

II.

JOHN WITNESSES THE ASCENSION.

Luke 24, 50. 51; Acts 1, 9—11.

When Jesus had spoken these things, He lifted up His hands and blessed them. And it came to pass, while He blessed them, while John and the others beheld, He was taken up, and a cloud received Him out of their sight. And while they looked steadfastly toward heaven as He went up, behold, two men stood by them in white apparel, who also said, Ye men of Galilee, why stand ye gazing up into heaven? This same Jesus who is taken up from you into heaven shall so come in like manner as ye have seen Him go into heaven. And they worshiped Him.

III.

JOHN IN CHRISTIAN FELLOWSHIP.

Acts 1, 12—14.

After the ascension, John, with the rest of the disciples, returned from the mount called Olivet, which is from Jerusalem a Sabbath-day's journey. When they were come in, they went up into an upper room. They all continued with one accord in prayer and supplication, with the women and Mary, the mother of Jesus, and with His brethren. They returned with great joy and were continually in the Temple, praising and blessing God.

As they, so we rejoice with great joy. Why? Let not your heart be troubled. I go to prepare a place for you. I will come again and

[67]

receive you unto Myself, that, where I am, ye may be also.   And your
joy no man taketh from you, John 14, 1—3; 16, 22.   O glorious hope!

O'er the distant mountains breaking	With my lamp well trimmed and burning,
Comes the redd'ning dawn of day;	Swift to hear and loath to roam,
Rise, my soul, from sleep awaking,	Watching for Thy glad returning
Rise and sing, and watch, and pray.	To restore me to my home.
'Tis thy Savior	Come, my Savior,
On His bright returning way.	Thou hast promised; quickly come.

IV.

JOHN HELPS ELECT AN APOSTLE.

Acts 1, 15—26.

In those days Peter stood up in the midst of the 120 disciples and
proposed the election of a successor to Judas Iscariot, one "to be a witness
with us of His resurrection."   They nominated Joseph, called Barsabas,
who was surnamed Justus, and Matthias.   After prayer they gave forth
their ballots, and the lot fell upon Matthias, and he was numbered with
the eleven apostles.

V.

JOHN AT PENTECOST.

Acts 2.

When the day of Pentecost was now come, fifty days after Easter,
they were all together in one place.   And suddenly there came from heaven
a sound as of the rushing of a mighty wind, and it filled all the house
where they were sitting.   And there appeared unto them tongues parting
asunder, like as of fire; and it sat upon each one of them.   And they
were all filled with the Holy Spirit and began to speak with other tongues,
as the Spirit gave them utterance.

Now, there were dwelling at Jerusalem, Jews, devout men, from every
nation under heaven.   And when this sound was heard, the multitude came
together and were confounded, because that every man heard them speaking
in his own language.   And they were all amazed and marveled, saying,
Behold, are not all these which speak Galileans?   And how hear we every
man in our own language wherein we were born?

Peter, standing up with the other eleven apostles, explained that this
miracle was that which had been spoken through the prophet Joel, chapter
2, 28. 29.   He preached the Law to show them their sins.   Let all the house

OUTPOURING OF THE HOLY SPIRIT.   P. P. RUBENS.

of Israel know assuredly that God hath made Him both Lord and Christ, this Jesus whom ye crucified.

When they heard this, they were pricked in their heart and said unto Peter and the rest of the apostles, Brethren, what shall we do?

Peter now preached the full Gospel, Repent ye and be baptized, every one of you, in the name of Jesus Christ unto the remission of your sins, and ye shall receive the gift of the Holy Ghost. For to you is the promise and to your children and to all that are afar off, even as many as the Lord, our God, shall call unto Him.

Then they that received his word were baptized; and there were added in that day about three thousand souls.

> Spirit of mercy, truth, and love,
> O shed Thine influence from above
> And still from age to age convey
> The wonders of this sacred day.
>
> In every clime, by every tongue,
> Be God's surpassing glory sung;
> Let all the listening earth be taught
> The wonders by our Savior wrought.

The prayer is heard. That day, in a way, is continued in our day. The Church preaches the same Gospel in most parts of the earth under heaven, preaches the Gospel in most languages in which men are born. The Church follows the spoken word with the written Word, translating the Gospel into most of the languages under heaven. The Church is the world's greatest Philological Institute. The Church follows the written Word with the school to teach reading the written Word the world over. The Church is the world's greatest Educational Institute. The Church follows with singing the Word and is the world's greatest Conservatory of Music, vocal and instrumental.

> All hail the day of Pentecost,
> The coming of the Holy Ghost!

CHAPTER XV.

JOHN IS PERSECUTED.

I.

THE FIRST APOSTOLIC MIRACLE:
A LAME MAN HEALED.

Acts 3, 1—11.

ETER and John were going up into the Temple at the hour of prayer, the ninth, and a lame man at the Beautiful Gate, seeing Peter and John, asked an alms. Peter, fastening his eyes upon him, with John, said, Look on us. Silver and gold have I none; but what I have, that I give thee. In the name of Jesus Christ of Nazareth, walk. "Poor, yet making many rich," 2 Cor. 6, 10. And leaping up, he stood and began to walk. And he entered with them into the Temple, walking and leaping and praising God. And as he held Peter and John, all the people ran together unto them in Solomon's Portico, greatly wondering. Pundita Ramabai says, "While the old Hindu Scriptures have given us some beautiful precepts of living, the New Dispensation of Christ has given us grace to carry these principles into practise, and that makes all the difference in the world. The precepts are like a steam engine on the track, beautiful and with great possibilities; Christ and His Gospel are the steam, the motive power that can make the engine move."

Peter and John again preached the Law and the Gospel.

II.

JOHN IN PRISON.

Acts 3, 12—4, 3.

Peter and John spoke to the wondering people who had run together to them in Solomon's Portico. And as they spake unto the people, the priests and the captain of the Temple and the Sadducees came upon them, being sore troubled because they taught the people and proclaimed in Jesus the resurrection from the dead. And they laid hands on Peter and John and put them in prison unto the morrow; for it was now eventide, too late to try them. Here was the first fulfilment of the prophesied persecutions.

III.

SUCCESSFUL PREACHING.

Acts 4, 4.

Although the preachers were in prison, many of them that heard the Word believed; and the number of the men came to be about five thousand.

IV.

JOHN IN COURT.

Acts 4, 5—22.

On the morrow Peter and John were haled before the Sanhedrin, the Supreme Court, and were asked, "By what power or by what name have you done this?" healed the lame man. Peter made a noble reply and ended, "Neither is there salvation in any other; for there is none other name under heaven given among men whereby we must be saved."

The learned judges were at their wit's end. They put their heads together and then tried to gag the preachers, commanding them not to speak at all nor teach in the name of Jesus. But Peter and John would not be gagged; they replied with astonishing boldness, "Whether it be right in the sight of God to hearken unto you more than unto God, judge ye. For we cannot but speak the things which we have seen and heard." Luther at Worms, in effect, said the same.

The Supreme Court judges were helpless; all they could do was to threaten the preachers some more and let them go. What a spectacle!

V.

REJOICING.

Acts 4, 23—31.

When Peter and John reported to their own company all that the court had said, the people lifted up their voice to God with one accord in praise and prayed Him to strengthen His servants "that with all boldness they may speak Thy Word." Do you pray like that for your pastor?

Said Mary, Queen of Scots, "I dread the prayer of John Knox more than an army of twenty thousand men."

VI.

JOHN AGAIN IN PRISON.

Acts 5, 1—40.

Despite prison, John and the other apostles kept on in the work of the Lord openly in Solomon's Portico, and the people magnified them, and the believers were the more added to the Lord, multitudes both of men and women. But the high priest and the other rulers rose up, filled with jealousy, and laid hands on the apostles and put them in the public prison. The second fulfilment of the prophesied persecutions. But an angel of the Lord by night opened the prison-doors and brought them out and said, Go ye and stand and speak in the Temple to the people all the words of this life. To hear it was to do it.

When the court sent for the prisoners, the officers reported, "The prison truly found we shut with all safety, and the keepers standing without before the doors; but when we had opened, we found no man within."

Imagine the faces of the judges! The bewildered judges wondered what would be the outcome. Then came one and reported, "Behold, the men whom ye put in prison are standing in the Temple and teaching the people." Again, imagine the faces of the judges!

When Peter and John were brought into court, the high priest thundered, "Did we not straitly charge you not to preach in this name? And, behold, ye have filled Jerusalem with your doctrine and intend to bring this man's blood upon us."

"This man" — they would not take the blessed name of Jesus into their mouths. "Bring this man's blood upon us," when they themselves had said, "His blood be on us and on our children." Now they blame it upon Peter and John. Yes, the lamb roiled the water for the wolf. "Ye have filled Jerusalem with your doctrine." Powerful preachers; the testimony is sure, coming from the enemy.

"We ought to obey God rather than men," quietly, but firmly replied Peter and John. Imagine the scene! How tense and dramatic! Thus Luther defied the Kaiser and the Reich at Worms in 1521. James Russell Lowell says: —

> And I honor the man who is willing to sink
> Half his present repute for the freedom to think
> And, when he has thought, be his cause strong or weak,
> Will risk t'other half for the freedom to speak.

The apostles would have been killed by the court but for the advice of the wily Gamaliel. Now the court scourged them, charged them not to speak in the name of Jesus, and let them go.

This is the third fulfilment of the prophecies of persecution.

VII.

REJOICING.

Acts 5, 41. 42.

Peter and John departed, blood streaming from their backs. And how did they depart? Rejoicing that they were counted worthy to suffer shame for the Name. And daily in the Temple and in every house they ceased not to teach and to preach Jesus Christ.

About 200, Tertullian, in his noble *Apology,* said to the heathen: "Every single drop of our blood springs up — in some, thirty; in some, sixty; and in some, a hundredfold." When Henry Voes and John Esch were killed at Brussels for being Lutherans, these young Augustinians went to heaven in their fiery chariot singing the *Te Deum!* When the saintly Samuel Rutherford was imprisoned in Aberdeen "for righteousness' sake," he wrote a friend: "The Lord is with me; I care not what man can do. My chains are overgilded with gold. No pen, no words, no engine, can express to you the loveliness of my only, only Lord Jesus."

CHAPTER XVI.

JOHN IN SAMARIA.

Acts 8, 5—25.

AFTER Stephen had become the first martyr for Christ, there was a great persecution against the church at Jerusalem, and they were all scattered abroad, preaching the Word. The persecution of the Church hastened the prosecution of the work of the Church. Then Philip went down to the city of Samaria and preached Christ unto them. What! In hopeless Samaria?

The people with one accord gave heed to those things which Philip spake, and there was great joy in that city. Hopeless Samaria was not hopeless. Wonders never cease. No, they do not. Hope on! We have successful missions in the slums. Our institutional pastors have success preaching in prisons, reformatories, houses of correction.

When the apostles at Jerusalem heard Samaria had received the Word of God, they sent unto them Peter and John. That strange report needed looking into. When Peter and John were come down, they prayed that the Samaritans might receive the Holy Ghost. They laid their hands on the Samaritans, and they received the Holy Ghost. Peter and John preached the Gospel in many villages of the Samaritans and returned to Jerusalem.

How times change! 'Twas but a few days ago that John would pray for fire from heaven to burn the Samaritans; now he prayed for fire, the fire of the Holy Ghost, to bless the Samaritans. It does matter of what spirit ye are. The Spirit of Christ certainly did make a change in John, the Son of Thunder.

Does the Spirit of God dwell in you? If any man have not the Spirit of Christ, he is none of His, Rom. 8, 9.

Dr. James Macdonald of Princeton University finds in St. John a counterpart of Luther. "Regenerating grace takes the iron will of a Luther and bends it to that of the divine mind and infuses into it a principle of new obedience without impairing its inherent firmness and strength."

[75]

CHAPTER XVII.

JOHN LOSES HIS BROTHER JAMES.

Acts 12, 1—3.

HEROD AGRIPPA I was the son of Aristobulus, killed by his own father, Herod the Great, butcher of the Innocents at Bethlehem. His sister was the adulterous Herodias, who demanded the head of John the Baptist. He was brought up in Rome, favorite of Antonia, mother of Germanicus, and led a most dissolute life. He made uncomplimentary remarks about the Emperor Tiberius and fell from favor into iron chains. When the slowly dying Tiberius was choked to death, in 37, Caius Caligula, Little Boots, freed Agrippa and made him king of Galilee and Perea. When Caligula ordered his statue set up in the Temple, Agrippa got him to cancel the order. When Caligula was stabbed to death, Agrippa favored Claudius, who made him king of all Palestine. A treaty of alliance, filled with his praise, was graven on a brazen tablet and set up in the Roman Forum.

On the death of Cymbeline his son Bericus appealed to Claudius, who sent Aulus Plautius and Vespasian to conquer Britain, and Vespasian fought and won thirty battles. Claudius rode into London and named his little son Britannicus. After six months Claudius returned and celebrated his triumph over eleven British kings.

"Now, about that time Herod the king put forth his hand to afflict certain of the Church. And he killed James, the brother of John, with the sword. And he saw that it pleased the Jews," Acts 12, 1—3.

Now James partook of the cup and the baptism of Jesus. He had said he could, and Christ had said he would, Matt. 20, 20—28; Mark 10, 35—45. This took place on March 25, 44, not very many years after the Passover days in which Christ had been crucified in the same city which stoned the righteous men and slew the prophets.

At Caesarea, Agrippa celebrated the British victories of Claudius and sat upon a throne and in his shining armor made a speech to the people. "It is the voice of a god and not of a man!" shouted the people. And at once the angel of the Lord smote him because he gave not God the glory; and he was eaten of worms and gave up the ghost," Acts 12, 21—23. This was in the summer of 44.

ANCIENT CAESAREA.

Breakwater with turrets topped with statues, the Sebasteum (circular temple), to the right of it the Praetorium, the former royal palace, where Paul was imprisoned, and the amphitheater.

CHAPTER XVIII.

JOHN AND PAUL.

AUL received into the Church uncircumcised Gentiles on the same footing as the circumcised Jews. This practise was fiercely denounced. False brethren sneaked in to spy out our liberty which we have in Christ Jesus that they might bring us into bondage. The Judaizers kept on saying, "Except ye be circumcised after the manner of Moses, ye cannot be saved," Acts 15, 1. 5. Also, they attacked Paul personally, saying he was no apostle at all and his gospel no Gospel. Of course, this created "no small dissension and disputation" among Paul's young converts.

Here was the crisis of Christianity. Is a man saved by faith in Jesus Christ or by good works and ceremonies? Paul had to stop the gospel of works, which is not another gospel, but the perversion of the Gospel of Christ, and he had to stop the slanders hurled at him personally.

Paul was an apostle, not of men, neither by man, but by Jesus Christ, and his Gospel was not after man, neither received he it of man nor was taught by man, but he received it by the revelation of Jesus Christ, Gal. 1, 1. 12. Paul had to fight for the truth of the Gospel, and fight to a finish. He carried the war into Jerusalem, the enemy's country, the headquarters of the Judaizers. He did not go for favors or patronage to get anything lacking added unto him; no, he demanded to be recognized as independent of the rest and equal with the best; and he gained what he wanted. Paul demanded his rights from the men who "were of reputation," of those who seemed "to be somewhat." Paul told them what Gospel he preached among the Gentiles and what success God had given him among the Gentiles.

"When James, Cephas, and John, who seemed to be pillars, perceived the grace that was given unto me," they had their doubts and scruples removed; they gave to Paul "the right hand of fellowship." Then they peaceably partitioned the world among themselves — Paul should go to the Gentiles and they to the Jews. With a little quiet irony Paul adds: "Only they would that we should remember the poor; the same which I also was forward to do." He was half amused to be prodded to do what he of his own accord was only all too eager to do. And he gathered a collection from his heathen converts for the needy Jewish brethren at Jerusalem. This was about the year 50, when Ventidius Cumanus was the procurator of Judea.

PETER.   ARTIST AND PUBLISHER UNKNOWN.

PAUL.   PAINTER AND PUBLISHER NOT KNOWN.

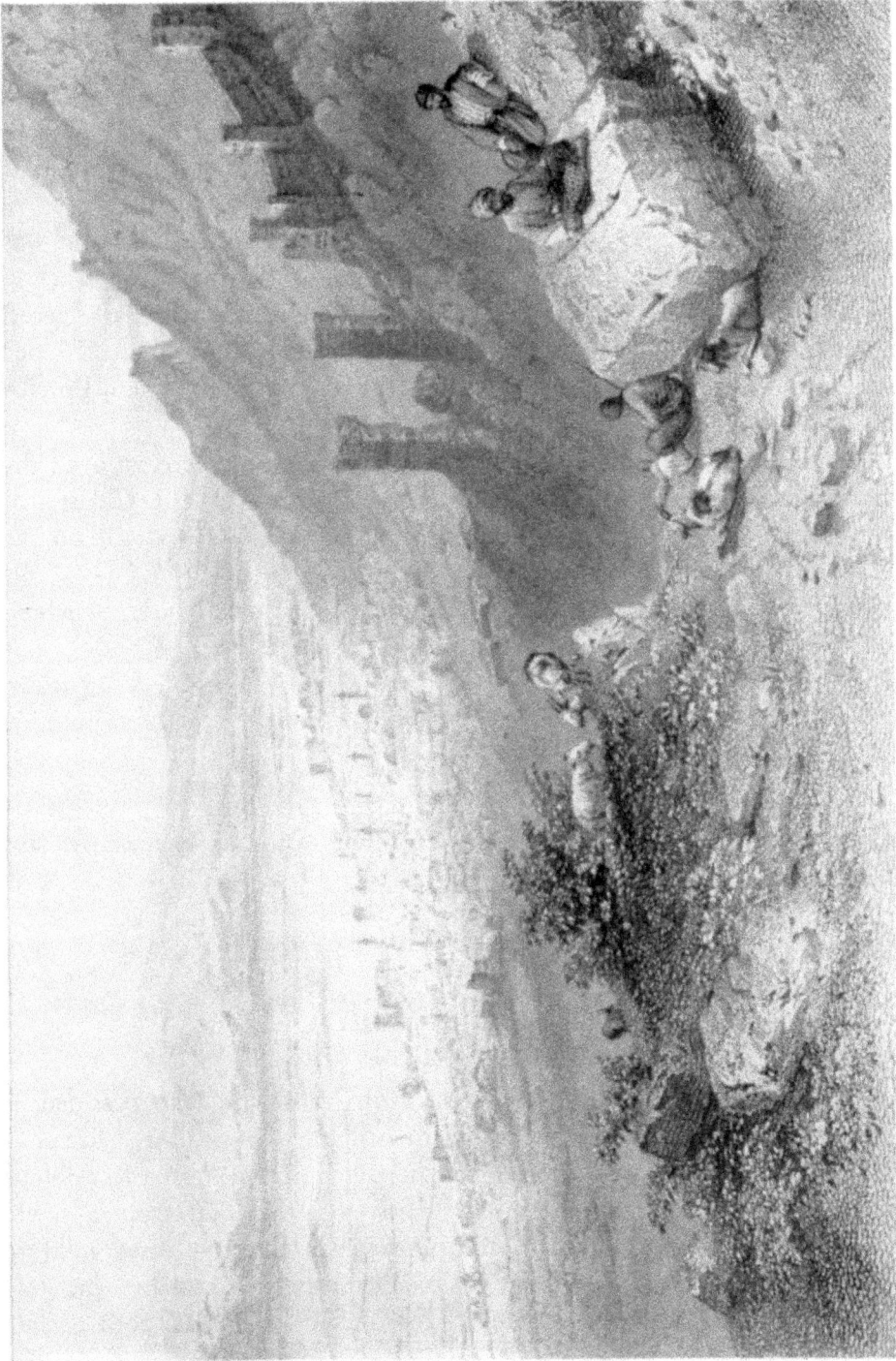

SYRIAN ANTIOCH, WHERE THE DISCIPLES WERE FIRST CALLED CHRISTIANS.

CHAPTER XIX.

JOHN'S LAST DAYS.

FROM now on we must rely largely upon tradition, hearsay, what has been handed down from mouth to mouth.

Claudius killed his wife Messalina, and in 54 he was killed by his wife Agrippina, who would make her darling Nero emperor. The procurator Felix took Drusilla, the daughter of Herod Agrippa I, from her husband, King Azizus of Emesa, and about 58 put Paul into prison at Caesarea. About 60 Paul appealed from Porcius Festus to Caesar Nero.

Rome burned July 19—24 and 28—30, in 64, and Nero enjoyed the fire and sang and fiddled. He blamed the calamity on the Christians; he persecuted them; he burned them alive as torches in his circus on the Vatican Hill.

Paul was put into prison, where he called for John Mark, to whom Keble says: —

> Companion of the saints! 'Twas thine
> To taste that drop of peace divine,
> When the great soldier of the Lord
>   Called thee to take his last farewell,
>   Teaching the Church with joy to tell
> The story of your love restored.

And Prof. William Cleaver Wilkinson of the Chicago University says of Paul: —

> But they condemned the guiltless man to die;
> And, like his Lord, he died without the gates.
> They led him to a chosen spot not far
> Beyond the city walls, he all the way
> Seen walking like one meekly triumphing;
> For a train followed and attended him
> Before whom he was as a conqueror.

James, the Lord's brother, the pastor of Jerusalem, who presided at the council about 50, who wrote the Epistle of James, was killed. Josephus writes the Sadducees stoned him during the change from Festus to Albinus in 62 or 63. Hegesippus writes the Pharisees hurled him from a tower about 66. The rule of Albinus was most cruel, but it seemed mild to that of Gessius Florus, 64—66. He made robbery a system; he stole about $20,000,000 from the Temple. Josephus and Tacitus both declare

[82]

he kindled the rebellion of set purpose to cover his crimes. The Jews drove him from the Temple and shut him up in the Castle of Antonia.

King Herod Agrippa II, the last of the Herods, who heard Paul, Acts 25 and 26, tried hard to patch up a peace, but he was pelted with stones out of the city. The zealots put to the sword the garrison of strong Masada. Eleazar, captain of the Temple, refused sacrifices for the emperor.

CLAUDIUS. MESSALINA. BRITANNICUS. OCTAVIA.

On July 5 the garrison of Antonia was killed, though promised under oath their lives would be spared. The high priest Ananias (Acts 23, 2; 24, 1) was dragged out of a sewer of the Asmonean Palace and killed; his palace and that of Agrippa and Bernice were burned. Strong Machaerus fell; Cyprus was taken; in five months all Palestine was in open rebellion. Then began that horrible epidemic of massacre among Jews and Syrians, without parallel in all history.

The legate of Syria, Cestius Gallus, marched south with Agrippa and

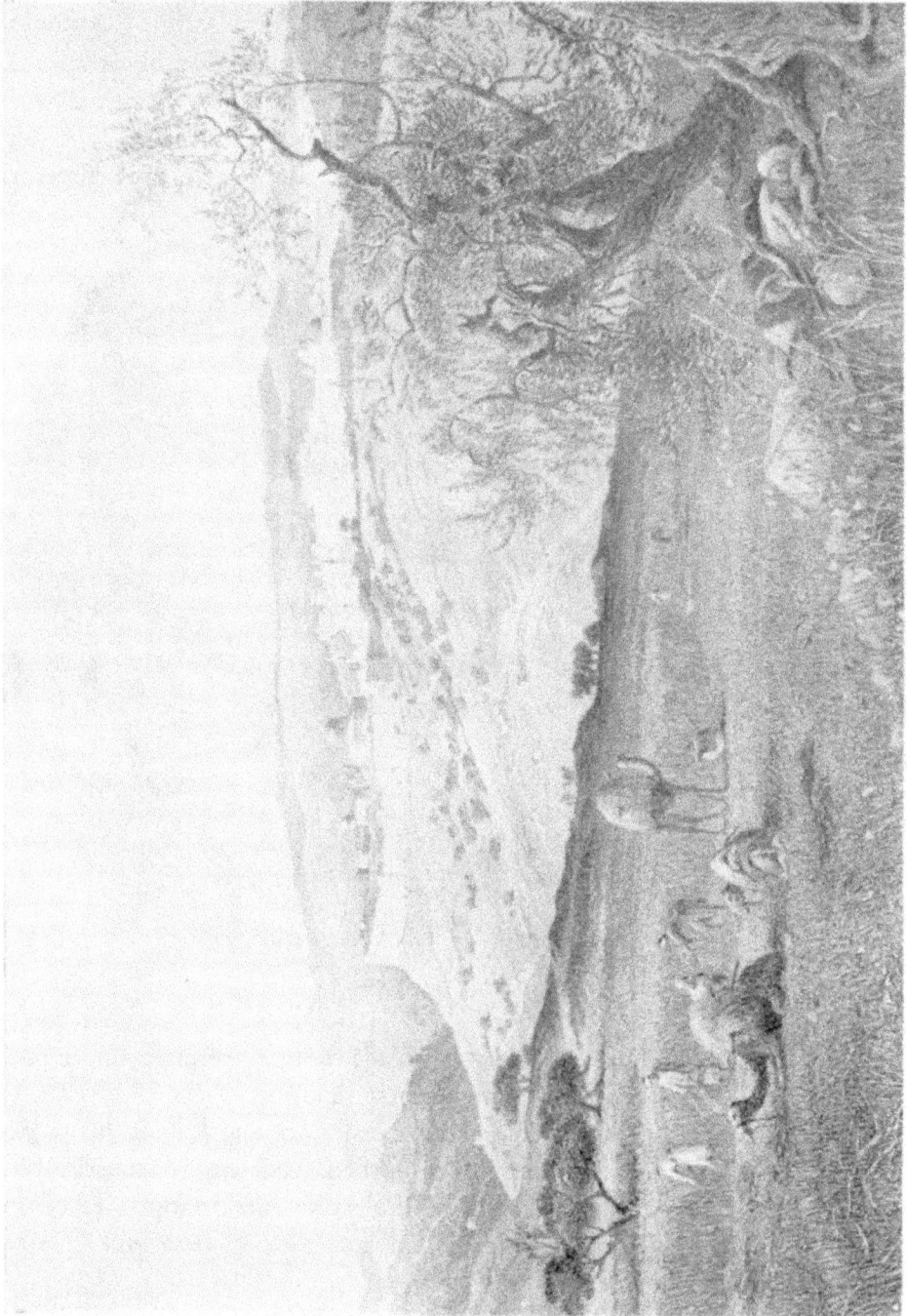

JERUSALEM, FROM SCOPUS.

left desolation in his tracks. On a Sabbath the Jews inflicted losses on him at Gibeon. On October 30 he advanced to Mount Scopus, seized Bezetha, the northern suburb, and drove the rebels within the second wall. Then he retreated and was defeated at Bethoron, where in days of old Joshua had lifted up his spear and bidden the sun "stand still upon Gibeon and thou, moon, in the valley of Ajalon." Cestius lost 5,300 foot, 380 horse, an eagle, his tents, his money, his engines of war.

News of the defeat reached Nero while on a theatrical tour at the

NERO.   TITUS.

Olympian games in Greece. He had disgraced Vespasian for yawning or sleeping during imperial singing, but now he ordered that able general of humble origin to recover the country fortune-tellers had promised him as his future empire. Early in 67 Vespasian landed at Ptolemais. He had the fifteenth legion; his son, Titus, brought the famous fifth and tenth legions from Alexandria; horsemen came from Syria, horse and archers from the king of Arabia; other troops from Kings Antiochus, Agrippa, and Sohenus — 60,000 warriors besides the slaves trained to arms. In March, Vespasian marched from Antioch, marched "from Dan to Beersheba"; it was like Sherman's "marching through Georgia, from Atlanta to the sea."

JERUSALEM, FROM THE MOUNT OF OLIVES.

"These are the beginnings of sorrows; let them which be in Judea flee to the mountains," Matt. 24, 8. To the mountains of Gilead the Christians fled, to Pella, in the Decapolis, on a small eastern branch of the Jordan. Josephus writes: "Many of the most eminent Jews swam away from the city as from a ship that was sinking." John may have been among them.

Gadara was the first to fall; even the infants were slain. Josephus defended Jotapata for forty-six days; the next it was betrayed and burned; Josephus was taken prisoner on July 20. Titus promised safety to strongly fortified Taricheae — Magdala? Yet 2,200 were massacred in the gymnasium, 6,000 were sent to Nero to cut through the Isthmus of Corinth, 30,400 were sold as slaves. Agrippa was wounded in the siege of Gamala; Vespasian took it on October 23; even the infants were slain, only two women escaped. And so forth and so on. The Romans rested in their winter quarters and enjoyed their watchful waiting. They had seen many a Roman holiday, but never such a Jewish holiday as was made for them by John of Giscala and Simon, son of Giora, in the most ferocious civil war known to history.

Nero stabbed himself on June 9, 68. The blue-eyed Galba was killed by the Romans on January 15, 69. The bewigged Otho, after three months, killed himself in April, 69. The giant Vitellius was tortured and flung into the Tiber in December. In 69 news of Nero's death reached Gadara on the eastern shore of Galilee, where Vespasian was camping, and the legions saluted him emperor. He hastened to Rome, leaving Titus to reduce Jerusalem.

About April 14, 70, Titus began the siege. On the west was the fifth legion under Sextus Cerealis, where the Assyrians had camped, 2 Kings 19, 33; Is. 37, 36.

In the plain just north of the city Abraham was greeted by the kings of the plain, Gen. 14, 17. And a little beyond, on Mount Scopus, the high priest Jaddua greeted Alexander the Great. Here Cestius Gallus had camped in 66, and here Titus had two legions and a third a little beyond. On the east was the famous tenth legion, on the Mount of Olives, the headquarters of Titus. In the city whole houses were filled with unburied corpses, which caused a pestilence. So great the famine that mothers killed and devoured their own children.

On July 5 Antonia was razed; on the 17th the daily sacrifice was

THE ENTRY OF TITUS INTO JERUSALEM.

WALL OF WAILING, JERUSALEM.

ended for all time; on August 8 the city was stormed; on the 10th the
Temple was burned; on September 8 Jerusalem was destroyed, only two-
score years after Christ's prophecy. The killed were estimated at 1,337,490,
the prisoners at 101,700; some of these built the Collosseum.

A medal was struck, with a woman under a palm-tree and the legend
Judaea Capta. At the shrine of Pan up at Caesarea Philippi Neronias,
Titus celebrated his victory with gladiatorial combats.

In 71 Titus celebrated his triumph; 700 Jews graced it, also the holy
vessels from the Temple. Bar Goria was hurled from the Tarpeian Rock.
Josephus wrote his *Jewish War* and delivered it to Vespasian; Titus and
Agrippa II wrote recommendations of it.

On June 23, 79, Titus became emperor and dismissed his mistress —
he unwilling, she unwilling — Berenice, daughter of Herod Agrippa I.

On August 24 Pom-
peii and Herculaneum
were buried by Vesu-
vius, and Pliny, Sr., lost
his life.

Some time during
that war of ferocities
and atrocities John and
Evangelist Philip and

MEDALS STRUCK BY VESPASIAN TO CELEBRATE THE
CAPTURE OF JERUSALEM.

one Ariston left their homeland and after shipwreck reached Ephesus,
the metropolis, mother city, of five hundred cities strewn around the heroic
country made immortal in history by Herodotus and in poetry by Homer.

The harbor was ornamented with a colonnade having a tripylon,
a triple gate, opening on Main Street. Near the dock, to the north, is
the luxurious hot bath with its marble mosaic floor of thirteen colors.

Farther north will rise the double Church of St. Mary, who will here
be proclaimed "Mother of God."

Main Street was a broad way of twenty meters, flanked by a colonnade
five meters deep, running straight east from the port into a mountain.
On the slope was Lysimachus's theater of three stories, with sixty rows of
marble seats for 30,000 people. Here Demetrius staged that dramatic
demonstration against Paul of which Luke tells us most graphically in Acts.

On the other side of the mountain is the Cave of the Seven Sleepers,
where Emperor Julian will become "the Apostate." In front of the theater

CAESAREA PHILIPPI.

a colonnaded street leads north to the large stadium and to the huge aqueduct. Seven columns are still standing, and on the top of each the storks built their nests and at the bottom stalk silently about in great gravity. Towards the south of the theater is the magnificent market, trodden by the feet of Paul, who preached in the hired hall of Tyrannus near by.

Southeast is the magnificent Magnesian Gate, flanked with strong towers and offering two broad openings for vehicles and between them one

SPOILS FROM THE TEMPLE AT JERUSALEM.
From the Arch of Titus.

for pedestrians. It had a figure of Nemesis, with wings and wheels, showing she was at home equally on earth and in the air. Under her the name of Vespasian appeared. In honor of his wife the rhetor Damianus built a marble colonnade over the Via Sacra a mile long to the temple of Artemis, or Diana.

Croesus gave golden bulls and columns to the temple. Cyrus took Ephesus, but spared the temple, Artemis being related to his own home goddess. When the temple was partly destroyed, it was rebuilt

FACADE OF ST. PAUL'S OUTSIDE THE WALLS OF ROME.

THE FLAVIAN THEATER.
Built by captive Jews after the destruction of Jerusalem on the site of Nero's Golden House.

ANCIENT EPHESUS.

The inner port, the market-place (Agora), and the amphitheater.

on a grand scale. In 480 Xerxes spared it, though he destroyed all other Ionian temples.

On the night Alexander the Great was born, Herostratus fired the Ephesian dome in order to make himself immortal. It was forbidden to mention his name under penalty of death, but everybody knows his name, while nobody really knows the name of the genius who built the

RUINS OF THE THEATER AT EPHESUS.

Artemision, which, Pausanias declares, surpassed all the temples of all other nations; it was held the greatest of the seven wonders of the world.

On a platform 418×239 feet stood the temple, 342×163. Purest Ionian columns rose to fifty-five feet and eight inches, 127 of them, thirty-six with sculptured drums, one by Scopas. In this marble forest stood such a crowd of gods and goddesses that it looked like Olympus. Above all towered Artemis, the "image which fell down from Jupiter," "whom Asia and all the world worshipeth." It was a large block of black wood coarsely carved, swaddled like an Egyptian mummy, covered with breasts, types of reproduction. On altars carved by Praxiteles and Thraso, priests fed the fires day and night and continuously threw on living animals. Everybody helped rebuild the temple, the men giving their money and the women their jewels.

After the battle of Granicus in 334 B. C., Alexander came to worship here and offered to pay the whole cost if his name were inscribed as the dedicator. The patriotic priests refused, but with the diplomatic compliment, "It is not fit for one god to build a temple to another god."

THE TEMPLE OF DIANA AT EPHESUS.

Alexander employed his architect of Alexandria to superintend the building of the temple, and Apelles's portrait of the conqueror with the thunderbolt of sovereignty in his hand was consecrated as Alexander's special gift to the temple at the cost of twenty gold talents, about $400,000 in our money. Here's a good one on the conqueror of the world. He complained the portrait did not look like him, but Bucephalus neighed in recognition of it. "The horse knows more of art than Alexander," said the artist. The people said there were two Alexanders, one given by Philip and invincible, the other painted by Apelles and inimitable.

The people of the whole Ionic confederation came here to adore. Dionysius of Halicarnassus tells us: "On certain days men, women, and children gathered thither for religion and for business. There were horse races and contests in gymnastics and music, for which prizes were given to the winners. Cities likewise offered their rich gifts to the gods. Then, spectacles and business having terminated, festivals and public rejoicing at an end, if any city had a quarrel with another, the magistrates were there to judge the cause."

Ephesus was the home of the great philosopher Heraclitus. It was the home of Balbilus, whom Nero and Vespasian had to tell their fortunes. And it was known for the Ephesian Letters, or charms. Clement of Alexandria gives them as Askeion, Kataskeion, Lix, Tetras, Damnameneos, Aision. He adds Androkydes, the Pythagorean, said they meant Darkness, Light, the Earth, the Year

ARTEMIS, THE DIANA OF EPHESUS.

THE "EPHESIAN LETTERS," OR CHARMS.

DALLMANN, JOHN. 7

(with its four seasons), the Sun (as subduing all things), and Truth. (*Stromateis,* V, p. 46.)

What was the moral result of the religion of Artemis? Philostratus relates Ephesus was utterly buried in idleness and in arrogance. She abounded in fiddlers and similar players upon instruments, seekers after depravity and pleasure. The streets were crowded with effeminate, dissolute, and lascivious men, and the night resounded with serenades, alarms, and music." They drove out the sage Hermodorus — "We want no good

RUINS OF ST. JOHN'S CHURCH AT EPHESUS.
Erected by Emperor Justinian.

men amongst us. If there be any such, let them go to live in other lands amid other nations." We may well apply to Ephesus the words of Shakespeare: —

They say this town is full of cozenage,
As, nimble jugglers that deceive the eye,
Dark-working sorcerers that change the mind,
Soul-killing witches that deform the body,
Disguised cheaters, prating mountebanks,
And many such like liberties of sin.

Such was the Ephesus to which John came. He found many Jews. When Pompey conquered Judea in 63 B. C., many left Jerusalem, and more Jews were in Ephesus than in any other heathen city outside of Alexandria. During the dictatorship of Julius Caesar the Maccabean priest-king, John Hyrcanus, asked Dolabella to free them from military service and allow them religious liberty; and Josephus recorded the decree of exemption on the grounds 1) that it was unlawful to bear arms in a foreign army, 2) that they could not march on the Sabbath, 3) that their *kosher* laws hindered them from sharing the common rations of the soldiers. This was confirmed by the Consul Lucius Lentulus and after Caesar's death by the Ephesians themselves.

Making laws and keeping laws are two different things. About fifty years before John came, Herod with his friend and patron Agrippa, son-in-law and minister of Augustus, came here. Nicholas of Damascus, courtier and historian of Herod, pleaded the cause of the oppressed Jews.

RUINS OF COUNCIL CHURCH AT EPHESUS.

Agrippa restored to them some of their rights at the prayer of Herod, whom he publicly embraced in token of his friendship with the whole nation.

Here John found Christians. Apollo of Alexandria, "full of learning and mighty in the Scriptures," Acts 18, 24, had preached the Gospel here. Aquila and Priscilla had worked and taught here. Paul had preached here so successfully as to alarm the followers of Artemis, Acts 18, 25—28. Onesiphorus had refreshed the soul of Paul and had not been ashamed of his chains, 2 Tim. 1, 16. Tychicus, Paul's "dearest brother and faithful minister in the Lord," Eph. 6, 21. Trophimus and Tychicus, who had gone with Paul to Rome, Acts 20, 4; 2 Tim. 4, 12. 20. Timothy, Paul's "own son in the faith," "the good soldier of Christ," whom Paul "besought to abide still at Ephesus," 1 Tim. 1, 2. 3. No doubt some of these remained and joyously welcomed John.

ENTRANCE TO THE THERMAE AT EPHESUS.

The only living apostle of the Lord naturally became the leader in the work of the Lord, and streams of living water flowed from him, according to the promise of Christ, John 7, 38.

Titus, "the Darling of Mankind," died September 13, 81, and was followed by his brother Domitian, who reared the arch of Titus. Tertullian calls him "a portion of Nero in cruelty." "Every public document as well as every discourse authorized by his name was to be headed 'Our Lord and God commands so and so,'" writes Suetonius. His statues were placed in the holiest temples, and whole hecatombs were sacrificed upon his altars.

This worthy "Lord and God" wished all Romans had but one head, then he could strike it off at one blow. The most clement emperor rarely deprived himself of the pleasure of witnessing the execution of a man. Flavius Clemens was Domitian's first cousin and was named consul, ordinary consul, and consul with the emperor, a triple honor. His wife was Flavia Domitilla, a niece of Domitian. The emperor named their two sons Vespasian and Domitian, had them brought up at court under Quintilian, and appointed heirs to the throne. Suddenly they were accused of being "tainted with atheism and of Judaizing," the common charge against Christians. Horrors! After the death of Domitian the Roman emperor would be a Christian!

AGRIPPA, SON-IN-LAW OF AUGUSTUS, BUILDER OF THE PANTHEON.

DIANA OR CHRIST?

Flavius Clemens was beheaded, his wife banished to Pandataria, an obscure island, their sons disappeared. The brave consul Acilius Glabrio was sent to the arena, but be overcame the wild beasts; he was sent into exile and killed.

Domitian "feared the coming of Christ," says Eusebius and on the authority of Hegesippus declares he sent for two Christians of Judea, grandsons of the Apostle Jude. They owned but $1,800 and eight acres

PITTI, FLORENCE.   CARLO, DOLCI, 1616—1686.
VISION OF ST. JOHN THE EVANGELIST ON THE ISLE OF PATMOS.

and toiled for their living, showing their horny hands. And they said Christ's kingdom was not of this world. Domitian felt his throne was in no danger from them and dismissed them. But he banished John to rocky Patmos, 60 miles from Ephesus, in 95, says Eusebius. An old Latin hymn says: —

> To desert islands banished,
>   With God the exile dwells
> And sees the future glory
>   His mystic writing tells.

That is, here John wrote his Apocalypse, or Revelation, to the seven churches of Asia — Ephesus, Smyrna, Pergamos, Thyatira, Sardis, Philadelphia, and Laodicea.

Agricola conquered Britain, defeating Galgacus at Aberfoyle in the Grampian Hills in Perthshire, killing 10,000 Scots with a loss of but 360 Romans. For this brilliant victory Domitian gave him a kiss with a stony look and an icy silence. Agricola's son-in-law, Tacitus, tells us about it. When Domitian was stabbed by the freedman Stephanus on September 18 of 96, Nerva followed and freed all whom Domitian had banished for "impiety," as Dio Cassius calls Christianity, which he did not know.

John returned to Ephesus and kept on laboring. He asked about a youth whom he had given in charge of a minister. "He is dead." "Dead? How did he die?" "He is dead to God. He became a robber chief."

John takes a horse to the mountains, is captured, and taken to the captain, who recognizes John and turns to flee. "Why do you flee from me? Be not afraid. If need be, I'll gladly die for you as

PATMOS.

Christ died for us. I will lay down my life for you. Stop, stop! Believe Christ hath sent me." The robber repented.

As strong as his love of Christ was his hate of Antichrist. Hearing Cerinthus was in the bath, John would not go in and be under the same roof with a denier of Christ.

The Son of Thunder was human and unbent from his labors by playing with a pet partridge, at which a hunter was rather surprised and a bit offended. "Do you always keep your bow bent?"

"No, that would make it useless."

"If you unbend your bow to keep it useful, I unbend my mind for the same reason."

John kept the Lord's Supper and Easter as he had learned it from his Lord at Jerusalem, on the 14th of Nisan and the resurrection three days after, no matter on which day of the week it might fall, — and here began the great split between the Greek and the Latin Church.

The aged seer was robed like the Old Testament priest, with a fair miter on his head, and over his brow was the petalon, a plate of gold engraved with the words, "Holiness unto the Lord."

Professor Tyndall admired Copernicus for publishing his great astronomical discovery only after pondering it for thirty-three years. For over fifty years John pondered before writing his Gospel of the Son of God.

When too feeble to walk, John was carried to church; too weak to preach, he lifted up his trembling hands and simply said, "Little children, love one another." Why ever and only this?

"Because it is the Lord's command, and nothing is done unless this is done." Eastwood beautifully tells the story thus: —

What say you, friends?
That this is Ephesus, and Christ has gone
Back to His kingdom? Ay, 'tis so, 'tis so;
I know it all; and yet, just now I seemed
To stand once more upon my native hills

And touch my Master. . . .
Up! Bear me to my church once more,
There let me tell them of a Savior's love;
For by the sweetness of my Master's voice
I think He must be very near. . . .

So raise up my head;
How dark it is! I cannot seem to see
The faces of my flock. Is that the sea
That murmurs so, or is it weeping? Hush!
My little children! God so loved the world
He gave His Son; so love ye one another,
Love God and men. Amen.

In this age Apollonius of Tyana was preaching, Epictetus was teaching, and Governor Pliny of Bithynia was writing his letters to his emperor Trajan. Where are they and their writings? Of John our Longfellow says: —

And Him evermore I behold
    Walking in Galilee,
Through the corn-field's waving gold,
In hamlet, in wood, and in wold.
    By the shores of the Beautiful Sea
He toucheth the sightless eyes;

Before Him the demons flee;
To the dead He sayeth, 'Arise!'
    To the living, 'Follow Me!'
And that Voice still soundeth on
From the centuries that are gone
    To the centuries that shall be.

Irenaeus writes: "John remained among them up to the times of Trajan," in 98, and died when he was a hundred years old, says Jerome.

THE SUCCESS OF THE GOSPEL.

When Paul and John came to Ephesus, it was perhaps the strongest stronghold of heathenism in all the Roman world; but it became the missionary headquarters of the Church. With what result?

Governor Pliny, Jr., of Bithynia wrote Emperor Trajan the heathen temples were about deserted, and what was he to do about the many Christians?

The Emperor Trajan tried to help along the worship of Artemis by presenting bronze doors; the Emperors Hadrian and Valerian greatly favored the goddess; the Emperor Diocletian fiercely persecuted the Christians. Seven brothers condemned to death fled into a cave to the east of the theater. After a sleep of two hundred years they awoke to find the city converted.

Possibly to this cave of the Seven Sleepers came Julian from Athens to see Maximus, the aged philosopher. Specters of fire appeared in the darkness, and a mysterious voice declared, "The gods have given you the soul of Alexander."

PITTI, FLORENCE.   CARLO DOLCI, 1616—1686.
ST. JOHN THE EVANGELIST.

Julian made the sign of the cross. Darkness and silence followed. The same voice said from afar, "That sign is impotent, but it marks a blasphemer to whom the gods will not speak." Julian fell on his face and swore to enthrone the old gods or die in the attempt. He died in the attempt and said, in Swinburne's verse: —

Thou hast conquered, O pale Galilean!
The world has grown gray with Thy breath,
We have drunken of things Lethean
And fed on the fulness of death.

Clement of Alexandria quoted the Sibylline Oracles: —

> And Ephesus shall wail along her shore
> And seek her temple — temple found no more.

Milton says: —

> From haunted spring and dale,
> Edged with poplar pale,
> The parting genius is with sighing sent;
> With flower-enwoven tresses torn,
> The nymphs in twilight shade of tangled thickets mourn.

And Browning says: —

> O ye vain false gods of Hellas,
> Ye are silent evermore.

And the stones of Diana's temple were used to build Christian churches.

CAVE OF THE SEVEN SLEEPERS OF EPHESUS.

In 431 the Emperor Theodosius called a synod to Ephesus, which met in the double church of Mary, on the north side of the city. Here Mary was given the title *Theotokos*, Mother of God. This was meant to teach that Christ had really the divine nature. In time the Virgin Mary was put into the place of Artemis.

In 449 the emperor called another General Council to Ephesus and made Dioscurus of Alexandria president. The 135 or 150 bishops met again in St. Mary's, but behaved so disgracefully that they were called a "Band of Brigands," and the synod is known in history as the "Ephesian Robber Synod." This in the city where Paul and John had labored and preached the love of God and man!

The church built over John's grave was likely rebuilt by Constantine the Great in the fourth century. In 530 the Emperor Justinian replaced it with a most splendid sanctuary in the form of a cross, one hundred meters east and west, with three naves and six main domes. The columns were erected out of solid rock, with white marble shafts. The capitals of the principal nave were covered with gold and decorated with the monograms of the Emperor Justinian and Theodora. For a thousand years it was one of the greatest sanctuaries of the Christian Orient.

In time the great metropolis was lost to the world under a cover of mud about twenty-five feet deep. On a hill is a squalid village called Ayasolouk, from Hagios Theologos, the Holy Theologian, meaning John the Divine.

After spending about nine years and much money, J. T. Wood, working for the British Museum, in 1871 found the site of the temple of Artemis about twenty-five feet under a barley-field. In August, 1922, Prof. Georgios Sotiriu found the ruins of Justinian's Church of John. In 1926 the Ephesus Excavations Board of Trustees was organized at Berlin, financed in part by John D. Rockefeller, Jr. Since then Prof. Josef Keil of Greifswald has been uncovering the Basilica of St. John on Ayasolouk Hill, over which soar the eagles as they soared in the days of Heraclitus and Alexander, and Paul and John.

CHAPTER XX.

JOHN'S PUPILS

RENAEUS tells us John taught "presbyters in Asia," the Roman province. The wise men of Ephesus might spin their ingenious theories and win worldly fame as philosophers, but John taught religion, religion based on solid facts of history. Christ was born in Bethlehem under Caesar Augustus, He suffered under Pontius Pilate, was crucified, dead, and buried, the third day He rose again from the dead, and ascended into heaven. "This thing was not done in a corner," as Paul said, but in Jerusalem. John taught what he had heard, what he had seen with his eyes, what he had looked upon, what his hands had handled.

Browning has him

Saying, "It is so; so I heard and saw,"
Speaking as the case asked: and men believed.

1. IGNATIUS.

Legend says the little child of Matt. 18, 2 was Ignatius, Fiery, also called Theoph'orus, God-carried, and Theopho'rus, God-carrier. He was taught by John, and about 65, between thirty and forty years of age, he was sent to be bishop of Antioch in Syria, where the disciples were first called Christians. In 115 the great city was almost destroyed by an earthquake. Blame it on the Christians! Kill them! The bishop appealed to Trajan. The weather-beaten old emperor asked bitterly, "Who art thou, Kakodemon [bad demon, miserable wretch], who dost dare to break my commands and make others perish miserably?"

"I am Ignatius Theophorus."

"What is this, 'Theophorus'?"

"It means one who beareth God in his heart."

"Do you mean *we* bear not in our hearts the gods who help us conquer our enemies?"

"The demons whom you adore are no gods, for there is but one God and one Jesus Christ, His only Son, to whose kingdom I long to come."

"You mean Him who was crucified under Pontius Pilate?"

"Even so. He it is who by His death crucified sin with the origin

[108]

of sin, triumphed over the malice of demons, and cast them down beneath the feet of those who bear Him in their heart."

"Then you carry this Christ in your heart?"

"Assuredly; for is it not written, 'I will dwell in them and walk in them'?"

"We decree that Ignatius, who says he bears the Crucified within him, should be bound and carried to Rome to be thrown to the beasts and become a spectacle to the people."

"I thank Thee, Lord, that Thou hast given me love for Thee and hast granted me to be bound with chains, even as was Thine Apostle Paul." And he helped put the chains on himself.

He wrote some letters. In a roundabout way he was taken to Rome. It was a great triumphal procession. He saw Nero's colossal marble statue, 112 feet high, now changed by a few touches into Apollo, the god of the sun and of poetry. Near by the great Flavian

THE EMPEROR TRAJAN.

Amphitheater, built by Titus with Jews dragged from Jerusalem. Being near to Nero's colossus, this huge theater was called the Colosseum. Into this place Ignatius was brought. "I am the Lord's wheat. I must be ground by the teeth of beasts to become the pure bread of Jesus Christ." Out bounded two hungry lions. In a minute the earthly remains of Ignatius were a few bones, which were wrapped in linen and sent to Antioch. "Now, these things took place on the thirteenth day before the kalends of January, that is, on the twentieth day of December, Sura and Senecio being then the consuls of the Romans for the second time, having ourselves been eye-witnesses."

Bishop Heber asks: —

> They met the tyrant's brandished steel,
>   The lion's gory mane;
> They bowed their necks the death to feel.
>   Who follows in their train?

THE LAST PRAYER.

GEROME.

2. QUADRATUS.

Quadratus, Kodratos, a Greek philosopher, became a pupil of John and presented the first Apology, or Defense, of Christianity to Hadrian when that emperor came to Athens in 125. In the shade of the portico Hadrian listened with great respect. Shortly after, the proconsul of Asia wrote how cruelly the Christians were persecuted. Hadrian ordered they should suffer only for direct violations of the law; spiteful accusations should be ignored.

3. POLYCARP.

Another one of John's disciples was Polycarp, Much Fruit, who became bishop of Smyrna. He went to Rome to see Bishop Anicetus about the proper day for keeping Easter. Though they could not agree, there was no division, and Polycarp was courteously invited to consecrate the Holy Eucharist. Shocked at various loose teachings which he heard at Rome, he would stop his ears and cry, "Good God, to what times hast Thou reserved me that I should hear such things as these!" Marcion, a notorious false teacher, met Polycarp and asked, "Do you know who I am?" "I know thee for the eldest son of Satan."

After Polycarp's return to Smyrna there was an earthquake and a pestilence. "Away with the atheists! Seek for Polycarp!" The proconsul of Asia, Statius Quadratus, did not check the worst persecution that had yet raged. In the crowded amphitheater he said, "I will release thee when thou hast denied thy Christ."

"Eighty and six years have I served Him, nor hath He ever done me wrong. Why, then, should I denounce my King and Savior?"

The proconsul kept the ceremony of sending around a herald to announce, "Polycarp has confessed himself a Christian."

"The beast for Polycarp!" roared the beasts, pagan and Jewish, old and young, male and female.

Too late for the beasts. "Fire!" cried the crowd and hurried out to bring in the needed fagots. The wind swelled out the flame like the sail of a ship into an arch or canopy of glory, in the midst of which Polycarp stood still praying, but untouched. The disappointed crowd yelled to a confector to kill, and he plunged his short sword into Polycarp's left side, and the blood quenched the fire. It was Sunday, February 23, 155.

God's elements are merciful,   The raging fire had spared the saint,
   Man only mocks His will;   The sword had power to kill.

The proconsul bade the centurion bury the body, but the Christians got
a few bones and buried them, over which a small church is still standing.

> I bless Thee, holiest Father,
>   I thank Thee, blessed Son,
> Because the golden crown is near,
>   The race is nearly run.
> God of all things created,
>   Angels and earthly power,
> I praise Thee for the agony
>   Of this departing hour. — *Mrs. Alexander.*

4. PAPIAS.

Papias, Fatherly, bishop of Hierapolis, likewise a pupil of John, also
was martyred in the same persecution as Polycarp.

5. POTHINUS.

Trophimus of Ephesus, the companion of Paul, is counted the earliest
bishop of the grand old city of Arelate, or Arles, in Gaul.   An amphitheater, an arch of triumph, two temples, and other relics still witness to
Rome's rule after Caesar's Gallic War.   The amphitheater was the scene
of the death of the martyrs who served for heathen sport and derision.
And so the amphitheater at Nimes, the city watered by the wonderful
Pont de Gard, built by Agrippa, son-in-law of Caesar Augustus.

Pothinus, an intimate friend of Polycarp and about the same age
and likely also a pupil of John, became bishop of Lugdunum, or Lyons,
almost entirely Greek-speaking.   He was helped by young Irenaeus,
Peaceful, a pupil of Polycarp.   Earthquakes — pestilence — famine.
"Perish the Christians!   Their defiance of the gods has brought this evil
upon us."   Under Marcus Aurelius the blow fell on Provincia, the province
curving around the Mediterranean.   Under torture, slaves in their agony
confess everything they were expected to confess: The Christians slew
infants, devoured human flesh, practised all kinds of abominations in their
meetings, and so forth and so on.

The ninety-year-old Bishop Pothinus was dragged to court, stoned,
and beaten by the crowd.   With clothes torn and covered with mire, he
was dragged to the dungeon, where he died two days later, the last of the
pupils of John.

Vettius Epigathus, a first senator of the Gauls, Sanctus, a deacon
of Vienne, Attalus of Pergamos, Maturus, a recent convert, Alexander,

FAITHFUL UNTO DEATH.   A. LELOIR.

A CHRISTIAN MOTHER STRENGTHENING HER DAUGHTER TO BE FAITHFUL UNTO DEATH.

LOUIS SOUZAY.

a physician of Phrygia, Marcellus, Valerian, the fifteen-year-old Ponticus and his sister Blandina — all were cruelly tortured and butchered. The foundations of the amphitheater may be seen to-day.

The ancient Bibracte, then called Augustodunum, now shortened to Autun, likewise suffered.

While the Christians of Lyons were suffering in prison in 177, they sent their presbyter Irenaeus to Rome with a letter to Bishop Eleutherus. On his return Irenaeus was made bishop to follow the murdered Pothinus. He learned the "barbarous tongue" in order to preach to the Celts of Gaul, more akin to the Scottish than to the Welsh Celts.

Aurelius was followed by his dissolute son, Commodus, who did not bother the Christians; in fact, they were protected by Marcia, a woman who had influence with the emperor.

While the Christians had peace from the pagans, they had no peace among themselves. Bishop Polycrates of Ephesus, of gray head and slender frame, but mighty spirit, would not depart from the custom of John in celebrating Easter. Bishop Victor of Rome

THE EMPEROR CONSTANTINE THE GREAT.

declared "the Church should have nothing in common with the Jews" and excommunicated the churches of all Asia. About 190 Irenaeus wrote a vigorous protest to the despotic Roman bishop.

When Marcia found her name in a list of those whom Commodus intended to kill, she beat him to it by poisoning the emperor, and the years of peace, 180—192, came to an end.

Septimius Severus, in 197, killed his rival, Clodius Albinus, in a terrible battle at the very gates of Lyons, and the Rhone ran red. While games were celebrated in the emperor's honor, the Christians were persecuted, the streets of Lyons ran red, and, it is said, Irenaeus died by the sword in 202.

A Latin verse in the mosaic pavement of St. Irenaeus in Lyons puts the number of his fellow-martyrs at 19,000.

> From new-born Lyons of thy memory turned
> Unto the earlier East and fondly yearned
> For Polycarp and Smyrna and the youth
> Of grave religion fair. — *J. Williams.*

Barely a hundred years after the Christians had been butchered at Lyons, the Roman emperor himself, in 314, invited Western bishops to meet him at Arles, each attended by two priests and three servants, bills footed by the emperor, to talk over church matters.

Up to the sixth century Greek hymns were sung in public worship at Arles, where also the *Te Deum* was first sung. The *Veni Creator* and the litanies also come from Gaul.

The Celtic churches in Britain and Ireland counted Easter by the fourteenth day of the new moon, appealing to John and Polycarp.

Ireland loved to build her churches in clusters of seven tiny churches, commemorating the seven stars and seven lamps of the seven churches of John's Revelation. Ruins of such may be seen at the twin lakes of Glendalough, among the rocks of Connemara, and in the wild vale Clonmacnoise.

The Celts of the West of Britain had their ancient liturgy no doubt through Pothinus from John at Ephesus, and it had Polycarp's dying Eucharistic hymn.

PART TWO.

JOHN THE EVANGELIST.

HIS GOSPEL.

CHAPTER I.

THE PROLOG.

THE WORD.

John 1, 1—18.

ILLIONS of books are in the libraries, but not one will be found to compare in vigor and sublimity with the prolog of John's Gospel," says Adolf von Harnack in the Christmas supplement to the *Vossische Zeitung* of 1902.

1. THE WORD IN ETERNITY.

"In the beginning was the Word" — already in existence at the beginning, hence eternal, as God was already in existence, and so eternal, when in the beginning He created the heaven and the earth, Gen. 1, 1; Ps. 90, 2; Col. 1, 17; Heb. 4, 12; John 17, 5. 24; 1 John 1, 1; Rev. 19, 13; 22, 13.

"And the Word was with God" — toward God and in relation with God and distinct from God.

"And the Word was God" — in being or essence as truly as the Father is God, John 10, 30.

This first majestic sentence of three clauses of stately symmetry tells us the Word is eternal, a person, and God.

"The same was existing in the beginning with God" — sums up the foregoing three statements and stresses the fact that each of them was true in the beginning.

Of this first sentence Chrysostom says, "Hear how he thunders!" And Augustine, "John has opened his words, as it were, with a burst of thunder." And the Lutheran Bengel, "This is the thunder brought down to us by a son of thunder."

This confutes the Arians, who say Christ is inferior to God; it confutes the Sabellians, who deny any distinction in the Holy Trinity; it confutes the Unitarians, who deny the deity of Christ.

Of this mystery Bernard says devoutly and sensibly: "It is rashness to search too far into it. It is piety to believe it. It is life eternal to know it. And we can never have a full understanding of it till we come to enjoy it."

A young French infidel read this verse and was converted. He preached the Gospel at Antwerp, and the pestilence in 1602 swept him from Leyden to glory — the famous Prof. Francis Junius.

2. THE WORD IN CREATION.

"All things severally came into being through Him, and apart from Him not a single thing came into being that came into being." Ps. 33, 6; Col. 1, 17; Heb. 11, 3; 1, 10. The Jehovah, who is praised as the change-less Creator in Ps. 102, 25—27, is none other than Christ. Heb. 1, 10—12; 13, 8. "The universe is God's language, the transformation of language into life."

This confutes the materialists, who say matter is eternal; it confutes the Manichees, who say the world was formed by an evil spirit; it confutes the Platonists, who say the world in part was made by angels and demons.

How noble is nature, the creation of the Word! Let us become devout naturalists. The great astronomer Kepler ends his *Harmony of Worlds* with the words: "I thank Thee, O my Creator and Lord, that Thou hast given me this joy in Thy creation, this delight in the work of Thy hands. I have shown the excellency of Thy works unto men, so far as my finite mind was able to comprehend Thine infinity. If I have said aught unworthy of Thee or aught in which I may have sought my own glory, graciously forgive it."

"In Him was life, and the Life was the light of men."

Thank God! It was sorely needed. Pythagoras admitted the need of divine help to teach man his duty. Socrates admitted his ignorance and the need of divine direction. The mighty Aristotle's last words were, "I entered the world corruptly, I have lived in it anxiously, I quit it in perturbation." So Cicero, so Seneca, so Xenophanes, so Hierocles, so many more. In the first century Varro found no fewer than 300 different gods in Rome, and he found 320 different answers to the one question, "What is the supreme good?"

"In Him was life, and the Life was the light of men."

Christ is the Life, the Living One, having life in Himself and giving life and light to others, John 5, 21. 26; 1 John 1, 1; 5, 11; Acts 13, 47; Rev. 1, 17; Ps. 27, 1; 36, 9; Deut. 30, 20; Is. 49, 6.

Tennyson says: —

> Our little systems have their day;
> They have their day and cease to be;
> They are but broken lights of Thee;
> And Thou, O Lord, art more than they.

In Christ alone is light, life, and salvation; outside of Christ is darkness, death, and damnation.

"The Life was the light of men." Christ is the Light of the world, and He makes Christians to be lights of the world.

We read on the grave of Albrecht Duerer: "The light of the arts and the sun of the artists."

Yes, but he got his light from Christ and used it to glorify Him.

3. THE WORD IN THE FLESH.

"The Word became flesh." 1 John 4, 2; Rom. 1, 3; 8, 3; Phil. 2, 7; Gal. 4, 4; Heb. 2, 14.

The Word *was,* and the Word *became.* God He *was,* man He *became.* God He was from eternity, man He became in time — the God-man! "Great is the mystery of godliness: God was manifest in the flesh," 1 Tim. 3, 16. As Luther sings: —

In our poor mortal flesh and blood
Disguised Himself the eternal Good.

In one person the divine and the human nature were united *truly,* to oppose the Arians; *perfectly,* to

CORREGGIO, † 1534.
"THE WORD BECAME FLESH."

oppose the Apollinarians; *undividedly,* to oppose the Nestorians; *unmixedly,* to oppose the Eutychians.

"The Word became flesh." What honor for us! Surely we ought to treat the human body with the greatest reverence. Novalis thinks "there is but one temple in the world, and that temple is the body of man."

"The Word became flesh." What comfort for us! For all his learning and holiness, Thomas Aquinas was in great terror of thunder and lightning. At all such times he would comfort himself with the sacred words, "The Word became flesh and dwelt among us."

Very good, for the angel had said, "Fear not; for unto you is born this day, in the city of David, a Savior, which is Christ the Lord." And so Dinah M. M. Craik carols: —

> God rest you merry, gentlemen,
> Let nothing you affright;
> For Christ is born of Mary
> Upon this Christmas night.

And Luther exults: —

> What harm can sin and death then do?
> The true God now abides with you.
> Let hell and Satan rage and chafe,
> God is your Brother, ye are safe.

"The Word became flesh."

Ben Jonson says: —

> The Father's wisdom willed it so,
> The Son's obedience knew no No,
>   Both wills were in one stature;
> And as that wisdom had decreed,
> The Word was now made flesh indeed
>   And took on Him our nature.

We join in the greeting of Richard Crashaw: —

> Welcome to our wondering sight,
>   Eternity shut in a span!
> Summer in winter; day in night!
>   Heaven in earth! and God in man!
> Great Little One, whose glorious birth
> Lifts earth to heaven, stoops heaven to earth.

"The Word dwelt among us" — as in a tent.

As Jehovah dwelt in a tabernacle, or tent, with the wanderers in the wilderness, so the Word dwelt with us in the tent of our human body. As Jehovah tented with Israel to lead the wanderers on their way into the wilderness and to hallow their resting-places, so Christ tented with us to teach and guide us and bless us in all our doings. Ex. 25, 8; 29, 45. 46; Is. 4, 5; 57, 15.

Philo says the tent in the wilderness was a symbol of God's intention to send to earth the perfection of His divine virtue. He certainly did so in Christ. The Word tented with us and also revealed Himself to us.

To the Israelites and even to Moses the sight of God's glory was terrible, Ex. 33. Not so the glory of Christ to His disciples. "And with delight we beheld His glory." And what glory! "Glory worthy of the Only-begotten and worthy of the Father that gave the glory."

Jehovah was in the Word made flesh, John 12, 41; Is. 40, 5; 66, 2. 18; 60, 2. The Jewish Targums also say that the Word is the Shekinah, or glory, of Jehovah made known in the Messiah. As the light shines through the lantern, so Christ's glory flashed through Him in His miracles, John 2, 11; 11, 40, in His words, in His transfiguration, passion, resurrection, and ascension.

The Tabernacle was "the tent of meeting." "There will I meet with you to speak there unto thee, and there will I meet with the *children of Israel*," Ex. 29, 42. In Christ, the Word, God meets with us. "And He will tabernacle with us in heaven and on the new earth," Rev. 7, 15; 21, 3.

The Word was "full of grace and truth" — faithfulness. He radiated grace and truthfulness, they shone out of Him. People "wondered at the gracious words which proceeded out of His mouth," Luke 4, 22. And they were impressed by His truthfulness. "Master, we know that Thou art true and teachest the way of God in truth," Matt. 22, 16.

In the Gospel we still behold Him "full of grace and truth." His grace is truthful, and His truth is gracious; the two streams meet and mingle their waters into one. His grace and truth beget trust and love in us. "May He who was full of grace and truth impress His character upon mine! Grace — eagerness to show favor; truth — truthfulness, sincerity, honor, for His mercy's sake" — found in the diary of Livingstone.

4. THE WORD REJECTED.

There was a man sent from God whose name was John. The same came for testimony, to bear witness of the Light that all men through Him might believe. He was not that Light, but was sent to bear witness of the Light. John beareth witness of Him — "Was it less true of Luther?" asks F. D. Maurice — and crieth with emotion, "This was He of whom I spake, The One coming after me is come before me because He was before I was."

Did the world gladly accept that Light? The world madly rejected that Light.

That was the true Light, which, coming into the world, lighted every man.

Christ was the *true* Light — opposed to all false light of the Gentiles.

Christ was the *true* Light — opposed to all types and shadows.

Christ was the *true* Light — opposed to all derived light.

Christ was the *true* Light — opposed to all that is ordinary and common.

He was in the world, and the world was made by Him, and yet the world acknowledged Him not. He came into His own home, and yet His own home folks did not receive Him in welcome.

His own "brethren" at first refused Him; His own home town, Nazareth, would kill Him; His own nation crucified Him. The Jews cut their own Jehovah.

Can we not see a tear drop as John pens these words? Does not our heart break as we read these words? Writing the music for "He was despised," Handel burst out weeping.

"Coming events cast their shadows before." This has been called "the Gospel of the Rejection."

Francesco Basily, director of the Conservatory of Music at Milan, rejected an applicant "who showed no disposition for music" — and it was the great Verdi!

"I have swept the heavens with my telescope and have found no God," said the supremely silly Lalande. He was like the cat that dissected a nightingale and found no song.

"And the Light shineth in darkness; and the darkness comprehended it not" — tragic. If we read "overcame it not," the opposition is also tragic, but the Light is victorious.

5. THE WORD RECEIVED.

"But whosoever received Him, to them gave He the power, right, privilege, to become children of God, to them that believe on His name."

The dying Melanchthon said to his friends, "I have those words always before me, 'As many as received Him, to them gave He power to become children of God, to them that believe on His name.'"

Yes, what a Christmas-gift Christ gives us — the right to become children of God! What Christmas-gift Christians give Christ — as dear children be ye imitators of God!

"Who was begotten, not of bloods, father and mother, nor of the will of the flesh, the natural strong sex impulse, nor of the will of a husband, but of God."

Clear as crystal and clear as a clarion is John's testimony to the miraculous virgin birth of Christ, Matt. 1, 18—25; Luke 1, 20—28.

Some manuscripts read: "Who were begotten, not of blood nor by the will of the flesh nor by the will of man, but by God." 1 Pet. 1, 23; 1 John 3, 9; John 1, 18; 3, 16; Eph. 1, 5.

This is the first mention of regeneration, and note how carefully John fences it off against errors. Negatively he states what is *not* the source, not man in any degree or manner. Positively he states what *is* the source, God alone. And that is true in the very nature of birth — as in natural generation, so in spiritual generation. This wonderful birth of the Christians is patterned after the miraculous virgin birth of Christ, Matt. 1, 18—25; Luke 1, 26—38.

"For out of His fulness we, all of us, have received."

What a picture! On the one side Christ, the great Giver; on the other are we, the receivers. On October 17, 1830, Dr. Andrew Bonar had a "secret joyful hope" that he really believed in Christ, and fulness and freeness of God's grace filled his heart. "I did nothing but receive."

And what are all we receiving?

"Grace for grace," one gift of grace in place of another and each gift bigger and better than the other, ever flowing and ever growing.

And we get as much as we take by faith. And the very best is yet to come in heaven — "We shall see Him as He is."

The Duchess of Gordon heard a Scotch pedler pray, "O Lord, give us grace to feel our need of grace. O Lord, give us grace to receive grace. O Lord, give us grace to ask for grace. O Lord, give us grace to use grace when grace is given."

We pray with W. M. Czamanske: —

> Dear Father, Fount of every grace,
>   Give grace that I may feel
> My need of grace in every place —
>   To me this grace reveal.
>
> Oh, grant me grace to ask for grace
>   And grace Thy gift to take,
> Then grace for grace to use Thy grace,
>   For my Redeemer's sake.

"For the Law was given through Moses; the grace and the truth came into being through Jesus Christ." Rom. 4, 16; 6, 14. 15; Gal. 5, 4.

For the first time, at last, He who is named the Word is introduced by His personal name, Jesus, and by His official title, Christ. And here we find a triple contrast.

1. Law and grace. Law demands perfection as God is perfect, and it worketh wrath and condemns.

Grace quickens the dead, helps the helpless, and saves the sinner.

2. The Law was laid down as a lifeless statute, dead and deadening.

Grace came into being, living and life-giving.

3. The Law was laid down through Moses, a messenger with a message which he delivered, but to which he had no personal relation.

Grace came through Jesus Christ, and He is Himself the grace and Gospel He brought. He is Himself the Way, the Truth, and the Life which He gives to us.

Ruskin declares all his "later writings, without exception have been directed to maintain and illustrate the great truth expressed in this passage." And he says "the root of almost every heresy from which the Church of Rome has suffered has been the effort of man to *earn,* rather than to *receive,* his salvation."

"God none hath ever yet seen; one, only-begotten God, who is in the bosom of the Father, He it is who interpreted Him."

When on earth, Christ was God's Exegete, official Spokesman. True God, Jesus knew all about God. As an eye-witness and ear-witness He could talk with full understanding of the Father; being man, He knew all about man, and He could talk intelligently about him. He knew *what* to talk, and He knew *how* to talk. "Hear ye Him!" Hear and heed!

He talked with words, and He talked with works, and actions speak louder than words. The whole earthly life of Christ was an exegesis of the Father, revealed the innermost heart of the Father to us poor sinners, proved plainly that God is Love.

In Prov. 8, 22—30 the eternal Wisdom is the Word of God; and this Word is the Law, *Thora,* in Ecclus. 24. There is a striking likeness between that Word and John's Word; all that is said of that Word is fufilled in the true Word, Jesus Christ. Christ is the Wisdom of God, 1 Cor. 1, 31. Cyprian of Carthage in his *Testimonia* calls Christ the Wisdom and the *Word of God.* In his "Hymn to Heavenly Beauty" Edmund Spenser says: —

> There in His bosome Sapience doth sit,
> The soueraine dearling of the Deitie.

The Word explains God, and that explains why "His name is called the Word of God," Rev. 19, 13; 1 John 1, 1. I reveal myself by my word — "Thy speech bewrayeth thee," Matt. 26, 73. "The style is the man," says Buffon. My word is myself uttered. God as a Person reveals Himself to us as persons by His Word. The Word is God-uttered. God in Christ is shown to the world in this Gospel.

On April 2, 1650, Oliver Cromwell wrote his son Richard: "Seek the Lord and His face continually; let this be the business of your life and strength and let all things be subservient and in order to this. You cannot find nor behold the face of God but in Christ; therefore labor to know God in Christ; which the Scripture makes to be the sum of all, even life eternal."

Arnold of Rugby and Charles Kingsley confessed they could only comprehend God as revealed in Jesus Christ. James Russell Lowell, our American poet, in his last days turned from Unitarianism to Christ for salvation. Joseph H. Choate, the great lawyer and ambassador to Great Britain, turned from Unitarianism to Christianity. Justice Miller of the Supreme Court renounced Unitarianism and joined a Christian Church. William Cullen Bryant, the American poet and editor, in his late seventies at Naples made a formal confession of his faith in Christ. Prof. Barrett Wendell of Harvard was wont to tell his students how his relative Oliver Wendell Holmes regretted he had slurred his father's Christian faith. He lost all interest in Unitarianism and attended a Christian church. A. Bronson Alcott called a meeting on April 14, 1870, at the house of Dr. Withrow and in the presence of Unitarians, Universalists, Sweden-borgians, Free Religionists, and Evangelicals confessed his faith in Christ and His atonement. President Warren of Boston University reported the whole in the *New York Christian Advocate* of April 17, 1870. Schleier-macher was a rationalist, but at death turned to Christ for salvation. Ritschl could not bear Paul Gerhardt's "O Bleeding Head and Wounded," but at death turned to it for comfort. The dying Horace Bushnell feared his Ritschlian writing would do great harm and then prayed, "O Lord Jesus, I trust for mercy only in the shed blood that Thou didst offer on Calvary." Lord Kelvin, the great scientist, confessed his greatest discovery was the discovery of God in Christ. The physician Abraham Capadose and the poet Isaac da Costa were baptized the same day at Leyden in Holland. What had brought these Jews to faith in their Savior? They told Rudolf Koegel it was the study of this prolog.

Have you by faith received Christ into your heart?

> Though Christ a thousand times in Bethlehem be born,
> If He's not born in thee, thy heart is still forlorn;
> The Christ on Golgotha alone can never save thy soul,
> The Christ in thine own heart alone can make thee whole.

That is true, and so we preach to you till Christ is formed in you.
And with the great Luther we'll pray his touching cradle carol: —

> Ah! dearest Jesus, holy Child,
> Make Thee a bed, soft, undefiled,
> Within my heart that it may be
> A quiet chamber kept for Thee.

CHAPTER II

THE BAPTIST'S WITNESS.

John 1, 19—51.

I.

THE TESTIMONY.

1. TO A COMMITTEE OF THE RULERS.

THE Baptist's testimony stirred the nation mightily. Might he be the Messiah?

The Jews, the Judeans, the Sanhedrin, the rulers, were alert and promptly sent a committee of priests and Levites in order to question him about his doings.

"Thou, who art thou?"

And he confessed and denied not, but confessed, *"I am not the Christ."*

"What, then? Art thou Elias?" Mal. 4, 5.

"I am not" — not the one you expect.

"Art thou that prophet?" Deut. 18, 15.

"No" — not the one you mean.

"Who art thou? — that we may give an answer to them that sent us. What sayest thou of thyself?"

"I am the voice of one crying in the wilderness, 'Make straight the way of the Lord,' as said the prophet Isaias," 40, 3.

2. TO PHARISEES.

And Pharisees were sent. And they asked him, "Why baptizest thou, then, if thou be not that Christ nor Elias, neither that prophet?"

"I baptize with water; among you standeth One whom ye know not; He it is who is coming after me, whose sandal strap to unloose I am not worthy."

These things were done in Bethabara, beyond Jordan, where John was baptizing. Jerome says it was the place where Joshua had crossed over into the Promised Land, the southern ford of the Jordan. Bethabara means "the House of Crossing," or "Fordtown." It is also called Bethany, "the House of the Boat," or "Ferrytown."

3. TO OTHERS.

1. The next day John gazed at Jesus coming unto him and saith, "Behold the Lamb of God, which taketh away the sin of the world. This is He of whom I said, After me cometh a man who is come before me. And I knew Him not; but that He should be made manifest to Israel, therefore am I come, baptizing with water."

And John bare record, "I saw the Spirit descending from heaven like a dove, and it abode upon Him. And I knew Him not; but He that sent me to baptize with water, the same said unto me, Upon whom

JOHN AND THE PHARISEES. John 1, 24—26.   W. STEINHAUSEN.

thou shalt see the Spirit descending and remaining on Him, the same is He which baptizeth with the Holy Ghost, and I bare record that this is the Son of God" — Elect of God.

2. Again, the next day after, the Baptist stood and two of his disciples, and looking upon Jesus as He was walking about, he saith, "Behold the Lamb of God!"

II.

THE TESTIMONY EXAMINED.

It is positive and fivefold.

a. Jesus is superior. "He that cometh after me is preferred before me, whose shoe's latchet I am not worthy to unloose," vv. 15. 27. 30.

According to the Rabbis it was too mean for a scholar to untie the sandal-string of his teacher, but the Baptist held himself too mean to do so mean a service; so superior is Jesus.

b. Jesus is eternal. "He was before me," vv. 15. 30. He is eternal — "In the beginning was the Word," v. 3. "He is before all things," Col. 1, 17. The superiority is in the priority.

c. Jesus is the Source of spiritual life. "He baptizeth with the Holy Ghost," v. 33. Acts 1, 5; 2, 4; 10, 44; 19, 6.

d. Jesus is the Savior. The great Isaiah in his great fifty-third chapter made the great prophecy about the Servant of the Lord who would be sacrificed for the sins of the people; the greater John baptized Him, laid his finger upon Him, and testified, "Behold the Lamb of God, which taketh away the sin of the world." He is the great, the divine Lamb; the true Passover Lamb; the Lamb of God, provided by God and acceptable to God, Jer. 11, 19; 1 Pet. 1, 19; 1 Cor. 5, 7. He beareth the sin by taking it upon Himself in our stead; He taketh it away by His death as our Substitute; He was made a curse for us, He made a vicarious sacrifice for sin. He taketh away and keeps on taking away, keeps on applying the eternal, once-made sacrifice. He taketh away the sin of the world. He made a universal atonement. He died for all. All have been pardoned; they that refuse to accept the pardon deny the Lord that bought them, 2 Pet. 2, 1.

> Chief of sinners though I be,
> Jesus shed His blood for me.

e. Jesus "is the Son of God," the Elect of God, v. 34.

III.

THE RESULT.

1. TWO FOLLOW JESUS.

"Behold the Lamb of God!" The two disciples that stood with the Baptist understood the Baptist and followed Jesus.

Jesus turned around and, seeing them following Him, asked, —

"What seek ye?"

"Rabbi, where art Thou staying?"

"Come, and ye shall see."

So they came and saw where He lodged, and they remained with Him that day; it was about the tenth hour. A fruitful interview.

2. THE TWO DISCIPLES BRING TWO MORE.

One of the two disciples who heard John and followed Jesus was Andrew, Simon Peter's brother. He first findeth his own brother Simon and saith to him, "We have found the Messiah," which means Christ, the Anointed, and brought him to Jesus. The Great Discovery — Christ!

Having looked intently upon him, Jesus said, "Thou art Simon, the son of John; thou shalt be called Cephas," which means Peter, a Stone, a part of a rock.

Nifanius names three Popes so ignorant to think Cephas comes from

THE FIRST DISCIPLES.   S. ITTENBACH.

Cephalus, a head, showing Peter's headship of the Church. Abraham Calov charges Cardinal Bellarmine with the same foolishness. Lightfoot says "the Christian Church has known nothing more sad and destructive" than the Romish attempt to make Peter the "rock" on which the Church is built.

From this "first" some think John next brought his brother James to Jesus. That is the way the Church grew — one brought the other. One and one make two. Two and two make four. Have you found Christ? Have you sought and taught and brought your brother? If not, why not?

A London Sunday-school was told, "I want each of you to bring a new scholar next Sunday." Little Mary Wood saw two dirty, ragged, barefooted boys fighting. She brought them to Sunday-school. Thirty years after 10,000 people in Exeter Hall were told, "We are those boys" — Moody and Sankey, who had brought many sinners to Christ. Sankey wrote: —

> Little Mary Wood
> Did the very best she could;
> Let us follow Mary's plan
> And do the very best we can.

Now, will *you?*

3. TWO MORE ARE "FOUND."

The next day Jesus would go forth into Galilee and findeth Philip of Bethsaida and saith, "Follow Me." Did he?

Philip findeth Nathanael — of Cana in Galilee, John 21, 2, likely the son of Tolmai, Bartholomew — and saith to him, "We have found Him of whom Moses in the Law, and the prophets, wrote, Jesus, son of Joseph, the man from Nazareth."

"Can any good thing come out of Nazareth?" All Galileans were despised boors, and Nazareth had a bad name.

"Come and see." "Taste and see that the Lord is good," Ps. 34, 8.

Jesus saw Nathanael coming to Him and saith about him, "Behold a real Israelite, in whom is no guile." Ps. 32, 2; Is. 53, 9.

What a compliment! A fierce papist said to Bishop Jewel, "I should love thee if thou wast not a Lutheran. In thy faith thou art a heretic, but surely in thy life thou art an angel." The infidel Lord Peterborough visited Fénelon and said, "If I stay here much longer, I shall become a Christian in spite of myself."

Says Nathanael to Jesus, "Whence dost Thou know me?"

"Before Philip called you, being under the fig-tree, I knew you." Prov. 15, 3.

"Rabbi, Thou art the Son of God, Thou art the King of Israel!" Luke 1, 32, 33; Matt. 2, 2. He came, he saw, he was conquered.

"Because I said to you, 'I saw you under the fig-tree,' do you believe? Greater things than this you shall see."

And He said to him, "Amen, amen," "Verily, verily," the first of twenty-five times these words are used by Christ, by Christ only, in this gospel only, and only to introduce something solemn. When repeated, "yes" and "no" are oaths, the Talmud tells us.

"Verily, verily, I say unto you, Ye shall see heaven open and the angels of God ascending and descending upon the Son of Man."

Jacob, the original Israelite, in a dream saw a ladder and the angels of God ascending and descending, and he called the place Bethel, House of God, Gen. 28, 13.

What Jacob saw in a dream Nathanael and all other real Israelites, in whom is no guile, shall see in reality.

Here the Son of God uses His favorite title of Himself — Son of Man. Dan. 7, 13. 14; Acts 7, 56. He is true God and true Man, the ladder between earth and heaven, the ladder upon which God came to man and man can come to God and find his true Father and heavenly home; He is the true *Scala Santa*. We shall see this Son of Man come in the glory of His Father with His angels, Matt. 16, 27; 26, 64; Mark 14, 62.

Aretius counts twenty-one names of Christ in this one chapter: 1. The Word. 2. God. 3. Life. 4. Light. 5. The true Light. 6. The only-Begotten of the Father. 7. Full of grace and truth. 8. Jesus Christ. 9. The only-begotten Son. 10. The Lord. 11. The Lamb of God. 12. Jesus. 13. A Man. 14. Son of God. 15. Rabbi. 16. Teacher. 17. Messiah. 18. Christ. 19. The Son of Joseph. 20. The King of Israel. 21. The Son of Man.

CHAPTER III

JESUS AT THE MARRIAGE AT CANA.

John 2, 1—12.

Lord, who at Cana's wedding-feast
Didst as a Guest appear,
Thou dearer far than earthly guest,
Vouchsafe Thy presence here;
For holy Thou indeed dost prove
The marriage vow to be,
Proclaiming it a type of love
Between the Church and Thee.

I.

JESUS HONORS MARRIAGE WITH HIS PRESENCE.

THE third day there was a wedding in Cana of Galilee, likely on a Wednesday, according to the Talmud.

The mother of Jesus was there, and Jesus also was bidden, and His disciples, to the marriage.

II.

JESUS BLESSES MARRIAGE WITH HIS FIRST MIRACLE.

All went merry as a marriage-bell, when suddenly a dark specter loomed up — the wine gave out! How embarrassing! That Oriental couple would feel disgraced all the days of their lives. Wine did not flow like water; they were temperate people.

Now the mother of Jesus saith unto Him, "They have no wine."

Jesus saith unto her, "Woman." A tender word in Greek; He uses the same word to her from the cross when He gives her into the care of the disciple whom He loved, John 19, 26. Ulysses used it to his wife Penelope and Caesar Augustus to Queen Cleopatra: "Take courage, O woman, and keep a good heart."

"What to Me and thee?" — a phrase from the Hebrew gently putting her aside, as we would say, "Leave that to me." These words are dead against the immaculate conception of Mary and against all prayers to her to pray for us.

"Mine hour is not yet come." Is that an implied promise His help would come when His hour was come? Mary seems to take it that way, for she said to the servants, "Whatsoever He may say to you do."

Follow Mary — tell your wants to Jesus and leave the rest to Him.

Obey Mary — "Whatsoever He saith unto you do." Whatsoever — do. Said the Duke of Wellington to an objecting officer, "Sir, I did not ask your opinion; I gave you my orders, and I expect to have them obeyed."

Now, six stone water-jars were there, set after the manner of the ceremonial washing of the Jews, holding two or three firkins apiece, about twenty-two gallons to a jar. Mark 7, 3.

Jesus saith to them, "Fill the water-pots with water." And they filled them up to the brim. He saith unto them, "Draw out now and bear to the ruler of the feast." And they bare.

Looks like a practical wedding joke; looks are deceiving.

Again: —
> The conscious water saw its God and blushed.

> The modest water, touched by grace divine,
> Confessed its God and blushed itself to wine.

When the ruler of the feast had tasted the water that had been made wine and knew not whence it was, (but the servants who had drawn the water knew,) the ruler of the feast called to the bridegroom and with mock gravity in the form of a complaint paid him a fine compliment — "Every man setteth forth the good wine first, and when men have well drunk, then that which is inferior. Thou hast kept the good wine until now."

No doubt the merry company hilariously applauded the merry remark.

Bengel observes: "The ignorance of the ruler proves the goodness of the wine; the knowledge of the servants, the reality of the miracle."

This beginning of signs did Jesus in Cana of Galilee and manifested forth His glory; and His disciples believed in Him — more firmly.

The Savior at a marriage — what a glad surprise! Jesus was not a stern, austere ascetic like that rough desert preacher John the Baptist. Jesus was not an Oriental despot, coming along in pomp and pride and power, too haughty to deign to mingle with His people. Busy as He was with the weighty matters of His Father's business, the holy Son of God yet took time to go to a marriage. Marriage was God's first institution, in Paradise, before sin had yet entered the world. Though sin had woefully corrupted this blessed state, yet marriage itself is honorable in all and the bed undefiled.

11   THE CLEANSING OF THE TEMPLE

St. John 2:15

Jesus honored this honorable institution by His holy presence. The Son of Man was human, and nothing human was foreign to Him. In all things it behooved Him to be made like His brethren, Heb. 2, 17. He rejoiced with them that do rejoice. It was a small town wedding, a homely and homespun affair, and He entered fully into the spirit of the festive occasion. He was one of them, genial, jovial, joyful with the merry-makers. He came eating and drinking, and for that some sneered at Him as a glutton and wine-bibber.

"Forbidding to marry" is a "doctrine of devils," not from Christ, but from Antichrist, 1 Tim. 4, 3.

Jesus hallowed our common life, especially our family life. Jesus rescued marriage and the family from polygamy and celibacy and restored it to its original purity and made the relation of husband and wife a type of the sacred union of Christ and His bride, the Church. The family is God's first institution, and it is to be the nursery of Church and State.

Invite Jesus to your wedding and keep Him as the best Friend and Guest of the family.

Jesus turned water into wine. This was the Savior's first sign — sign of what? He manifested forth His glory — what glory? Glory as of the Only-begotten of the Father, the Son of God. Also glory of the Son of Man, our Brother in the flesh. It was a sign of His divine power, also a sign of His human brotherly sympathy. He forestalled the sadness with gladness. His first sign was not to multiply loaves and fishes to still hunger, but to create wine to greaten joy; for wine maketh glad the heart of man. He did not give a bare necessity, but a luxury.

God's first institution in Paradise is honored by Christ's first miracle. Christ could fast, and He could feast. He would not turn stones into bread for Himself, but He turned water into wine for others.

How human! How winsome! Who is not delighted with this de-liciously delicate trait in His character? What a lovely view we get of the heart of our Lord! How this charm draws us close to Him! Luther truly says: "We cannot draw Christ too deeply into the flesh." Jesus hallowed our common, earthly joys. Jesus a kill-joy? Jesus is the true Joy-bringer! The sunny Son of Man brings sunshine into our lives, brings flowers into our homes, sets the birds and hearts a-singing.

> . . . the best is yet to be,
> The last of life for which the first was made.

We just can't help singing the Crusaders' Hymn: —

> Beautiful Savior,
> King of creation,
>   Son of God and Son of Man!
> Truly I'd love Thee,
> Truly I'd serve Thee,
>   Light of my soul, my Joy, my Crown!

Let us pray in the words of J. F. Clarke: —

> Dear Friend, whose presence in the house,
>   Whose gracious word benign,
> Could once, at Cana's wedding-feast,
>   Change water into wine,
>
> Come, visit us, and when dull work
>   Grows weary, line on line,
> Revive our souls and make us see
>   Life's water glow as wine.
>
> Gay mirth shall deepen into joy,
>   Earth's hopes shall grow divine,
> When Jesus visits us to turn
>   Life's water into wine.
>
> The social talk, the evening fire,
>   The homely household shrine,
> Shall glow with angel-visits when
>   The Lord pours out the wine.
>
> For when self-seeking turns to love,
>   Which knows not mine and thine,
> The miracle again is wrought
>   And water changed to wine.

And we add: —

> O blest the house, whate'er befall,
> Where Jesus Christ is all in all;
> Yea, if He were not dwelling there,
> How poor and dark and void it were!
>
> Then here will I and mine to-day
> A solemn cov'nant make and say:
> "Though all the world forsake Thy Word,
> I and my house will serve the Lord.

It is believed this Cana is Kefr Kenna, still a prosperous village of about 1,000. In 722 the English St. Wilibald spent a day there, and four hundred years later another English pilgrim, Saewulf, spoke of the convent of "Holy Architriclinos," named in honor of the "ruler of the feast," built by the Empress Helena, mother of Constantine the Great. It is six miles north of Nazareth. Josephus with two hundred men marched in one night to Tiberias from Cana. A little west is Jotapata, which Josephus defended against Vespasian. Near by is Gath-Hepher, where Jonah was born, 2 Kings 14, 25.

This miracle has been most popular from the first. Of the fifty-two marble sarcophagi found in the catacombs and now in the Lateran sixteen have carvings of this wedding. Frescoes and mosaics in many churches show this scene. Tintoretto's genius is shown in his great picture of the wedding in Santa Maria della Salute in Venice. Rudolf Schaefer has a fine "Wedding of Cana" and Edward von Gebhardt a gripping "Christ and the Bridal Couple."

After the wedding, Jesus and His mother and His brothers and His disciples went down to Capernaum, where they stayed "not many days."

Who were His "brothers"? Stepbrothers, children of Joseph by a former wife, says Epiphanius — the oldest and simplest answer. They were Joseph, Simon, Jude, and James, "the Lord's brother," the first pastor of Jerusalem, Acts 1, 14; 12, 17; 15, 13; 1 Cor. 15, 7. Grandsons of Jude were leaders of the Church under Domitian, says Eusebius.

CHAPTER IV.

JESUS CLEARS THE TEMPLE-COURT.

John 2, 13—25.

I.

THE NEED.

THE Jews paid their yearly Temple-tax, and they had to pay it in the sacred Jewish half-shekel. And so the Jews from all parts of the world had to exchange their foreign money for the Jewish money. Bankers, or money-changers, were needed, and many of them, to serve the millions crowding the Holy City at the Passover. That was quite necessary, — but not their usury of ten to twelve per cent.! Instead of bringing their Passover lamb from Rome, Babylonia, and the rest of the world, the people would buy it at Jerusalem; also the needed salt, oil, meal, herbs, etc., Deut. 14, 24. So cattle-dealers were needed, many of them. These bankers and merchants crowded the Court of the Gentiles on the fourteen-acre Temple area and the surrounding colonnades.

The worst thing is the corruption of the best thing. The sons of Annas, the former high priest, held concessions which gave them a monopoly of all the business transacted in that place. They received the rental of the stalls and booths placed there for traders and money-changers. To what extent they shared the profits of the extortions levied there cannot now be known precisely. But the extortions were prodigious and notorious, and they fell most heavily upon the poor. Usurious charges were exacted by the money-changers. One dealer charged $4 for a pair of pigeons worth eight cents.

What are you going to do about it?

One did something.

II.

THE ACTION.

The Lord of the Temple came suddenly to His Temple and found His Temple profaned. His rich red blood boiled with righteous wrath. He made a scourge of small cords, and drove them all out of the Temple-court, and poured out the changers' money, and overthrew the tables, or banks.

III.

THE AUTHORITY.

"Take these hence; make not My Father's house a business house."

His disciples later remembered that it was written, "The zeal of Thine house hath eaten Me up," Ps. 69, 9.

Have you a zeal for God's house? Then why do you not send more missionaries? That is what a heathen Hindu asked. What is your answer?

Jesus fulfilled what had been foretold long ago: "Behold, the Lord whom ye seek, shall suddenly come to His Temple; and He shall sit as a refiner and purifier of silver," Mal. 3, 1. 2. And He will come again, and sit, and sift, and shift — some to His left hand, some to His right.

Where will you be?

We rub our eyes in wonder at the violence of this radical and robust Reformer. We are astounded at the dash and daring of the strange countryman in the Holy City. We are mystified that this young carpenter got out without a scratch. Why didn't one of the many ruined bankers and cattlemen rise up in fury and club, floor, and brain Him on the spot? On the one hand, "My strength is as the strength of ten because my heart is pure." On the other hand, "Conscience doth make cowards of us all." Richard III says: —

> My conscience hath a thousand tongues,
> And every tongue brings in a several tale,
> And every tale condemns me for a villain.

The majesty of His moral grandeur awed the mob, and they cowered in the corners. To clear the Temple was the king's right and duty. King Hezekiah and King Josiah had done this, and the saying went they would return as the Messiah. By His work Christ honored His Father, and by His Word He offered Himself to His nation as their Messiah.

IV.

THE CHALLENGE.

The Jews, likely the Temple police, demanded His warrant for His revolutionary act.

"What sign showest Thou to us, seeing that Thou doest these things?" Do some miracle to prove yourself the Messiah, having the right to clear the Temple-court.

BIRD'S-EYE VIEW OF PRESENT-DAY JERUSALEM.

V.

THE REPLY.

Jesus replied, "Destroy this temple, and in three days I will raise it up."

"Forty and six years was this Temple in building, and wilt Thou rear it up in three days?" But He was speaking of the temple of His body. 1 Cor. 3, 16. 17; 6, 19; 2 Cor. 6, 16.

Christ clearly foresaw His death and His resurrection; and He foresaw the end of the Temple service and the rise of the Christian Church.

When therefore He was risen from the dead, His disciples remembered that He had said this unto them; and they believed the Scripture and the word which Jesus had said. Ps. 16, 10.

Godet says: "It is in Christ's person this great drama is enacted. The Messiah perishes; the Temple falls. The Messiah lives again; the true temple rises on the ruins of the symbolical Temple. For in the kingdom of God there is no simple restoration. Every revival is at the same time an advance."

VI.

THE RESULT.

"The Jews," the profiteering rulers, never forgave Jesus for this act and plotted to destroy Him.

On the other hand, "many believed in His name when they saw the signs which He did." But Jesus was not trusting Himself to them because He knew all men and needed not that any should testify of man; for He knew what was in man. Jer. 17, 10; 20, 12.

In the course of time shameful abuses had crept into the Church of God. In the crassest way forgiveness of sins was sold for cold cash. The corruption was deep and wide. It was deplored and denounced privately and publicly, by priest and prince, by preacher and professor, by Council and Reichstag. All to no avail. This is history. Martin Luther made a scourge of Rom. 1, 16. 17: "The just shall live by faith" and drove out the merchants of the "holy business" and turned the den of thieves into a house of prayer.

Has Christ driven the thieves out of your heart and made it a house of prayer?

Are you driving the thieves out of the house of prayer and keeping clean the Church of God?

In clearing the Temple-court, Jesus claimed lordship. His lordship was proved by His oversight of the Temple; by His foresight of the destruction and raising of the temple of His body; by His insight of men. His lordship was accepted by His disciples and by the Jews that believed on Him.

Do I submit to Him? Do I admit Him into my heart? Do I permit Him to rule me? Do I commit myself wholly in trust to Him? Do I transmit His Gospel to others?

> Enter in, Lord, cleanse Thy temple,
> Give the grace to put away
> All that hinders, all that's doubtful;
> O'er my life hold blessed sway.

CHAPTER V.

JESUS AND NICODEMUS.

John 3, 1—21.

ICODEMUS was a scribe, a Rabbi, a professor of theology; he was a Pharisee, a strict church-member, and also a patriotic Jew; he was a ruler of the Jews, a member of the Supreme Court, the Sanhedrin. This personage came to Jesus by night. Why by night? We are not told, and so we do not know. Be the reason what it may, he went by night; but he went.

Jesus is greeted by the great Rabbi — "Rabbi, we know that Thou art a Teacher come from God; for no man is able to do these signs which Thou art working except God be with him."

Truly astounding words from a great Rabbi to a young country carpenter. At any rate, they prove the deep impression Christ had already made upon Jerusalem. Was he paying a sincere compliment? Was he flattering or patronizing? Was he saying something just to break the ice and open the conversation?

Whatever it was, the young carpenter Rabbi of Galilee of the Gentiles coldly ignored the remark of the important personage; without a warm word of welcome, grateful recognition, or inviting encouragement He looked him straight in the eye and went straight to the heart of the matter by seriously saying, "Verily, verily, I say unto thee, Except a man be born again, he is not able to see the kingdom of God." Mark 10, 15; Matt. 18, 3; Luke 18, 17.

A teacher is not needed; needed is a Savior.

In 1752 Whitefield wrote to Benjamin Franklin: "I bid you, my friend, remember that One at whose bar we shall both presently appear hath solemnly declared that without it [the new birth] we shall in no wise see His kingdom."

That was a staggering blow to Nicodemus. Gentiles, to be sure, had to be "born again," but an orthodox Jew? An insult! Nicodemus tried to hide his confusion by retorting with a sickly smile, "How can a man be born when he is old? Can he enter a second time into his mother's womb and be born?"

DALLMANN, JOHN.   [145]   10

How supremely silly even great officers and learned men can be when they try to avoid facing squarely a personal demand of Christ! They actually try to make out Christ a fool. Wesley complained: "Oh, how hard it is to be shallow enough for a polite audience!" Westcott says: "The great mystery of religion is not the punishment, but the forgiveness, of sins; not the natural permanence of character, but spiritual regeneration."

Jesus could very properly have broken off the talk right here, but He

JESUS AND NICODEMUS.

calmly passed over the clumsy joke and simply and solemnly repeated, "Verily, verily, I say unto thee, 'Except a man have been born of water and the Spirit, he cannot enter into the kingdom of God.'"

Even a man with so much civil morality as Nicodemus was yet outside the kingdom of God. Even he had need to be born anew in order to enter God's kingdom. That news was indeed humiliating.

Why the need?

"That which hath been born of the flesh is flesh; and that which hath been born of the Spirit is spirit."

Nicodemus was born of the "flesh," of sinful parents, and so was "flesh," was sinful. In order to enter the spiritual kingdom of God, he had to be spiritual, born again, of the Spirit of God, in the water of Holy Baptism. Nicodemus was staggered, he marveled.

"Marvel not that I said unto thee, 'Ye must be born again.' The wind bloweth where it listeth, and thou hearest the sound thereof, but knowest not whence it cometh and whither it goeth. So is every one that hath been born of the Spirit."

In connection with Eccl. 11, 5 we see the way of the wind and natural birth is a mystery. So is also the new birth, the spiritual birth. And the new reborn is free; he only is free from the slavery of sin and come into the glorious freedom of God. "Where the Spirit of the Lord is, there is liberty," 2 Cor. 3, 17.

When Summerfield came to America, he was asked where he was born. "In Dublin and in Liverpool," answered the wise and witty Irishman. In Dublin he was born of the flesh, in Liverpool he was born again of the Spirit. You really begin to live when you are born again.

Nicodemus was now thoroughly chastened; he dropped his airy manner and meekly asked, "How can these things be?"

Jesus does not let up, but shows up the specialist's ignorance in his own department. "Art thou the teacher of Israel and understandest thou not these things?" If the teacher himself flunks in so important a matter, what can we look for in the others?

Verily, verily, I say unto thee, We speak that we do know and testify that we have seen, and ye receive not our witness. They rejected the Baptist's baptism, Matt. 21, 26.

If I have told you earthly things and ye believe not, how shall ye believe if I tell you heavenly things? And no man hath ascended up to heaven but He that came down from heaven, the Son of Man, which is in heaven — therefore able to tell of heavenly things. And as Moses lifted up the serpent in the wilderness, Num. 21, 4—9, even so must the Son of Man be lifted up — on the cross and in the ascension, in order that every one that believeth may in Him have eternal life.

Christ is the only Life-giver to a serpent-bitten world. Dr. Cruciger said, "I die with weak faith, but yet with faith." Amid the splendor of a triumphal procession a courtier asked the king, "What is wanting?" "Continuance." We have continuance, life eternal, endless and glorious.

"For God so loved the world that He gave His only-begotten Son," — unique, unlike any other, — "that whosoever believeth in Him should not perish, but have everlasting life." The Gospel in a nutshell, says Luther.

A young college man read this verse. "God so loved the world" — that is big enough for me. "That He gave His only-begotten Son" — that is provision enough for me. "That whosoever believeth in Him" — that is definite enough for me. "Should not perish, but have everlasting life" — that is sure enough for me. This verse saved him.

Richard Baxter says: "I thank God for this word 'whosoever.' Did it read, there is mercy for Richard Baxter, I am so vile, so sinful, that I would have thought it must have meant some other Richard Baxter; but the word 'whosoever' includes the worst of all the Baxters that ever lived."

Luther says when his translation of the Bible was printed, a slip of paper fell to the floor. The printer's little daughter picked it up and read, "God so loved the world that He gave" — the rest was not printed. Taught to dread God, this new light on God filled her with joy. When the mother asked why she was so joyful, the girl handed her the paper. The mother was puzzled: "He gave — what was it He gave?" The girl was puzzled, but only for a moment; then she said quickly, "I don't know; but if God loved us well enough to give us *anything,* we need not be afraid of Him." Great logician and great theologian, that girl. But what did He give? His unique Son!

Plutarch says a king was taken to task for giving an enormous present to a friend. "What! would you not have me be liberal? Let the world know that, when the king gives, he gives generously, like a king." Very well; but God gives like God.

Luther and many other dying saints comforted themselves with this great verse.

After missionaries had labored in Tahiti for about fifteen years, and labored in vain, Mr. Hunt pressed this verse upon King Pomare II. At last he said, "We never heard of any God that loved us and loved everybody in that way." That convert is now the leader of a host of nearly a million in the South Seas.

And one said to Nott, "Oh, and thou canst speak of such love without tears?" — himself weeping from shame and joy. When Cyrus gave freedom to the Jews, they were like men that dreamed; it was too good to believe. They had to hear it again, and then were their mouths filled with laughter and their tongues with singing.

The pardon for a condemned forger had not come, and so Dr. Rippon hurried to Windsor, into the bedchamber of George III, to get a copy. He returned to London in the nick of time; for the forger was already being marched to the scaffold. What good would the pardon have been had it not been made known? For the sake of Christ, God has pardoned the whole world; but of what good is it if you do not make it known to the world? Do you love the world of sinners? Did you send your son to be a preacher that the world might not perish, but have everlasting life? Do you give money to send another man's son to become a preacher of the saving Gospel?

"For God sent not His Son into the world to judge the world, but that the world through Him might be saved" — the supreme purpose.

> Not to condemn the sons of men
> The Son of God appeared;
> No weapons in His hand are seen
> Nor voice of terror heard.
> He came to raise our fallen state
> And our lost hopes restore;
> Faith leads us to the Mercy-seat
> And bids us fear no more.

"He that believeth on Him is not condemned; but he that believeth not is condemned already because he hath not believed in the name of the only-begotten Son of God" — the supreme separation. Condemned, or not condemned — there is no middle ground. Only two classes — to which do you belong?

"This is the judgment, that the Light came into the world, and men loved the darkness rather than the Light because their deeds were evil" — the supreme explanation.

Said the dying infidel Thomas Hobbes, "I am going to take a leap in the dark." "I am going to take a leap in the light," said the dying Thomas Jewett. You are going to take a leap — whither?

"For every one that doeth evil hateth the light, neither cometh to the light, lest his deeds should be reproved" — the supreme sadness.

When the original gas company in 1807 lighted Pall-Mall, it was at first derided and then treated in Parliament as a rapacious monopoly, ruining established industry. The adventurers in gaslight did more for the prevention of crime than the government had done since the days of Alfred, we read in Knight's *England*. More so the light of the Gospel.

Two miracles: first, God gave His Son, the Light of the world; second, the world rejected the Son of God.

"But he that doeth the truth cometh to the light that his deeds may be made manifest, that they are wrought in God" — the supreme test. Ps. 139, 23. 24. Are you practising what you have learned from Christ?

What effect had that night sermon on Nicodemus? He confessed Jesus was a teacher come from God. On his own showing he should have accepted the heavenly teaching. Jesus taught him he was a helpless and hopeless sinner. Jesus, the Son of God, became the Son of Man to die in the stead of sinners in order to save them from perishing everlastingly. Whosoever believeth in that Savior shall have life eternal. Jesus taught as the Teacher come from God — and more. He is the Savior sent by God. Christ preached Christ — and Him crucified. Christ preached justification by faith, without the deeds of the Law, as the only salvation for a sinner like Nicodemus with all his morality. Christ preached heaven and hell, but no purgatory.

Did Nicodemus accept that saving Gospel? We are not told. We are told when the Jews later would kill Christ, he stood up for Jesus and protested, "Does our Law judge any man before it hear him?" That lone and feeble voice was fiercely hushed by his ferocious fellow-judges. Later he saw Jesus lifted up on the cross and no doubt remembered that memorable night talk when Jesus told him the Son of Man must be lifted up. When Joseph boldly went to Pilate and "craved the body of Jesus," Nicodemus brought spices to embalm it and helped give it honorable burial in the new tomb of Joseph of Arimathea.

Are you born again, regenerated? Do you believe Christ died for your sins as your Substitute? Do you cast aside all trust in your good works and put your whole trust in Christ alone? Eternal life is provided by the love of God, offered in the Gospel, received by faith.

When Parmenides was reading a philosophical discourse at Athens, one after the other left, until only Plato remained. Yet Parmenides went on, saying Plato alone was audience enough for him. One Nicodemus was audience enough for Christ Himself. If so, is one single soul not enough for you to work on? Christ sacrificed the time to sleep in order to talk to Nicodemus. Do you sacrifice anything to talk to your neighbor about his soul?

CHAPTER VI.

THE BAPTIST'S CANTICLE.

John 3, 22—4, 4.

I.

THE OCCASION.

FTER these things came Jesus and His disciples into the land of Judea, outside of Jerusalem; and there He tarried with them and baptized. John also was baptizing in Enon, near Salim, because there was much water there, — a spring in Enon and five just south, — and people came and were baptized. For John had not yet been cast into prison.

Then there arose a dispute on the part of John's disciples with a Jew about purifying — whether John's was as good as that of Jesus — the first sacramental controversy.

They said to John, Rabbi, He that was with thee beyond the Jordan, to whom thou barest witness, behold, the same baptizeth, and all come to Him.

The disciples of John were very jealous of their beloved master's fame and also of their own honor, and their bitter complaint might easily kindle the hellish fires of that green-eyed monster jealousy even in the heart of the big-hearted John.

If there was any danger of this, the Baptist overcame the temptation and quieted his indignant disciples by explaining for the last time his place over against Christ.

II.

THE CANTICLE.

"A man can take nothing unless it be given him from heaven."

It is God that gave to John, and it is God that gave to Jesus. That ends it. It is God that gave to you and to me and to all others. How simple! How important to remember! Will you quarrel with God Himself?

"Ye yourselves bear me witness that I said, I am not the Christ, but that I am one sent before Him.

[151]

"He that hath the bride is the Bridegroom: but the friend of the Bride-groom, which standeth and heareth Him, rejoiceth greatly because of the Bridegroom's voice. This my joy therefore hath been made full. He must increase, but I decrease." Ex. 34, 15; Deut. 31, 16; Ps. 73, 27; Is. 54, 5; Hos. 2, 19; Song of Sol. 2, 8; 5, 2; Matt. 22, 1; 25, 1; Mark 2, 19; 2 Cor. 11, 2; Eph. 5, 32; Rev. 19, 7; 21, 2. 9; 22, 17.

Such tender, sweet, heavenly music from this rough desert preacher! Should not every pastor and every Christian sing it with all his heart? "Let Christ live, let Martin perish!" said Luther. Bismarck wished to be nothing but his king's man, and he devoted his titanic powers to make his king William the German emperor. Lord Beaconsfield devoted his great powers to make his beloved Queen Victoria the Empress of India. A candle consumes itself in order to give light to others. Let us consume ourselves in order to glorify Christ. He must increase, I decrease.

"He that cometh from above is above all; he that is of the earth is earthly and speaketh of the earth; He that cometh from heaven is above all. What He hath seen and heard, that He testifieth; and no man receiveth His testimony." Yes, the mass of men reject Christ.

Henry IV of France asked the Duke of Alva had he observed the eclipse? No, the Spaniard had so much business on earth he had no time to look up to heaven. You? You so busy on earth no time to look up to Christ?

"He that hath received His testimony hath set to his seal that God is true." The fact that he has become a Christian through faith in God's Gospel is a proof that God is true, is faithful. That is a proof for himself, and it is to be a proof for others. A Christian is a seal stamped upon God's truth, or faithfulness, and he testifies to that truth to others.

"Swear, curse Christ, and I release you." Polycarp replied, "Eighty-six years have I served Him, and He has done me nothing but good; how, then, can I curse Him, my Lord and Savior?" And with a firm step he went to the stake to be burned alive.

"For He whom God sent speaketh the words of God; for He giveth not the Spirit by measure." The Spirit gives to whom He pleases and in the measure that He pleases. And the messenger of God speaks not his own words, but the words of God.

Paul says: "When ye received from us the word of the message, even the Word of God, ye accepted it not as the word of men, but, as it is in truth, the Word of God, which also worketh in you that believe," 1 Thess. 2, 13. 1 Cor. 2, 13; 2 Tim. 3, 15—17; 2 Pet. 1, 21. Do you accept the word of the Gospel-preacher as the Word of God?

What is true of all preachers sent by God is, of course, most especially true of *the* Messenger of God, Jesus Christ, whom He has sent.

"The Father loveth the Son and hath given all things into His hand. He that believeth in the Son hath everlasting life; and He that disobeyeth the Son shall not see life, but the wrath of God abideth on him."

What a solemn and severe final testimony of the Baptist! By nature we are all under the wrath of God, Eph. 5, 6. What a hopeful and helpful parting word! By faith in Christ we may all escape the wrath of God and enjoy the grace of God. Christ is the only way of escape from the wrath of God to the heart of God.

Are you walking this Way?

III.

THE ACTION OF CHRIST.

When the Lord knew that the Pharisees had heard that Jesus made and baptized more disciples than John, — though Jesus Himself baptized not, but His disciples, — He left Judea again for Galilee. And He must needs go through Samaria, the shortest way.

Behold the delicate tact of the Savior! He would not add fuel to the flames; He would remove the fuel from the flames; He removed Himself from the scene of dispute that the flames of dispute might die down and out.

What a divine example for all Christians to avoid unseemly rivalry!

CHAPTER VII.

JESUS AND THE SAMARITANS.

John 4, 5—42.

ESUS left Jerusalem by a northern gate and soon saw on the left the Nob of 1 Sam. 21, 1; a little on to the right the Gibeah of Benjamin and Saul and God, Judg. 19, 12; 1 Sam. 15, 34; 10, 3; to the left the Mizpah of Samuel, and to the right the Ramah of Benjamin, 1 Kings 15, 20. 17. To the left Ataroth-Addar, then Beeroth, and Gophnah, which Vespasian will take in 69, and Timnath-Serah, where Joshua's grave is shown, Josh. 16, 5; 9, 17; 19, 50; 24, 30. Beyond will rise the castle of Baldwin, the Crusader. Next comes Bethel, Jacob's House of God, Gen. 28, 19; Judg. 1, 23; Josh. 18, 13; next Shiloh, the home of old Eli and young Samuel, 1 Sam. 2 and 3; Jer. 7, 12; 26, 6; Judg. 21, 19. On to Lebonah and then a view of Gerizim, the mount of blessing on the south, and Ebal, the mount of cursing on the north, and beyond the Great Hermon with his cap of ice.

At the northeast corner of Gerizim is Jacob's Well, a half mile north is Joseph's tomb, Acts 7, 16; beyond is Sychar. To the west of the well stood the oak of Shechem and the pillar of Abimelech, Judg. 9, 6; Josh. 24, 26. Between the feet of the two mountains the plain of Sichem or Shechem is not more than 500 yards wide; it is 1,800 feet above the sea, and Gerizim rises 800 feet still higher. Here God first appeared to Abraham; here Jacob dwelt on his return from Padan-Aram; here Dinah was disgraced; here Joseph was sold into Egypt, Gen. 12, 7; 34, 2; 37, 36. Here was one of the cities of refuge, and here Joshua addressed the gathered tribes for the last time, Josh. 20, 24. Here in B. C. 933 Jeroboam rent the kingdom and made Shechem his capital, 1 Kings 12. About fifty years later Omri moved the capital to the new city of Samaria, which gave the name to the whole country.

Shalmaneser IV besieged Samaria in 724, and Sargon, in 722, destroyed the capital and dragged 27,290 Samaritans to Assyria and colonized Samaria with heathen Assyrians under Esarhaddon. These found the deserted country overrun with lions, sure proof the local god was displeased. They asked the return of an Israelitish priest to teach

VIEW FROM NEBY SAMWIL (MIZPAH).

them the religion of Jehovah. The priest came to Bethel, and a corrupted Judaism was grafted on the heathen religion, 2 Kings 17 and 23.

When Ezra led the Jews back to Jerusalem and built the Temple, the Samaritans begged, "Let us build with you, for we seek your God as ye do, and we sacrifice unto Him since the days of Esarhaddon." They were curtly refused, Ezra 4; Neh. 3 and 4.

In B. C. 409 Sanballat built on Mount Gerizim a rival temple, patterned after the one at Jerusalem, and copied the worship of the Jews.

SAMARIA.

Their first high priest was Manasseh, grandson of the Jewish high priest Eliashib, whom Nehemiah chased away for marrying a heathen woman, the daughter of Sanballat, Neh. 13, 28.

After the death of Antiochus VII in 128, the Jewish priest-king John Hyrcanus destroyed the temple and the city. In 63 Pompey freed the city, and the Legate Gabinius rebuilt it in 56, Augustus gave it to Herod in 30, who named it Sebaste and rebuilt the temple in grand style, as the ruins prove. From east to west ran the street of columns a mile long and twenty yards wide; without the lost capitals the columns are sixteen feet high, some monoliths. On the top of the hill, called a crown in Is. 28, 1, which is

1,455 feet above the sea, stood the temple Herod built to Augustus, with an altar and the colossal statue. Under this temple were the palaces of Omri, Ahab, and Jehu. Professor Sellin of Berlin excavated here.

The Samaritans looked upon Jacob, Joseph, and Ephraim as their fathers, and they looked for a Messiah from their own ranks, from Joseph, not from Judah. The Judeans accused the Samaritans of worshiping the idols Rachel had stolen from her father and buried on Mount Gerizim. The Samaritans replied by calling Jerusalem a dung-heap! The verb to dung is also used for sacrificing to idols. The sacrifices at Jerusalem were

RUINS OF BETHEL.
The site of Jacob's vision.

not to the true God, who was at Gerizim, but to idols! And thus Beelzebul is the god of dung, of idols.

Rabbi Chuda said the Samaritans were heathens, yet Simon ben Gamaliel treated them as Israelites.

During a night about 8 A. D. Samaritans sneaked into the Temple at Jerusalem and strewed dead men's bones around, and this pollution greatly disturbed the Passover festival.

When a crowd gathered at the village of Tirathana to go up Mount Gerizim to worship, Pontius Pilate suspected a revolution and killed some and arrested many and executed most cruelly the most prominent prisoners. For this atrocity Pilate was deposed by Vitellius, the legate of Syria.

Under the procurator Cumanus, 48—52 A. D., Galilean Jews on their way to the Passover were massacred in the Samaritan village of Ginaea.

MOUNT GERIZIM.   NABLUS, THE ANCIENT SHECHEM.   MOUNT EBAL.

The bribed procurator refused to punish the murderers. The Jewish Zealots Eleazar and Alexander invaded Samaria, plundering and murdering. The procurator Cumanus and the Syrian legate Ammidius Quadratus had to adopt stern measures, and after much bloodshed quiet was restored by the decision of the emperor.

When the Jewish War broke out in 66, the Samaritans thought the cat would jump towards the Jews, and in June, 67, a strong armed mob met on Mount Gerizim. But they bet on the wrong horse. Vespasian sent the legate Cerealis, who stormed them with 60 horse and 3,000 foot. Refusing to surrender, 11,600 were put to the sword. After the war, in 72, Shechem was rebuilt and named for the Flavian emperor Flavia Neapolis, corrupted now into Nablus. Dean Stanley calls it one of the most beautiful spots in all Palestine, and Dr. Robinson writes: "It came upon us suddenly like a scene of fairy enchantment. We saw nothing to compare with it in all Palestine."

In 333 a pilgrim of Bordeaux found the plantain-trees around the well so old the natives claimed they were planted by Jacob.

Of the 150,000 pounds of olive-oil produced at Nablus, nine-tenths is used for soap.

In 1904 there were only 175 souls of Samaritans left. They still worship on their Mount Gerizim, and they have one of the oldest manuscripts of the Pentateuch.

> Here springs of sacred pleasure rise
> To ease your every pain.
> Immortal fountains! Full supplies!
> Nor shall ye thirst in vain.
>
> Dear Savior, draw reluctant hearts;
> To Thee let sinners fly
> And take the bliss Thy love imparts
> And drink and never die.

Jesus was wearied with His journey and sat thus, just as He was, by the well; it was about the sixth hour.

There cometh a woman of Samaria to draw water. Jesus saith unto her, Give me to drink. (For His disciples were gone away unto the city to buy food.) Then saith the woman of Samaria unto Him, How is it that Thou, being a Jew, askest drink of me, which am a woman of Samaria? (For Jews use not anything together with Samaritans, drink not out of the same cup, eat not from the same dish, etc.) The Rabbis ruled, "Let no one talk with a woman in the street; no, not with his own wife. Talking with a woman is one of the six things which make a disciple impure." When Niebuhr politely saluted a woman in Arabia, she turned her back upon him. Now, here was a strange man talking to a strange woman; still worse, a Jew

THE ROLL OF THE LAW.

talking to a Samaritan. Horrors! As a man and a Jew, Jesus humbled Himself to beg a favor of a Samaritan woman. The Savior resolutely, in utter disregard of all conventions, broke through the rules of etiquette to get near to a sinful soul. He says, "Learn of Me." Shall we?

The woman thought the Jew was so friendly because so helpless;

He was thirsty, and at the well, but had nothing to draw with. So near and yet so far. The joke was on the Jew, and the Samaritan enjoyed the sorry plight of the man and poked a little fun at Him.

The Jew did not wince at the thrust, offered no excuse, but replied with great gravity, "If thou knewest the gift of God and *who* it is that saith to thee, Give Me to drink, thou wouldest have asked of Him, and He would have given thee living water." God Himself is the Fountain of living waters. Ps. 36, 9; Jer. 2, 13; 17, 13; Rev. 22, 1. So there is an implied claim to Godhead.

"The gift of God!" cries the Eastern water-carrier, peddling his precious fluid in the hot and dusty streets. Jesus asks a small favor in order to grant a great favor, Himself, the Gift of God, the real Theodore.

A soldier found a jewel on Duke Charles of Burgundy, slain in 1476 at Nantes by the Swiss, and sold it for one crown in money; it was sold again for two crowns; again for 700 florins; once more for 12,000 ducats; at last for 20,000 ducats; you may see it in the Pope's tiara. "If thou knewest."

The woman did not grasp the meaning of these deep words and said, somewhat saucily, "Sir, Thou hast nothing to draw with, and the well is deep [about 100 feet]; whence hast Thou that living water? Art Thou greater than our father Jacob, which gave us the well and drank thereof himself and his children and his cattle?"

Jesus overlooks the banter and goes on: "Whosoever drinketh of this water shall thirst again; but whosoever drinketh of the water that I shall give him shall never thirst; but the water that I shall give him shall become in him a fountain of water springing up into everlasting life."

Let us pray with Charles Wesley: —

> Thou of life the Fountain art,
>   Freely let me take of Thee;
> Spring Thou up within my heart,
>   Rise to all eternity.

Let us have done with

> . . . dropping buckets into empty wells
> And growing old in drawing nothing up.

The simple Samaritan entirely misses the meaning of Christ, but her appetite is whetted, and she eagerly cries, "Sir, give me this water that I thirst not, neither come all the way hither to draw."

DALLMANN, JOHN.   11

Certainly a fine brand of water that will for all time save you the drudgery of daily trudging out of town to the well and lugging home the needful water-supply for the whole family.

Intent only on her bodily comfort, she hears only of water and hears not at all about the water of "everlasting life."

> Ho! ye that pant for streams
>   And pine away and die,
> Here you may quench your raging thirst
>   With springs that never dry.
>
> Rivers of mercy here
>   In a rich ocean join;
> Salvation in abundance flows
>   Like floods of milk and wine.

Jesus seems to change the subject and makes a sudden and startling flank attack: —

"Go, call thy husband and come hither."

"I have no husband."

"Thou hast well said, 'Husband have I not'; for thou hast had five husbands; and he whom thou now hast is not thy husband; in that saidst thou truly."

Before he can see the Savior, a sinner must see his sins.

That thrust went home. Her flippancy has left her, and in her voice we can detect the tone of awe, "Sir, I perceive that Thou art a prophet!" That was her way of confessing her sin. She was uneasy, and she asked for more information on a fundamental question.

"Our fathers worshiped in this mountain, Gerizim; and ye say that in Jerusalem is the place where men ought to worship."

Jesus tells her it does not matter *where* you worship, but *whom* you worship and *how* you worship.

"Woman, believe Me, an hour is coming when ye shall neither in this mountain nor yet at Jerusalem worship the Father. Ye worship that which ye know not." Zeph. 2, 11; Mal. 1, 1.

That was true; themselves had written in a letter to Antiochus Epiphanes they had built on Gerizim "an anonymous temple," to a nameless god.

"We worship that which we know, for the salvation is of the Jews." Rom. 9, 4. The salvation is in the Savior. Coming to Zacchaeus, Christ said, "To-day is salvation come to this house. Luke 19, 9. "But an hour is coming, and now is, when the true worshipers shall worship the Father in spirit and in truth; for the Father seeketh such to worship Him. God is Spirit: and they that worship Him must worship Him in spirit and in truth" — without hypocrisy and idolatry.

That, too, went over her head, and she said, "I know that Messias cometh (which is called Christ); when He is come, He will declare us all things." Deut. 18, 15—19.

So eagerly did the Samaritans expect the Messiah that they rose in rebellion and gathered on Mount Gerizim to await the Deliverer. At the end of his term Pilate crushed them.

Jesus saith, "I that speak unto thee am He."

The first full flood of revelation of the Savior. He roused in her the sense of sin, and then He gave her "the gift of God, a well of living water springing up into eternal life."

Not in Jerusalem, but to a simple, sinful woman of detested Samaria. "And His name shall be called 'Wonderful.'"

"Lord, give me this water that I thirst not."

Upon this came His disciples and were wondering that He talked with a woman. Yet no man said, "What seekest Thou? Why talkest Thou with her?"

When we see the Lord doing strange things, at which we must wonder, let us follow the example of the disciples — not call Him to account, but keep a reverent silence.

> Judge not the Lord by feeble sense,
> But trust Him for His grace;
> Behind a frowning providence
> He hides a smiling face.

Socrates, the best of the Greeks, also talked with a sinful woman. From his knowledge of human nature he taught that bad woman how to have more success in luring men to adultery. Yes, there is a difference between Christ and Socrates — wider than the poles.

THE FIRST WOMAN MISSIONARY.

The woman then left her water-pot and went her way into the city and saith to the men, "Come, see a man who told me all things that ever I did; is this perhaps the Christ?" Then they went out of the city and were coming unto Him.

"Let him that heareth say, 'Come,'" Rev. 22, 17. The woman heard Christ and said to others, "Come to Christ." Origen calls her "The Apostle of the Samaritans."

THE SAVIOR'S FOOD.

In the mean while His disciples were asking Him, "Master, eat." But He said unto them, "I have meat to eat that ye know not of." Therefore said the disciples to one another, "Hath any man brought Him aught to eat?" Jesus saith unto them, "My meat is to do the will of Him that sent Me and to finish His work." In the joy of doing God's work, Jesus had forgotten all about His hunger. There is genuine joy in doing your duty to God.

"Say not ye, There are yet four months, and then cometh harvest? Behold, I say unto you, Lift up your eyes and look on the fields, for they are white already to harvest" — likely the Samaritans coming to Him.

When Leonard Kaiser was burned for a Lutheran at Scherding in 1527 and saw the crowds, he cried, "Behold the harvest! O Master, send forth Thy laborers!" When J. Hudson Taylor preached at Ningpo, a Chinaman asked how long the good news had been known in England. "Some hundreds of years." "What! Why did you not come sooner?"

Says W. G. Polack: —

The fields are white to harvest
With living, human grain;
Go forth, ye chosen servants,
To garner in Christ's name.

The Church has prayed for reapers
To bring the harvest in,
And you she now commissions
The souls of men to win.

God bless your earnest labors
And let His kingdom come
And in His goodness hasten
The heavenly harvest-home.

"And he that reapeth receiveth wages and gathereth fruit unto life eternal that both he that soweth and he that reapeth may rejoice together. And herein is that saying wholly true, One soweth, and another reapeth. I have sent you to reap that whereon ye bestowed no labor; other men labored, and ye are entered into their labors."

Livingstone reaped little in Africa, but he stirred up many to Gospel the Africans.

MANY BELIEVE.

And many of the Samaritans of that city believed on Him for the sayings of the woman, which testified, He told me all that ever I did. So when the Samaritans were come unto Him, they besought Him that He would tarry with them; and He abode there two days.

The Jews cast out Jesus, the Samaritans invite Him.

And very many more believed because of His own word and said unto the woman, "No longer do we believe because of thy speaking, for we have ourselves heard, and we know, that this is indeed the Savior of the world."

"A Light to lighten the Gentiles and the Glory of Thy people Israel."

The testimony of a Christian is very precious to us, but we must go on and know for ourselves that Jesus is indeed the Christ, the Savior of the world. "The Spirit itself beareth witness with our spirit that we are the children of God," Rom. 8, 16.

What an unconventional Preacher! What an unconventional church! What an unconventional congregation — a single sinful Samaritan woman! What an unconventional sermon! What an effect — the sinful woman at once became an active missionary! She brought many Samaritans to hear Jesus. Many Samaritans believed in Christ, the Savior of the world.

Go thou and do likewise.

Great oaks from little acorns grow. A pedler sold Richard Sibbes's *Bruised Reed* in a Shropshire village. The farmer's son read it and found the Savior. That farmer's son was Richard Baxter, who wrote *The Saints' Everlasting Rest*. It converted Dr. Doddridge, who wrote *The Rise and Progress of Religion in the Soul*. It converted William Wilberforce, who freed the slaves and wrote *A Practical View of Christianity*. It converted Legh Richmond, who wrote *The Dairyman's Daughter*, which converted hundreds of Englishmen.

CHAPTER VIII.

JESUS AND THE COURTIER OF CAPERNAUM.

John 4, 43—54.

AFTER two days Jesus departed into Galilee — Upper Galilee, with Capernaum.

For Jesus Himself testified to the truth of the proverb that a prophet hath no honor in his own country. His own country, Lower Galilee, with His own city, Nazareth, tried to kill Him.

John Sebastian Bach, the mightiest master of music among men, was not appreciated until long dead. Carlyle of Scotland found his first honor in far-away America. Montaigne said, "The farther off I am read from my home, the better I am esteemed."

When, then, Jesus had come into Upper Galilee, the Galileans received Him with honor, having seen all that He did at Jerusalem at the feast; for they also had come for the feast. So Jesus came again into Cana of Galilee, where He made the water wine.

I.

THE COURTIER'S PRAYER.

There was a certain royal officer whose son was sick at Capernaum.

It is a pleasing guess that it was Chuza, steward of Herod Antipas, sometimes called king of Galilee; for Chuza's wife, Joanna, was one of the women supporting Jesus, Luke 8, 3.

The same, having heard Jesus is coming from Judea into Galilee, went to Him and besought Him that He would come down and heal his son; for he was at the point of death. To this day the place is known for its many malignant fevers.

"Lord, in trouble have they visited Thee," Is. 26, 16. "In the day of my trouble I sought the Lord," Ps. 77, 2.

Philip Jacob Spener had a wayward son, for whom he could only pray, pray, pray. When the prodigal fell sick unto death, he suddenly started up and cried, "My father's prayers surround me like mountains!" His body and soul were saved.

II.

THE LORD'S REBUKE.

Then said Jesus to him, "Except ye see signs and wonders, ye will not believe."

Here was a sigh of sadness and sorrow. The people of Sychar believed Jesus' word only, without signs; but most people had no eyes to see His character, and they had no ears to hear His Gospel; they had eyes and ears only for signs and wonders and ever clamored for more signs and wonders. They did not want Him, they wanted His; and not help for the soul, but only help for the body. Because men see not the miracles they demand, they reject the Savior. The Lord rebukes the craving for seeing miracles. "Blessed are they that have not seen and yet have believed," John 14, 11; 20, 29.

III.

THE COURTIER'S PERSISTENT PLEA.

The courtier said unto Him, "Sir, come down ere my little boy die."

The courtier showed no hurt feeling at the rebuke, neither did he lose heart. He did not try to defend or excuse himself. He did not make any demand as to time or manner. He did not argue the case. His case was desperate, a matter of life and death, and he simply, earnestly, repeated his piteous plea.

Christ Himself spoke the two very human and rather humorous parables of the Selfish Neighbor and the Unjust Judge in order to drive home the truth that men ought always to pray and not to faint, Luke 11, 5—10; 18, 1—8. And Paul writes: "Be patient in tribulation, continuing instant in prayer," Rom. 12, 12.

IV.

THE LORD'S GRACIOUS ANSWER.

Jesus saith unto him, "Go thy way; thy son liveth."

V.

THE COURTIER'S FAITH.

The man believeth the word that Jesus spake unto him and went his way.

This is Christian faith, trusting the bare word of Christ and acting upon that word. Without any other supports to lean on, our faith rests on the Word of Christ and relaxes on that in perfect peace. Abraham believed the almost unbelievable promise of God, and then he obeyed the almost unobeyable command of God. Hence he is called "the father of believers," and believers are called "the children of faithful Abraham."

Christ believed the Word of God and fought off the Tempter by saying, "It is written." Luther believed the Word of God and his characteristic pictures show him with his right forefinger pointing to chapter and verse of the open Bible, "It is written."

Believe the *word* "Baptism doth now save us."

Believe the *word* "Thy sins are forgiven thee."

Believe the *word* "My body, My blood, given and shed for thee for the remission of sins."

Believe the *word* "The just shall live by faith."

Believe the *word* "Thy dead shall live."

Believe the *word* "Where I am, there shall also My servant be."

VI.

FAITH CROWNED.

As he was now going down, his servants met him, saying, "Thy child liveth."

Then inquired he of them the hour in which he got better. They said to him, "Yesterday about the seventh hour the fever left him." So the father knew that it was that very hour in which Jesus said to him, "Thy son liveth"; and himself believed and his whole house.

The sickness of the son was a blessing in disguise — it led the whole family to faith in the Savior.

No chastening for the present seemeth to be joyous, but grievous; nevertheless afterward it yieldeth the peaceable fruit of righteousness unto them which are exercised thereby, Heb. 12, 5—11. The psalmist confessed: Before I was afflicted, I went astray; but now have I kept Thy Word. It is good for me that I have been afflicted that I might learn Thy statutes, Ps. 119, 67. 72.

This again, a second sign, wrought Jesus when He had come out of Judea into Galilee.

The first time He turned water into wine at a wedding and manifested forth His glory; and His disciples believed on Him. The second time He turned weeping into rejoicing at a case of mortal sickness and manifested forth His glory; and the whole family believed on Him. A glorious Savior, glorious in all conditions of our life. He rejoices with them that rejoice, and He weeps with them that weep.

He is what Dallas Gibson calls

MY ALL-WEATHER FRIEND.

In Cana's merry company
　My Savior takes His place;
Mid laughter gay and jollity
　I see His smile-kissed face.
'Tis good to think when spirits sink
　That laughter's nothing wrong,
To look the devil in the eye
　And chase him with a song.

I see Him at the city Nain
　Without the smile of cheer,
His gentle features clothed with pain,
　His eyes dimmed by a tear.
'Tis well to know that such a woe
　For me may be in line;
'Tis heaven to see that, if it be,
　I have a Friend so fine.

I see Him twisting on the tree,
　The lad who promised fame;
I learn that He is there for me,
　I bend my head in shame.
What if it be at Calvary
　Where ends the road I tread?
'Tis fitting so, for there I'll know
　How pain and glory wed.

CHAPTER IX.

JESUS AT BETHESDA.

John 5.

Not when Bethesda's pool a tranquil mirror lay,
  Kissed into radiance by an Orient sun,
But when the angel stirred its crystal depths,
  The wondrous power of healing was begun.
Calm and unruffled by a troublesome thought
  Like fair Bethesda's pool a soul may lie,
Bathed in the placid sunlight of content,
  While seasons of rich grace are passing by;
But when the Spirit stirs the sluggish depths
  Until its calm gives way to wild unrest,
Then comes sweet healing, and the sin-sick heart,
  Dropping its burden there, finds peace and rest.—*Minnie E. Kenney.*

AT the northeast corner of Jerusalem is St. Stephen's Gate, through which sheep are brought into the city to this day, and this is likely the Sheep Gate named in this chapter. The quarter north of the Temple is called Bezetha to-day. In 1872 M. Clermont-Ganneau said here must be the site of Bethesda. In the fall of 1888 Algerian monks uncovered a cistern 55 by 12½ feet, with 24 steps leading down 30 feet in the rock, and a twin pool 60 feet long. The crusaders built a church with five arches and five porches. Herr Schick identifies this as the site of Bethesda.

I.

THE PHYSICIAN.

After these things there was a feast of the Jews, and Jesus went up to Jerusalem.

Now there is at Jerusalem by the Sheep Gate a pool called in Hebrew Bethesda, having five porches.

This Bethesda means House of Mercy, we may call it Mercy Hospital. It had five colonnades, like the one of the hot springs at Tiberias.

In these porches lay a multitude of sick, blind, halt, withered.

(They were waiting for the moving of the water. For an angel went down at certain seasons into the pool and troubled the water; whosoever then first after the troubling of the water stepped in was made whole of whatsoever disease he had.)

At Kissingen a spring begins to bubble about the same time every day and just then is most efficacious, especially for eye troubles.

And a certain man was there who had been thirty and eight years in his infirmity. When Jesus saw him lying and knew that he had been now a long time in that case, He saith to him, "Wouldest thou be made whole?"

The sick man answered Him, "Sir, I have no man, when the water

EL AKSA MOSQUE.   DOME OF THE ROCK.   POOL OF
On the site of   On the site of the Temple.   BETHESDA.
Solomon's palace.   Not a mosque; not built by Omar.

is troubled, to hurry me into the pool; but while I am coming, another steppeth down before me."

Jesus saith to him, "Rise, take up thy bed [a light mattress] and walk."

And at once the man was made whole and took up his bed and walked.

Now it was the Sabbath on that day.

Christ's powerful command to walk gave the powerless man the power to walk.

"Give what Thou commandest, and command what Thou wilt," says Augustine.

The grace of our Lord Jesus Christ! He did not wait to be asked; He really asked to be asked in order to bestow His help. "Behold, I stand at the door and knock."

Austin Dobson says: —

> "Arise and walk!" the One Voice said;
>   And, lo! the sinews, shrunk and dry,
>   Loosed, and the cripple leaped on high,
> Wondering, and bare aloft his bed.
> The age of miracle is fled:
>   Who at the halt to-day shall cry,
>   "Arise and walk!"?
>
> Yet though the Power to raise the dead
>   Treads earth no more, we still may try
>   To smooth the couch where sick men lie,
> Whispering to hopeless heart and head,
>   "Arise and walk!"

II.

THE MASTER.

The Jews therefore said to him that was cured, "It is the Sabbath-day; it is not lawful for thee to carry thy bed" — for that was "working," and that was the great sin of breaking the Sabbath, which was punished most severely, Ex. 23, 12; Jer. 17, 21.

He answered them, "He that made me whole, the same said to me, 'Take up the mattress and walk.'"

It seems he was afraid of the punishment and therefore tried to excuse himself by shifting the blame on his Healer. It seems the rulers accepted the excuse; but they tried to find the real offender.

Then asked they him, "Who is the fellow that said to thee, Take up and walk?" But he that was healed wist not who it was; for Jesus had turned aside, a multitude being in the place.

Afterward Jesus findeth him in the Temple and said to him, "Behold, thou art made whole; sin no more lest a worse thing befall thee."

The gracious and merciful Savior now sternly lifts a warning finger. If you abuse His mercy, He will surely punish. The hottest hell is for the backsliding Christian.

The man went away and told the Jews that it was Jesus who had made him whole.

III.

THE DEFENSE.

1. THE LORD OF THE SABBATH.

And for this cause the Judeans, the rulers, began to persecute Jesus, because He began to do these things on the Sabbath. He had "worked" by healing the man, and He got the man to "work" by carrying his bed — two clear cases of breaking the Sabbath.

But Jesus made His defense: "My Father worketh until now, and I also work."

My Father worketh all the time, even on the Sabbath, and does not break the Sabbath; He is Lord of the Sabbath. And I also, like my Father, work together with Him, even on the Sabbath, and I do not break the Sabbath, no more than My Father; I, too, am Lord of the Sabbath.

For this cause the Judeans sought the more to kill Him, because He not only had broken the Sabbath, but also was calling God His own Father, making Himself equal with God.

Here is a clear understanding: Jesus knew what He was saying, and the Judeans knew what He was saying, and they knew what they were doing and why they were doing it.

J. S. Blackie says: —

> Death is the price we pay on earth's green sod
> For God's free gift to live and work with God.

Then Jesus formally replied to them, "Verily, verily, I say to you, The Son can do nothing of Himself unless He be seeing the Father doing something; for what He, the Father, doeth, the Son doeth likewise. For the Father loveth the Son and showeth Him all things that Himself doeth; and greater things than these shall He show Him, that ye may marvel. For as the Father raiseth the dead and quickeneth them; so the Son quickeneth whom He will. For the Father judgeth no man, but hath given all judgment to the Son that all honor the Son even as they honor the Father. He that honoreth not the Son honoreth not the Father who hath sent Him."

The Jews thought they were honoring the Father by dishonoring the Son; on the contrary, by dishonoring the Son, they were dishonoring the Father. A most sublime claim! Without Christ men are without God, atheists. Outside the Holy Trinity all "gods" are idols, and an idol is nothing. Christ is a radical, He goes to the root. What Christ says Paul repeats, and we must repeat the solemn warning to an idolatrous world.

Bishop Amphilochus of Iconium bowed to Emperor Theodosius, but refused to bow to his son Arcadius, at which the emperor showed great displeasure. But the sturdy Christian replied, "O King, how much more will Jehovah abhor those rejecting His Son!"

More, and still more wonderful — "Verily, verily, I say unto you, He that heareth My Word and believeth Him that sent Me hath eternal life and cometh not into judgment, but hath passed out of death into life."

All men are by nature in the state of spiritual death, and only by faith in Christ do they enter the state of spiritual life. Christ is the Life-giver. There is no twilight zone, no middle ground, no "no man's land"; death or life.

"Verily, verily, I say unto you, The hour is coming, and now is, when the dead shall hear the voice of the Son of God; and they that hear shall live — Lazarus, for example. For as the Father hath life in Himself, so hath He given to the Son to have life in Himself, and hath given Him authority to execute Judgment also because He is the Son of Man.

"Marvel not at this; for the hour is coming in which all that are in the graves shall hear His voice and shall come forth — they that have done good, to the resurrection of life, and they that have done evil, to the resurrection of damnation." No purgatory and no annihilation of the wicked.

"I can of Mine own self do nothing; as I hear, I judge, and My judgment is just because I seek not Mine own will, but the will of the Father who sent Me. If I Myself bear witness of Myself, My witness is not true" — from the view-point of the opponents.

2. HE CITES HIS WITNESSES.

a. The Father.

"There is Another that beareth witness of Me; and I know that the witness which He witnesseth of Me is true." The Father is *the* Witness, enough even for Christ's opponents.

b. The Baptist.

"Ye have sent to John, and he hath borne witness to the truth. But the witness which I receive is not from man; howbeit, these things I say that ye may be saved. He was the lamp that burneth and shineth, and ye were willing to rejoice for a season in his light."

Since they accepted the Baptist, they should have accepted his testimony of Christ. Regeneration is better than admiration.

c. The Works.

"But I have *the* witness as a greater than John, — who did no miracles, — for the works which the Father hath given Me to finish, the very works that I do, bear witness of Me that the Father hath sent Me." The Father is the decisive witness.

d. The Father, in the Scriptures.

"And the Father, who sent Me, He Himself hath borne witness of Me. Ye have neither heard His voice at any time nor seen His form. And ye have not His Word abiding in you; for whom He sent, Him ye believe not. Ye search the Scriptures, because ye think that in them ye have eternal life; and these are they which bear witness of Me; [Is. 34, 16] and yet ye will not come to Me that ye may have life."

Mary Jones, born in 1782, was too poor to own a Bible; she walked two miles to learn large portions for her Sunday-school lessons. She saved every penny and, when sixteen, walked barefoot twenty-five miles to Bala, in Wales, to buy a Bible. The few copies left were promised. She wept bitterly. Mr. Charles was touched and sold her one. In Demember, 1802, he told the story to the Committee of the Religious Tract Society, and that started the great and blessed British and Foreign Bible Society.

Said the dying Dr. Samuel Johnson, "Young man, attend to the voice of one who has possessed a certain degree of fame in the world and who is about to stand before his Maker. Read the Bible every day of your life." Like words were said by Presidents Lincoln, John Quincy Adams, McKinley, Roosevelt, Wilson, Coolidge, and Hoover.

Do you search the Scriptures? Have you found your Savior? Are you spreading the Scriptures?

Though the Bible clearly portrays Christ as the Savior, many do not will to come to Him to get eternal life. They wilfully shut their eyes to Him. This is a fearful saying. It shows man's awful responsibility for his own destruction.

3. FROM DEFENSE THE LORD ADVANCES TO ATTACK.

A REASON FOR THE REJECTION OF CHRIST.

"I accept not honor from men," much less do I seek it. "But I know you that ye have not the love of God in you," — the love of God to men. If you had, you would not persecute Me for showing the love of God, mercy to men, to the suffering man I healed on the Sabbath.

MOSES WITH THE TABLES OF THE LAW.

"I am come in My Father's name, and ye receive Me not; if another shall come in his own name, him ye will receive."

The prophecy became history.

Simon Barkochba was hailed by Rabbi Akiba as the Star of Jacob, Num. 24, 17, and for this false Christ many thousands of the best of the Jews went into death, 132—135.

Many reject Christ and accept Darwinism, Eddyism, Spiritism, and other isms. Robert Owen rejected Christ, but died believing in spirit-rapping. The magnificent Cardinal Wolsey said bitterly, "Had I but served my God with half the zeal I served my king [Henry VIII], He would not in my old age have left me naked to mine enemies."

"How can ye believe who receive glory one of another, and the glory that cometh from the only God ye seek not?"

4. THE JUDGES WILL BE JUDGED.

"Do not think that I will accuse you to the Father; there is one that accuseth you, even Moses, on whom ye have set your hope. For if ye believed Moses, ye would believe Me; for he wrote of Me [Deut. 18, 15—19]. But if ye believe not his writings, how shall ye believe My words?"

"If they believe not Moses and the Prophets, neither will they believe though one rose from the dead."

What a defense! The prisoner at the bar turns prosecuting attorney and makes a deadly attack on His enemies.

How did the trial end? John does not say. Enough said. They did not succeed this time. If at first you don't succeed, try, try, again. They did try again.

DALLMANN, JOHN.

12

CHAPTER X

JESUS THE BREAD OF LIFE.

John 6—7, 1.

Guide me, O Thou great Jehovah,
　Pilgrim through this barren land;
I am weak, but Thou art mighty,
　Hold me by Thy powerful hand.
Bread of Heaven, Bread of Heaven,
　Feed me till I want no more.

I.

JESUS FEEDS FIVE THOUSAND.

AFTER these things, Jesus went over to the eastern shore of the Lake of Galilee, and a great multitude was following Him because they were noticing the signs He was doing on the sick. Jesus went up to the hill, and there He sat with His disciples.

Now the Passover, the feast of the Jews, was nigh, when the Messiah was expected to reveal Himself.

The mighty Xerxes looked upon his countless hosts and thought that even the youngest and stoutest would soon sleep with the dead, and he shed tears. Lifting up His eyes and seeing a great multitude coming to Him, Jesus was filled with compassion. Sydney Smith says that, when A sees B in trouble, he is quite sure C should help. Not so Jesus; He saith to Philip, "Whence shall *we* buy loaves that these may eat?"

This He said to prove him, for He Himself knew what He would do.

Philip answered, "Two hundred denarii worth of bread is not sufficient for them that every one of them may take a little."

A denarius was the pay for a day's work, about sixteen cents.

Andrew, Simon Peter's brother, saith to Him, "There is a little lad here who hath five barley loaves and two small fishes; but what are they among so many?" Yes, what? Five crackers and two sardines for 5,000 hungry men, not counting the women and children, children with bottomless stomachs! Ridiculous!

Man's extremity is God's opportunity.

Jesus said, "Make the people recline." Now there was much grass in the place. So the men reclined, in number about five thousand. They looked like beds in a garden, Mark notes.

Jesus took the loaves, looked up to heaven, and gave thanks.

Do you? Ponder the words of M. D. Babcock: —

> Back of the loaf is the snowy flour,
> And back of the flour the mill,
> And back of the mill is the wheat and the shower,
> The sun and the Father's will.

Commodore Foote invited the king of Siam and asked a blessing at the table. "Why, that is just as the missionaries do," said the surprised king. "Yes, and I am a missionary, too." And you?

Jesus blessed the coarse barley crackers and dried fish. Do you grumble at your hard fare?

We pray with W. G. Polack: —

> Jesus, lead me graciously,
> Show Thy beauty unto me;
> Let my sins be all forgiven,
> Feed me with the Bread of Heaven.

We pray with Mary A. Lathbury: —

> Break Thou the Bread of Life,
>   Dear Lord, to me,
> As Thou didst break the loaves
>   Beside the sea;
> Beyond the sacred page
>   I seek Thee, Lord;
> My spirit pants for Thee,
>   O living Word.

Having given thanks, Jesus distributed to them that were set down, likewise also of the fishes, as much as they would.

> 'Twas seed-time when He blessed the bread,
> 'Twas harvest when He brake.

When they were well filled, He said to His disciples, "Gather the remaining fragments that nothing be lost." So they gathered them and filled twelve baskets. These baskets were the lunch boxes specially provided for Jews to carry Levitically clean food on a journey.

Pythias was so rich he could entertain the million soldiers of Xerxes, but died lacking bread. Christ always has a surplus, but He does not

waste even a single crumb. Waste not, want not. Be liberal, also frugal.
What is thrown away may be very useful.

> There spread a cloud of dust along a plain;
> And underneath the cloud, or in it, raged
> A furious battle, and men yelled, and swords
> Shocked upon swords and shields. A prince's banner
> Wavered, then staggered back, hemmed by foes.
> A craven hung along the battle's edge
> And thought, "Had I a sword of keener steel, —
> That blue blade that the king's son bears, — but this
> Blunt thing!" He snapt and flung it from his hand
> And lowering crept away and left the field.
> Then came the king's son, wounded, sore bestead,
> And weaponless, and saw the broken sword,
> Hilt-buried in the dry and trodden sand,
> And ran and snatched it, and with battle-shout
> Lifted, afresh he hewed his enemy down
> And saved a great cause that heroic day.

Christ multiplied the loaves and fishes, but He used His disciples to
give to the hungry. Christ multiplies the loaves and fishes to you. Do you
keep for yourself what Christ intends for the needy? Mrs. Charles asks: —

> Is thy cruse of comfort failing?
>   Rise and share it with another,
> And through all the years of famine
>   It shall serve thee and thy brother.
> Love divine will fill thy storehouse
>   Or thy handful still renew;
> Scanty fare for one will often
>   Make a royal feast for two.
>
> For the heart grows rich by giving;
>   All its wealth is living grain;
> Seeds which mildew in the garner,
>   Scattered, fill with gold the plain.
> Is thy burden hard and heavy?
>   Do thy steps drag wearily?
> Help to bear thy brother's burden!
>   God will bless both it and thee.
>
> Is thy heart a well left empty?
>   None but God its void can fill;
> Nothing but a ceaseless fountain
>   Can its ceaseless longing still.
> Is the heart a living power?
>   Self-entwined, its strength sinks low;
> It can only live in living,
>   And by service love will grow.

Christ used the five crackers and two minnows of the little lad; and that is worth remembering.

Only five barley loaves!	Behold, with them, when Jesus speaks,
Only two fishes small!	The multitude is fed.
And shall I offer these poor gifts	And when thine eyes shall see
To Christ, the Lord of all?	The holy ransomed throng
To Him whose mighty word	In heavenly fields, by living streams,
Can still the angry sea,	By Jesus led along,
Can cleanse the lepers, raise the dead?	Unspeakable thy joy shall be
He hath no need of me.	And glorious thy reward
Yes, He hath need of thee;	If by thy barley loaves one soul
Then bring thy loaves of bread.	Has been brought home to God.

Theresa was going to build an orphanage with but three shillings. "What are three shillings!" the people scoffed. "With three shillings Theresa can do nothing; but with God and her three shillings there is nothing Theresa cannot do." Did she do it? She did. Zinzendorf started among his schoolfellows the "Order of the Grain of Mustard-seed"; it grew into the great Moravian mission-work. John Howard was a "dull, good man"; but Christ blessed his "barley loaves," and he reformed the prisons. William Carey was a humble cobbler; but Christ blessed his "barley loaves," and he began England's mission to India. Lutheran immigrants in the wilds of Perry County, Mo., built a rude log cabin, and God blessed these "barley loaves" into a great theological seminary.

II.

JESUS ACCLAIMED AS THE MESSIANIC KING.

When the people saw the sign which He did, they said, "This is of a truth *the* prophet that cometh into the world." Deut. 18, 18.

The free dinner made Jesus very popular with the crowd, and they would then and there make Him their king to have for all time the full dinner-pail. They would rebel against the foreign Roman tyrants. What a temptation!

III.

JESUS NIPS A REVOLT.

Jesus having perceived that they were about to come and by force seize Him in order that they might make Him king, He withdrew, this time farther into the mountains and this time Himself alone and to pray. And in order that His disciples might not catch the spirit of revolution, He straightway forced them to enter the boat and cross the lake.

What a spectacle! Jesus running away from a royal crown! All the world would give all the world for a crown, but this Man says, "My kingdom is not of this world."

IV.

JESUS DISPELS FEAR.

Now, when it became evening, His disciples went down to the lake and, having entered into a ship, were making for the other side of the lake toward Capernaum. And darkness had already come on, and Jesus had not yet come to them. And the lake was being roused by a high wind which was blowing. When they had rowed twenty-five or thirty stadia, — three or four miles, — they beheld Jesus walking on the lake and drawing near to the ship; and they were affrighted. But He saith to them, "It is I; be not afraid."

Therefore they were willing to receive Him into the ship; and soon the ship was at the land whither they were going.

As long as he did not know Christ, Luther was afraid of Him. When he died, John Wesley cried, "The best of all is, God is with us!"

> If Thou wert less than One Divine,
>   My soul should be dismayed;
> But through Thy human lips God says,
>   'Tis I; be not afraid.

Keble says truly: —

> Thou Framer of the light and dark,
> Steer through the tempest Thine own ark;
> Amid the howling wintry sea,
> We are in port if we have Thee.

V.

JESUS SOUGHT BY THE PEOPLE.

On the morrow the crowd which had stood on the eastern side of the lake and had seen that there was none other boat there save one and that Jesus had not entered with His disciples into the boat, but that His disciples had gone away alone (howbeit there came little boats from Tiberias near to the place where they had eaten the bread after the Lord had blessed it) — when the crowd therefore saw that Jesus was not there, neither His disciples, they themselves got into the little boats and came to Capernaum, seeking Jesus.

And when they had found Him on the western side of the sea, they said to Him, "Rabbi, when camest Thou hither?" Yes, and how?

Yes, another miracle — crossing the lake without a boat.

VI.

JESUS REBUKES THE PEOPLE.

Jesus does not satisfy the curious questions as to when and how. He does not thank them for trying to make Him king. He throws a wet blanket on their political and gastronomic enthusiasm. He says very gravely and bluntly, "Verily, verily, I say unto you, Ye seek Me, not because ye saw the signs, but because ye ate of the loaves and were filled."

What an outspoken, plain-speaking preacher, this Jesus! He does not mince words. He certainly does hurt their feelings. The divine Physician lays His holy finger on the sore spot. Instead of seeing in the bread the sign, they saw in the sign only the bread.

As then, so now. Henry Martyn at Dinapore soon saw the Hindus cared more for his loaves of bread than for the Bread of Life, and he was ready to give up. But he remembered verse 26 and said, "If the Lord Jesus was not ashamed of preaching to such bread-seekers, who am I that I should give them over in disgust?" Soon some began to ask, "What must we do to be saved?"

Many people care more for the ladies' supper than for the Lord's Supper.

Why do *you* seek Jesus? Are you looking for business? votes? a job? a husband? a wife? card parties? dances?

VII.

JESUS DIRECTS THE PEOPLE.

After the sharp rebuke for seeking the wrong thing, Jesus earnestly directs them to seek the right thing.

"Work" — do not look to Me for bread without working.

"Work, not for the food which perisheth, but for the food which abideth unto eternal life."

Of course, you must work for the food which perisheth, but that is not to be the aim of your life. You are not to live to eat, but to eat to live.

Seek ye first the kingdom of God and His righteousness, and the other things shall be added unto you.

This eternal life the Son of Man shall give to you.

> 'Tis heaven alone that is given away,
> 'Tis only God may be had for the asking,

says J. R. Lowell.

"For Him the Father, even God, hath sealed."

The Eastern bakers stamped their names on their loaves, and God stamped His seal of approval upon Christ — at His baptism.

VIII.

THE SUPREME QUESTION.

It seems the people were stirred by His words, for now they ask, "What shall we do that we may work the works of God" (pleasing to God)?

IX.

THE SUPREME ANSWER.

"This is the work of God [desired by God, 1 Cor. 15, 58], that ye may continually believe on Him whom He hath sent" — from heaven, the Savior.

Luther says, "To depend on God's Word, so that the heart is not terrified by sin and death, is a much severer and more difficult thing than the Carthusians or all orders of monks demand."

They asked about works — plural; Christ answers work — singular. Not do, but trust; not works, but faith. Christ here plainly teaches justification by faith without the deeds of the Law. That is the teaching of Paul, and that is the teaching of Luther. That is Christianity according to Christ.

That faith worketh by love. That faith is the one mother of a large family of good children. That faith is the good root bringing forth all kinds of good fruit. Faith in Christ is Christianity; good works are applied Christianity.

Kaiser Karl V, on whose lands the sun never set, gave up all and slunk into the cloister of San Geronimo on the Yuste. What for? To expiate his adulteries. "The Sun King," the profligate Louis XIV of France, at death asked for absolution. The confessor, Père Tellier, asked did he suffer much? "No; that's what troubles me. I should like to suffer more for the expiation of my sins."

They would be saved by their own sufferings, not by the sufferings of the Savior. Great kings? Poor things!

This is the most significant declaration, that all eternal life proceeds from nothing else than faith in Christ. And Luther is the one that opened this truth to the world and thereby made a new world.

Florence E. Johnson says: —

He held out His loving hand to me
    While He pleadingly said, Obey!
Make Me thy choice, for I love thee so, —
    And I could not say Him nay.
Crowned, not crucified — this must it be;
No other way was open to me.

I knelt in tears at the feet of Christ
    In the hush of the twilight dim
And all that I was or hoped or sought
    Surrendered unto Him.
Crowned, not crucified — my heart shall know
No king but Christ, who loveth me so.

X.

A SEVERE TEST.

Did the people gladly accept this glorious Gospel of the heavenly Teacher? They did not; they testily made a test.

"What, then, doest Thou for a sign that we may see and believe Thee? What workest Thou? Our fathers ate manna in the desert, as it is written, 'Bread from heaven gave He them to eat.'" Ps. 78, 23—25; Neh. 9, 15; Ex. 16, 15; Deut. 18, 15; Acts 3, 22. You did not do as much as Moses, and the Messiah must outdo Moses. Now go to it; show us a really big miracle. It is almost unbelievable people can be so unreasonable.

XI.

JESUS ACCEPTS THE CHALLENGE.

Jesus therefore said to them with the most solemn emphasis, "Verily, verily, I say unto you, It was not Moses that gave you the bread out of heaven; but My Father giveth you the true Bread out of heaven. For the Bread of God is that which is ever coming down out of heaven and giveth life unto the world."

XII.

A RUDE INTERRUPTION.

"Lord, evermore give us this bread!" — really better than manna. Ever eager to eat, never ready to believe. Just like Mrs. Pea — during the whole sermon her mind was on the dinner in the oven. "Bread and games!"

XIII.

A DEEP SAYING.

"I am the Bread of Life."

Moses was not the giver, only the instrument of God, the Giver. The manna came from heaven indeed; yet it did not give life, only nourished life, and only bodily life, and only for Israel. Christ, the genuine Bread of God, cometh down from heaven and actually giveth life, spiritual life, and for the whole world. In every way, then, Christ is far greater than Moses. Because no one could ascend, Christ would descend.

Christ here preaches the universal atonement, redemption for the whole world. Accused of false teaching, Ebenezer Erskine said, "Moderator, our Lord Jesus says of Himself, 'My Father giveth you the true Bread from heaven.' This He uttered to a promiscuous multitude; and let me see the man who dares to affirm that He said wrong." Christ goes on: —

"He that cometh to Me shall never hunger, and he that believeth on Me shall never thirst." Eccl. 24, 21. Christ is the Giver and the Gift.

"But I said unto you that ye have seen Me and yet believe not. All that the Father giveth Me shall come to Me; and him that cometh to Me I shall by no means cast out."

How may I come to Jesus? "Come to Him just as you are," answered the Rev. Caesar Malan. She came just as she was, and Charlotte Elliot wrote: "Just As I Am, without One Plea."

Dr. Durham, who wrote a good commentary on Solomon's Song, said, "For all that I have written or preached, there is but one scripture which I can now remember or dare grip unto now that I am hastening to the grave. It is this: 'Whosoever cometh unto Me, I will in no wise cast out.'" Only one, but enough. "Though I have tried to avoid sin and please God to the utmost of my power, yet from the consciousness of perpetual infirmities I am still afraid to die," said the great Bishop Butler. A friend read him this verse 37. "Ah, I have read this a thousand times, but I never felt its force till this moment, and now I die happy."

"Because I came down from heaven not to do Mine own will, but the will of Him that sent Me."

Abu Taher commanded one soldier to plunge a dagger into his breast, a second to leap into the Tigris, and a third to cast himself down a precipice. Each one obeyed on the instant. "Tell your commander what you have seen," said the Carmathian Imam, who had marched with 500 horses against Moctador's 30,000 soldiers. "Before evening your general shall be chained among my dogs." And it was so. If soldiers obey thus to destroy men's lives, should not the soldiers of Christ, like Christ, obey the Father to save men's lives?

"And this is the will of Him that sent Me, that of all which He hath given Me I should lose nothing, but should raise it up again at the Last Day. This, too, is the will of My Father, that every one who beholdeth the Son and believeth on Him should have eternal life; and I will raise him up at the Last Day."

Thank God! Even John Stuart Mill says, "Let rational criticism take from us what it may, it still leaves us the Christ."

Surely, these gracious words of the Lord's hearty invitation melted the hearts of the people, did they not? They did not.

XIV.

DISSATISFACTION.

The Jews then murmured at Him because He said, "I am the Bread which came down from heaven."

And they were saying, "Is not this Jesus, the son of Joseph, whose father and mother we know? How does He now say, 'I come down from heaven?'"

Jesus therefore answered, "Murmur not among yourselves. No man can come to Me except the Father, who hath sent Me, draw him; and I will raise him up at the Last Day. It is written in the prophets, And they shall be all taught of God. [Is. 54, 13; Jer. 31, 34; Micah 4, 2.] Every man therefore that hath heard and hath learned of the Father cometh unto Me. Not that any man hath seen the Father, save He who is from God, He hath seen the Father." That is Christ. "Verily, verily, I say unto you, He that believeth on Me hath eternal life.

"I am that Bread of Life. Your fathers did eat manna in the wilderness, and they died. This is the Bread which cometh down out of heaven that a man may eat thereof and not die. I am the living Bread which came out of heaven; if any one eat of this Bread, he shall live forever; and the Bread that I shall give is My flesh, which I will give for the life of the world."

XV.

DISSENSION.

The Jews therefore strove among themselves, saying, "How can this Man give us His flesh to eat?"

Then Jesus said unto them, "Verily, verily, I say unto you, Except ye eat the flesh of the Son of Man and drink His blood, ye have no life in you. Whoso continually eateth My flesh and drinketh My blood hath eternal life; and I will raise him up at the Last Day. For My flesh is true food, and My blood is true drink. He that eateth My flesh and drinketh My blood dwelleth in Me and I in him. As the living Father sent Me, and I live because of the Father, so he that eateth Me, he also shall live because of Me. This is that Bread which came down from heaven; not as your fathers did eat manna and are dead; he that eateth of this Bread shall live forever."

These things said He in the synagog, as he taught in Capernaum.

Among the ruins of this White Synagog, built by the Roman centurion, the Palestine Exploration Society found a stone engraved with a pot of manna. Christ may have pointed to this as He said, "Your fathers did eat manna." The synagog is now being rebuilt.

XVI.

DISGRUNTLED DISCIPLES.

Now, many of His disciples, when they heard this, said, "This is a hard saying; who can hear it?"

How modern! Do you know church-members who grumble at the "harsh" teaching of the "strict" preacher and start a "whispering campaign"?

When Jesus knew in Himself that His disciples murmured at it, He said, "This causeth you to stumble? And if ye should see the Son of Man ascending up where He was before? The Spirit is the Quickener, the flesh profiteth nothing; the words that I have spoken to you are spirit and are life. But there are some of you that believe not."

For Jesus knew from the beginning who they were that believed not and who it was that should betray Him.

And He said, "Therefore said I unto you, No man can come unto Me except it be given unto him of the Father."

Robert Speer says here, "Why God would give it some rather than others He did not say. Indeed, we may question whether the way in which He put it raised the inquiry which troubles us as to the seeming partiality of God. Was not His form of speech simply a way of stating the obvious fact that some hear and some do not, without raising the question as to why some do and some do not? That mystery, He says, is with God. Is not that the only possible way to leave it? Can any one say more than that?"

If only all Calvinists and Arminians had said this and become Lutherans, who say no more and no less than God reveals, who bravely say, I do not know, when God is silent.

Student Talmage persisted in pestering his professor about the great Bible mysteries, and at last the professor retorted, "Mr. Talmage, you will have to let God know some things you don't."

"If a difficulty meets thee which thou canst not solve, so let it go," said Luther. Says D. A. Hayes, "He was great enough to know that he could not know all things. He was humble enough to believe that there were some mysteries he must be content to leave unsolved. He was great enough and wise enough to say, 'So let it go.' "

XVII.

DEFECTION FROM THE RANKS.

Upon this many of His disciples went back and walked no more with Him.

How modern! People do not like the preaching of Christ and quickly quit Christ. "I resign." "Strike out my name." "Cancel my dues."

Did Jesus try to hold these disciples by coaxing and flattery? Did He promise to use the soft pedal? Did He lower His standard? Did He change His method or message? He did not. Take it, and be saved; leave it, and be lost.

XVIII.
DECISION DEMANDED.

Then said Jesus to the Twelve, — and we can hear the tender pleading in His tone, — "Ye would not also go away?"

We can easily imagine how His human heart fluttered as He anxiously awaited their decision. What pastor has not asked the same question in the same spirit of his confirmation class? So many have gone away; ye would not also go away?

XIX.
DEVOTION DECLARED.

Simon Peter answered Him, "Lord, to whom shall we go? Thou hast words of life eternal; and *we* have believed and know that Thou art the Holy One of God."

Yes, that is the question, To whom shall we go? And the answer is, Christ or chaos; there is no middle ground.

Peter was the spokesman for the Twelve; may he ever be our spokesman also! God grant us all His grace ever to make this glorious and victorious confession against all open enemies and all unfaithful church-members!

XX.
DETECTION OF A DEVIL.

Jesus answered them, "Did not I choose you, the Twelve? And one of you is a devil." Now He was speaking of Judas, the son of Simon Iscariot; for he it was that should betray Him, being one of the Twelve.

He may deceive others, the hypocrite cannot deceive Christ. But how heart-breaking! A serpent in the bosom.

XXI.
DEPARTURE.

After these things Jesus walked in Galilee; for He would not walk in Judea, because the Jews sought to kill Him.

The Christian does not in a foolhardy spirit rush into martyrdom. Christ did not; and He bids us, "When they persecute you in one city, flee ye into another."

CHAPTER XI.

JESUS AT THE FEAST OF TABERNACLES.

John 7, 2—8, 1.

IN their wanderings from Egypt to Palestine the Israelites lived in tabernacles, or booths of boughs. In memory of this they kept a yearly festival and lived in booths for seven days, beginning on the fifteenth of Tizri, late in September, Lev. 23, 42. 43. On the eighth day every man went into his own house; the wandering in the wilderness was over, he was home.

At the same time it was a Thanksgiving Day and Harvest Festival. A striking feature of the feast was the drawing of water from Siloam, carrying it in a golden vessel in procession to the Temple, pouring it out upon the altar to the blare of the silver trumpets of the Levites and the joyful hallelujahs, Ps. 113—118, of the jubilant multitudes. This pouring of the water was in memory of the miraculous supply of water in the wilderness and to thank the Lord for watering their fields and pastures. On the eighth day no water was poured; they were out of the arid desert and now in "a land of springs of water."

The feast was a mixture of religious service and social frolic with torch-dancing, singing, and music. It became a saying, "He who has not seen the rejoicing at the pouring out of the water from the pool of Siloam has never seen rejoicing in his life." What Josephus calls "the holiest and greatest" feast of the Jews was now at hand.

I.

BEFORE THE FEAST.

1. JESUS AND HIS BRETHREN.

a. The Taunt.

His brethren therefore said unto Him, "Depart hence and go into Judea that Thy disciples also may see the works that Thou doest. For no man doeth anything in secret and himself seeketh to be known openly. If Thou do these things, show Thyself to the world" — as the Messiah.

If you wish to be king, you are wasting your time doing your

THE MOUNT OF OLIVES, FROM MOUNT ZION.

miracles in Galilee, in the *hinterland*. If you wish to be king, go to Judea. Jerusalem is the city of the great King; on Mount Zion is the place to do your miracles and become king.

They talked this way "for neither did His brethren believe in Him" — as the Messiah. Later on they did.

Brethren, yet not believers. A true picture of many a home to-day. Some members of a family believers, others unbelievers. Sad, but true. "A man's foes shall be they of his own household," Matt. 10, 34—36.

b. The Retort.

Their taunts did not goad Him to do anything rash or wrong, but He retorted tartly, "My time is not yet come; but your time is always ready. The world cannot hate you; but Me it hateth because I testify of it that the works thereof are evil. Go ye up unto this feast; I am not yet going up to this feast, for My time is not yet full come" — to reveal Myself as the Messiah.

Every one that testifies against the evil works of the world will get the hate of the world. Do your duty and take what's due you.

c. The Departure.

And having said these words to them, He abode still in Galilee. But when His brethren had gone up, then went He also up to the feast, not openly, but, as it were, in secret — incognito, not proclaiming Himself as the Christ.

2. THE DISCUSSION AT JERUSALEM.

a. Among the Rulers.

Then the Jews sought Him at the feast and said, "Where is He?" — that fellow. Luther thinks their hate kept them from naming Him.

Spurgeon asked a young man in London how he had found Christ. "Through reading Luther on Galatians. I read it two or three times, and I saw the difference between the covenant of works and the covenant of grace; I saw how man was ruined by his works and how he must be saved by faith, and I found the Savior while reading that book."

b. Among the People.

And there was much murmuring among the people concerning Him. Some said, "He is a good man"; others said, "Nay; but He misleadeth the people." Howbeit no man spake openly of Him for fear of the Jews, the ruling Rabbis.

No free speech at Jerusalem; the people were cowed by the ruling clique.

II.
DURING THE FEAST.
FIRST SCENE.
Vv. 14—24.

Now, about the midst of the feast Jesus went up into the Temple and began to teach — at the risk of His life.

And the Jews, the rulers, therefore marveled, saying, "How knoweth this man letters, having never learned?" — in a theological seminary. He is a false teacher, and as such He ought to be killed. Deut. 17, 12. 13.

Jesus repels the sneer and slur. He shows that He studied theology in a good theological seminary, under a good theological Teacher, that He is a Theodidact, taught of God Himself. He is an eager and a faithful Pupil of God. He does not wish to be admired as an original genius, He demands acceptance of His teaching as the teaching of God.

"My doctrine is not Mine, but His that sent Me." Deut. 18, 18. Therefore My teaching is true.

And you can find out for yourselves.

"If any man willeth to do His will, he shall know of the doctrine whether it be of God or whether I speak from Myself."

"Were it not for that text, I think I should sometimes sit down astonished and pray to die," wrote Romanes to Kingsley.

"I wish I had your creed, then I would live your life," said one to Pascal. "Live my life, and you will soon have my creed," replied the great French thinker. Experience through experiment. Here is the real scientific theology.

Long ago Sophocles saw and stated this truth, "A heart of mildness, full of good intent, far sooner than acuteness will the truth behold." And Fichte testifies, "If the will be steadfastly and sincerely fixed on what is good, the understanding will of itself discover what is true." And so Pascal says, "The perception of truth is a moral act." And so say even Professors Tyndall and Huxley.

A lady said to her pastor, "No, don't come. You know more about it than I do, and you might persuade me. And I don't want to be persuaded." A man said, "No, even if you prove it out of the Bible, I will not leave the lodge."

"He that speaketh of himself seeketh his own glory; but He that seeketh His glory that sent Him, the same is true, and no unrighteousness is in Him. Did not Moses give you the Law, and yet none of you keepeth the Law? Why go ye about to kill Me?"

The people answered, "Thou hast a devil" — Thou art possessed, Thou art crazy; "who goeth about to kill Thee?"

Jesus answered them, "I have done one work, and ye all marvel." (Healing the sick on a Sabbath at Bethesda.)

"Moses therefore gave unto you circumcision (not because it is of Moses, but of the fathers); and ye on the Sabbath-day circumcise a man. If a man on the Sabbath-day receive circumcision that the Law of Moses should not be broken, are ye angry at Me because I have made a whole man well on the Sabbath-day? Judge not according to the appearance, but judge righteous judgment."

To this cutting, caustic demand the rulers remain sullenly silent.

Kant gleefully told this joke on himself; or was it on Lavater? Lavater was a physiognomist, who read a man's character from his features. He was shown portraits of Kant, the great philosopher, and of a criminal — and picked Kant for the criminal and the criminal for Kant! "Judge not by appearances."

SECOND SCENE.
Vv. 25—36.

1. RESISTANCE.

Then said some of them of Jerusalem, "Is not this He whom they seek to kill? But, lo, He speaketh boldly, and they say nothing unto Him. Do the rulers know indeed that this is the Christ? But we know this man whence He is; but when Christ cometh, no man knoweth whence He is."

2. REVELATION.

Then Jesus cried aloud in the Temple as He was teaching, "Ye both know Me and know whence I am [irony]; yet I am not come of Myself, but He that sent Me is true, whom ye know not. I know Him, because I am with Him, and He sent Me."

3. RESULTS.

1. Then they sought to arrest Him; and yet no man laid hands on Him, because His hour was not yet come.

2. And many of the people believed on Him and were saying, "When Christ cometh, will He do more or greater miracles than these which this man hath done?"

3. The Pharisees heard that the people murmured such things concerning Him; and the Pharisees and the chief priests sent Temple police officers to arrest Him.

After these parenthetical verses Jesus concludes: —

"Yet a little while am I with you, and then I go unto Him that sent Me. Ye shall seek Me and shall not find Me; and where I am, ye cannot come."

Then said the Jews among themselves, "Whither will He go that we shall not find Him? Will He go unto the dispersed among the Greeks and teach the Greeks? What is this word that He said, 'Ye shall seek Me and shall not find Me; and where I am, ye cannot come'?"

Yes, He did go to the Dispersion, more so than they ever dreamed. Their unconscious prophecy was recorded in the Greek language by a native of Palestine in a Greek city.

III.

THE END OF THE FEAST.

1. CHRIST'S GREAT PROMISE.
Vv. 37—39.

Now, on the last day, the great day of the feast, Jesus stood and cried aloud, "If any man thirst, let him come to Me and drink."

The pouring of the water on the altar was the type, Christ is the fulfilment of that type. Then was fulfilled the prophecy of Joel, chap. 3, 18, that a fountain should come forth of the house of the Lord; and the vision of Ezekiel, chap. 47, 1—12, of a river coming out of the threshold of the Lord's house and growing deeper and wider as it flowed; and the prophecy of Isaiah, chap. 12, 3, "With joy shall ye draw water out of the wells of salvation." 1 Cor. 10, 4; Is. 28, 16; 55, 1; Rom. 9, 33; Jer. 2, 13; Ps. 36, 10; 42, 2; Matt. 5, 6.

The waters of the world are salty; the more one drinks, the more raging becomes the thirst, and Christ is the only One able to slake the

JESUS AT THE FEAST OF TABERNACLES.

fierce thirst. Augustine tried all the philosophies and religions, but he was
still thirsty; his thirst was satisfied at last by Christ.

> The frail vessel Thou hast made
>   No hands but Thine can fill;
> For the waters of this world have failed,
>   And I am thirsty still.

> Water, water, everywhere,
> But not a drop to drink.

> I heard the voice of Jesus say,
>   "Behold, I freely give
> The living water; thirsty one,
>   Stoop down and drink and live!"
> I came to Jesus, and I drank
>   Of that life-giving stream;
> My thirst was quenched, my soul revived,
>   And now I live in Him.

Still more: —

"He that believeth on Me, as the Scripture hath said, out of his belly
shall flow rivers of living water." Is. 58, 11; Zech. 14, 8.

But this spake He of the Spirit which they that believe on Him should
receive; for the Holy Ghost was not yet given because that Jesus was not
yet glorified — in His death, resurrection, and ascension.

Like Christ, the Christian also becomes a living fountain. Millions
have drunk from Matthew, Mark, Luke, John, Peter, Paul; from Luther,
Paul Gerhardt, Dr. Walther, and many other smaller fountains.

2. THE EFFECT.

1. THE EFFECT ON THE PEOPLE.
Vv. 40—44.

a. Many of the people therefore, when they obediently heard this
saying, said, "Of a truth this is the Prophet." Deut. 18, 15.

b. Others said, "This is the Christ."

c. But some said, "Shall the Christ come out of Galilee? Hath not
the Scripture said that Christ cometh of the seed of David and out of the
town of Bethlehem, where David was?" 1 Sam. 17, 15; 2 Sam. 7, 12. 13;
Ps. 132, 11; Is. 11, 1; Jer. 23, 5; Micah 5, 2.

So there was a division among the people because of Him.

d. And some of them were inclined to arrest Him; but no man laid
hands on Him. Christ made friends and enemies. As then, so now;

as there, so here. To some a savor of life unto life, to others a savor of death unto death.

You — friend or enemy?

2. THE EFFECT ON THE POLICE.
Vv. 45. 46.

The Temple police officers that had been ordered to arrest Christ, v. 32, came to the chief priests and Pharisees, who demanded, "Why did ye not bring Him?"

The officers answered, "Never man spake like this man."

His eloquence had charmed and disarmed these hardened soldiers.

Sent to kill Mark Antony, the soldiers were melted to tears by Mark Antony's eloquence. "Can you kill Caius Marius?" "I cannot kill Caius Marius," cried the executioner and fled. Sent to arrest Christ, the soldiers did not arrest Christ. "Never man spake like this man."

What a perfect tribute to the eloquence of Christ from an unexpected quarter! What those ruffians said long ago still holds good to-day. The judgment of those ignorant soldiers has been confirmed by the world's

SERVANTS OF THE CHIEF PRIEST.

greatest and wisest minds. How do you account for that? So far, so good; but not good enough. It is not enough to praise the eloquent sermon; you are to give your soul to the Savior.

3. THE EFFECT ON THE PHARISEES.
Vv. 47—52.

Then answered them the Pharisees, "Are ye also led astray? Has a single one of the rulers or of the Pharisees believed on Him? But this rabble, who knoweth not the Law, are cursed."

Pretty poor and pretty popular "argument": What does this professor say? What does that doctor think? Everybody that does not follow these "big men," these "authorities," is, of course, every kind of a fool. All wrong. Let us be independent and original thinkers. Let us take our conscience and our Bible and stand up, if need be, against the world. A single Athanasius was right and the whole world wrong. A single Luther was right and the whole world wrong.

FAIR PLAY!

Nicodemus saith unto them (he that came to Him before, being one of them), "Doth our Law judge a man except it first hear from him and know what he doeth?" Deut. 1, 16. 17; Ex. 23, 1.

A manly demand for fair play, something due the worst criminal.

FAIR PLAY SCORNED.

What did the brave man get from the highest officials of God's chosen people? Biting sarcasm and personal insult. In blind rage they turned on him: "Art thou also of Galilee? Search and see that out of Galilee ariseth no prophet." Therefore He is a false prophet, and therefore He must die.

THE PARTING OF THE WAYS.

And every man went to his own house. Jesus went to the Mount of Olives.

Thus ended the Feast of Tabernacles.

CHAPTER XII.

THE BITER BITTEN.

John 8, 2—11.

I.

CHRIST AND HIS ENEMIES.

EARLY in the morning Jesus came again into the Temple, and all the people came unto Him; and He sat down and taught them. What a peaceful picture! Soon it was marred by an ugly incident.

The scribes and Pharisees brought unto Him a woman taken in adultery; and when they had set her in the midst, they say, "Master, this woman was taken in adultery, in the very act. Now Moses in the Law commanded us that such should be stoned; but what sayest *Thou?*"

This they said, tempting Him, that they might have to accuse Him.

What a disgusting scene! Doctors of Divinity and Pharisees, heads of the Church, appear zealous for God's Law only to trip and trap and destroy Him. In addition, these vile hypocrites dragged this miserable sinner into public view in a most fiendish manner to destroy Him. Would He say, No? Then the people would rise against Him for flouting the plain Law of God. Lev. 20, 10; Deut. 22, 22—24. Would He say, Yes? Then the people would stone her to death on the spot, and the Romans would arrest Him for a rebel against Rome rule. John 18, 28—31. In either case they would easily be well rid of Him.

But Jesus stooped down and with His finger wrote on the ground, as though He heard them not. So Eastern teachers do to-day.

Was it because His pure soul shrank from this dirty story? Was it because He would by this gesture show His utter contempt for heartless hypocrites? At any rate, He clearly showed He wished to have nothing to do with the case; let it go to the proper court. Luke 12, 14.

But they thought they had Him in a corner, and they would not let up. So when they continued asking Him, He lifted up Himself and said unto them, "He that is without sin among you, let him first cast a stone at her." Deut. 17, 7.

And again He stooped down and wrote on the ground.

He is through with the case.

JESUS OPPOSED BY THE PHARISEES

St. John 8:59

What a dramatic and surprising turn in the story. Jesus cleverly turned the tables on His enemies. They would put Him in a tight fix; He put them in a tight fix. He turned from the sin of the woman to their own sins of unchastity.

They which heard it, being convicted by their own conscience, went out one by one, beginning at the eldest, even unto the last. Christ forced the accusers to become self-accusers. What an impressive picture of the

THE WOMAN TAKEN IN ADULTERY.

power of conscience! "Conscience doth make cowards of us all." Like whipped spaniels they silently slunk away. They dug a ditch for Him and fell into it themselves.

II.

CHRIST AND THE WOMAN.

Jesus was left alone, and the woman standing in the midst.

Augustine says beautifully, "Two are left: *Miseria et Misericordia,* Misery and Mercy." The sinner and the Savior of sinners are face to face. What will He do?

When Jesus had lifted up Himself and saw none but the woman, He said unto her, "Woman, where are those thine accusers? Hath not a single man condemned thee?" — to be stoned.

She said, "No man, Lord."

Jesus said unto her, "Neither do I condemn thee" to be stoned. "Go, and sin no more."

The Lord came not to be a judge in earthly matters; He came not to condemn, but to seek and save the lost, to be a friend of sinners, John 3, 17; 12, 46; Matt. 18, 11; 11, 19. The Lord condemns the sin and refuses to condemn the sinner. The Savior is merciful, He graciously dismisses the poor sinner. The Savior is holy, He earnestly warns against sin. His last word rings out, "Go, and sin no more." Absolution and admonition.

> "Neither do I condemn thee!" O come, thou great transgressor,
>   Thy sins thou dost enumerate as grains upon the strand;
> Take heart and bring thy weight of crimes to Jesus, thy Confessor;
>   He all thy guilt will cancel as the script upon the sand,
> Shall cast the load behind His back and cause thee to adore
> The love that speaks the Gospel charge to "Go, and sin no more." — *A. Mueller.*

Has the Savior forgiven you? Are you heeding His warning? How often have you received the Lord's Supper for the forgiveness of sins? How often have you gone to "Go, and sin no more"? How much have you grown in holiness? How do you act toward sin and your sinful neighbor? Do you hate the sin and love the sinner? Do you act like the Savior?

CHAPTER XIII.

JESUS THE BENEFACTOR.

John 8, 12—59.

I.

THE LIGHT OF THE WORLD.

Vv. 12—30.

Thou Sun of our day, Thou Star of our night,
We walk by Thy ray, we live by Thy light;
Oh, shine on us ever, kind, gracious, and wise,
And nowhere and never be hid from our eyes.

"THE Lord went before them by day in a pillar of cloud to lead them the way, and by night in a pillar of fire to give them light," Ex. 13, 21. This leading of the Lord during the wanderings in the dreary desert the Israelites celebrated in the yearly Feast of Tabernacles, called also the Feast of Lights. In the Court of the Women, at the altar of burnt offering, there were great candelabra, each having four gold oil-tanks. On the first night of the feast young priests would climb ladders to light them, and the great illumination reached almost every house in Jerusalem. Even a venerable old Rabbi like the famous Hillel would deem it an honor to join in the joyous torch-light procession and show his skill in dancing. This great light was a type of the Messiah, and Christ claims it was fulfilled in Himself.

1. A TESTIMONY.

a. To Himself.

"The Lord is my Light, the everlasting Light, a Light to the Gentiles." Ps. 27, 1; Is. 60, 19; 42, 6; 49, 6; Luke 2, 32.

The Rabbis said, "Light is the name of the Messiah." The Baptist was not that Light, but he bore witness of that Light, John 1, 8. 9.

Christ said, "I am the Light of the world. He that followeth Me shall not walk in darkness, but shall have the light of life." Christ is the living Light, and He gives the light of life. Then we shall not walk in the darkness of ignorance and unbelief and sin. 1 Thess. 5, 4; 1 John 1, 6.

As God was present in the cloud, so God is present in the cloud of the human flesh of Christ. As God was present to light and to lead His people, so Christ is present to light and to lead us. He is the Shekinah, the Glory of God among men, to give the light of life, to bless us with life that is life indeed. Christ preached Christ. He is inclusive — the Light for the whole world; He is exclusive — the only Light in the whole world. Believe in Him, follow Him, and have the light of life everlasting. Believe not in Him, follow Him not, and have the darkness of death everlasting.

Said Lord Tennyson, "What the sun is to that flower, Jesus Christ is to my soul." What is He to you?

b. To the Father.

The Pharisees therefore said unto Him, "Thou bearest witness of Thyself; Thy witness is not true." One man's word does not count.

Jesus answered, "Though I bear witness of Myself, yet My witness is true; for I know whence I came and whither I go; but ye know not whence I come or whither I go.

"Ye judge after the flesh" — outward looks; not worthy of the name — "I judge no man.

"And yet if I judge, My judgment is true; for I am not alone, but I and the Father that sent Me.

"It is also written in your Law that the testimony of two men is true. Deut. 17, 6; 9, 15; Matt. 18, 16. I am One that bear witness of Myself, and the Father that sent Me beareth witness of Me." Is. 43, 10.

c. To the Jews.

They retorted in angry irony, "Where is Thy Father?"

Jesus replied with sublime pity and patience, "Ye neither know Me nor My Father; if ye knew Me, ye would know My Father also."

In Christ we know the Father. This was the clearest and boldest claim to Godhead Jesus had yet made. He taught God could be known in Christ, and could be known only in Christ. In the ears of His hearers this was horrible blasphemy. Why did they not up and stone Him to deserved death? John explains: These words spake Jesus in the treasury as He taught in the Temple; and yet no man arrested Him, for His hour was not yet come.

Jesus spoke the truth at the risk of His life. We should follow Him.

2. AN ANNOUNCEMENT.

a. About the Jews.

Murderous men though they were, Jesus in divine love warned them. Then said Jesus again to them, "I go My way, and ye shall seek Me and shall die in your sin; whither I go ye cannot come."

Dreadful words of the loving Savior. There comes a time when it will be too late. Charles IX, who ordered St. Bartholomew's Massacre in 1572, died bathed in the blood from his own veins, saying, "What blood! What murders! I know not where I am. How will all this end? What shall I do? I am lost forever. I know it."

After he had cast out the Christian faith, the dying Professor Clifford said these frosted words, "I have seen the spring sun shine out of an empty heaven upon a soulless earth, and I have felt with utter loneliness that the Great Companion was dead."

Winwood Reade wrote the *Martyrdom of Man,* in which he, with wild and whirling words, preached his atheism, "with the hand of death upon him," says his uncle, Charles Reade. But he often sighed for his old belief, when to him "God was semihuman, and man was half divine, and after death life began, and happiness never ceased, and my mother and my Margaret would be joined to me again. Now my heart rebels against the fate of the human race, doomed to work like coral insects of the sea."

The Italian apostate Francis Spiera wailed at death, "My sin is greater than the mercy of God. I have denied Christ of my own free will; I feel that He hardens me and allows me no hope."

"Be not deceived, God is not mocked."

Then said the Jews, "Will He kill Himself? because He saith, Whither I go ye cannot come."

Jesus ignored the scoff and said unto them, "Ye are from beneath, I am from above; ye are of this world, I am not of this world.

"I said therefore unto you that ye shall die in your sins; for if ye believe not that I am He, ye shall die in your sins."

By nature all men "are of this world," in a sinful state, and there is but one way to get out and be saved. "Believe that I am He, the Jehovah, Messiah." Deut. 32, 39; Is. 41, 13; 43, 10. 13. Outside this one Savior there is no salvation.

They said to Him, rather scornfully, "Who art Thou?"

"Even that which I have also spoken to you from the beginning." He is what He says; His words reveal His being; He is Himself His Gospel. When faith grasps His Word, faith grasps Christ Himself.

b. About the Father.

"I have many things to say and to judge of you, but He that sent Me is true; and what I have heard from Him, that I speak to the world."

They understood not that He spake to them of the Father. How sad that men should turn away from their *Father!*

c. About the Son.

"When ye have lifted up the Son of Man, then shall ye know that I am He" — the Savior — "and that I do nothing of Myself; but as My Father taught Me these things, I speak. And He that sent Me is with Me; He hath not left Me alone; for I do always those things that are pleasing to Him."

The rulers will lift Him up on the cross, but thereby they will lift Him up to heaven. And then they shall know who He is.

As He spake these things, many believed on Him. Since then many more Jews have believed on Him.

Do you believe on Him?

II.

THE LIBERATOR.

Vv. 31—59.

Then said Jesus to those Judeans that believed on Him, "If ye continue in My Word, ye are My disciples indeed; and ye shall know the truth, and the truth shall make you free."

We need to be made free. Even the heathen Plato calls lusts the hardest tyrants; and Seneca says the passions are the worst slavery; and Shakespeare says, "Vice is imprisonment"; Cicero says, "The wise man alone is free"; and Epictetus says, "Liberty is the name of virtue."

Cowper sings: —

> He is a freeman whom the truth makes free,
> And all are slaves beside. There's not a chain
> That hellish foes confederate for his harm
> Can wind around him, but he casts it off
> With as much ease as Samson his green withes.

The Son is free, and He makes us free. When Paul was made free, he freed the Church from Judaism. When Luther was made free, he freed the Church from Romanism.

The Son is the great Emancipator of the soul, and the emancipated soul will labor to emancipate the body.

Under the Emperor Trajan a rich Roman became Christ's freedman and on an Easter Sunday made his 12,500 slaves freedmen.

William Wilberforce was made free by the truth. "I never knew happiness until I found Christ as a Savior. Read the Bible! Read the Bible! Through all my perplexities and distresses I never read any other book, and I never knew the want of any other." As Christ's freedman he labored all his life to make the slaves free men. On his death-bed he heard the good news that Parliament on August 1, 1834, had passed his bill and all the 700,000 slaves throughout the British colonies were set free.

William of Orange headed the one million oppressed Protestants against Spain, then the world's mightiest state, whose banners the Pope had blessed. Had he made a treaty with a foreign power? "I made a close alliance with the King of kings; and I doubt not that He will give us the victory." He did.

The Judeans angrily objected with their proudest boast: "We be Abraham's seed and were never in bondage to any man; how sayest Thou, Ye shall be made free?" See Matt. 3, 7—9.

That's rich! What about the four hundred years in Egypt and the seventy years in Babylon? Never in bondage? Then why pay galling taxes to the hated Roman tyrant, whose soldiers are now standing on frowning Antonia, watching the very Temple-courts, where they were hissing their empty braggart vaunt? Never enslaved! How easy to shut your eyes to disagreeable facts! None so blind as they who *will* not see.

And they were in still sorer slavery than the one they were denying. Jesus goes on calmly and sternly, "Verily, verily, I say to you, Every one living a life of sin is the slave of sin. And the slave abideth not in the house forever, but the Son abideth forever. If, therefore, the Son shall make you free, ye shall be free indeed."

Man the slave of sin — here is pessimism. Man shall be free — here is optimism. Dying in our stead as our Substitute, Jesus freed us from our sin, from the fear of death and the devil; He gives us the glorious liberty of the children of God.

Says old Matthias Claudius: —

> There is a noble slave in thee
> To whom thou owest liberty.

We say with John Newton: —

> Now, Lord, I would be Thine alone;
> Come, take possession of Thine own,
>   For Thou hast set me free.
> Released from Satan's hard command,
> See all my powers waiting stand
>   To be employed by Thee.

"I know that ye are Abraham's seed; but ye seek to kill Me because My Word makes no headway in you. I speak the things which I have seen with My Father, and ye do the things which ye have heard from your father."

"Abraham is our father."

"If ye were Abraham's children, ye would do Abraham's works. But now ye seek to kill Me, a man that hath told you the truth, which I have heard of God; this did not Abraham. Ye do the deeds of your father."

They felt the sting and fired back, "We be not born of fornication; we have one Father, God."

"If God were your Father, ye would love Me; for I came forth and am come out of God; neither came I of Myself, but He sent Me."

Again Jesus clearly gives Himself out as the Son of God from eternity who came into the world as the Son of Man.

If they were really the children of God, they would readily understand and receive the Son of God. On the contrary, they treat Him as a foreigner. And so Jesus asks, "Why do ye not understand My speech? Because ye cannot hear My Word" — that is why I ask.

Very appositely Bogatzky and Woltersdorf here quietly remark very disquietingly, "We are not Lutherans unless we have Luther's mind, spirit, faith, and works." Hm! How about it?

Voltaire misused his gifts to ridicule the Christian religion. At death his conscience started up, and fury and despair succeeded each other by turns. The doctor told him, "Sir, you cannot live six weeks."

"Then I shall go to hell."

Having denied they are real children of Abraham or of God, Jesus now tells the Jews what they are by painting a portrait of them and their father. "Ye have the nature of your father, the devil, and it is your will to do the lusts of your father; he was a murderer from the beginning and stood not in the truth because there is no truth in him. When he speaketh a lie, he speaketh of his own innermost nature; for he is a liar and the father thereof. But because I tell the truth, ye believe Me not. Which of you convicteth Me of sin? And if I say the truth, why do ye not believe Me? He that is of God heareth God's words; ye therefore hear them not because ye are not of God."

We stand aghast as these thunderbolts are furiously hurled at the Jews. God graciously grant that we may never feel "the *wrath* of the *Lamb*"!

What a pedigree — children of the devil! What a characteristic — a devilish nature!

And who dares say all this? One who dares challenge the world, "Which of you convicteth Me of sin?"

Says W. E. H. Lecky: "It was reserved for Christianity to present to the world an ideal character, which through all the changes of eighteen centuries has filled the hearts of men with an impassioned love; has shown itself capable of acting on all ages, nations, temperaments, and conditions; has been not only the highest pattern of virtue, but the strongest incentive to its practise; and has exercised so deep an influence that it may be truly said that the simple record of three short years of active life has done more to regenerate and to soften mankind than all the disquisitions of philosophers and all the exhortations of moralists."

Did the hearers repent and reform? They gave a shout of derision — "Say we not well that Thou art a Samaritan and hast a devil?" A despicable foreigner and crazy. No argument — abuse. Christ's great apostle was also abused — "Paul, thou art mad." Paul's great disciple was also abused. Is there any vile name that has not been hurled at Luther? Are we not abused for being Lutherans? and "Missourians"? That is all in a day's work, it belongs to our business.

To the deadly insult Jesus replied, "I have not a devil; but I honor

My Father, and ye dishonor Me. And I seek not Mine own glory; there is One that seeketh and judgeth.

"Verily, verily, I say unto you, If a man keep My Word, he shall never see death."

What gifts! Besides liberty also immortality!

What does the Church do for you?

A SNEER.

Then said the Jews unto Him, "Now we know for certain that Thou hast a devil. Abraham is dead and the prophets, and Thou sayest, If a man keep My Word, he shall never taste of death. Art Thou greater than our father Abraham, which is dead? And the prophets are dead. Whom makest Thou Thyself?"

A HEAVY BLOW.

Jesus answered, "If I glorify Myself, My glory is nothing. It is My Father that glorifieth Me, of whom ye say that He is your God.

"Yet ye have not known Him; but I know Him; and if I should say, I know Him not, I shall be a liar like unto you; but I know Him and keep His Word.

"Your father Abraham triumphantly rejoiced that he should see My day; and he saw the day of My birth — and was glad."

Abraham rejoiced in the birth of Isaac and the "everlasting covenant" through which all Israel and all the world was to be blessed, in Christ, and so he rejoiced in the birthday of Christ, "having seen afar off," Heb. 11, 13.

AN INCREDULOUS QUESTION.

Then said the Jews unto Him, "Thou art not yet fifty years old, and hast Thou seen Abraham?"

A SOLEMN ASSERTION.

Jesus said unto them, "Verily, verily, I say unto you, Before Abraham came into being, I am."

Men come, and men go, but Christ is, is eternal, "the same yesterday, to-day, and forever."

Jesus preached the sermon; the Jews took up the collection — "They took up stones to cast at Him" — for blasphemy. Supreme Court judges would become "Judge Lynch."

But Jesus hid Himself and went out of the Temple-court.

Men still stone Him with their stony hearts. The greatest Benefactor is treated like the greatest malefactor.

When we study this most remarkable chapter, we are astonished at the fierce controversy raging between the lone Christ on the one side and on the other the mad crowd of the Jewish rulers, members of the Supreme Court. And we think of Heb. 12, 3: "Consider Him that endured such contradiction of sinners against Himself."

Yes, consider Him lest ye be wearied and faint in your minds when ye must endure such contradictions of sinners against yourselves.

CHAPTER XIV.

JESUS HEALS THE BLIND.

John 9.

Come to the Light: 'tis shining for thee;
Sweetly the Light has dawned upon me.
Once I was blind, but now I can see;
The Light of the world is Jesus.

I.

THE MIRACLE WORKED.

1. THE NEED.

HASTING away to save Himself from being stoned to death, Jesus yet halted as He saw a man blind from birth; halted to help at the risk of His life. His disciples asked, "Master, who did sin, this man or his parents, that he was born blind?"

An old, very old question. To be sure, all afflictions are the result of sin, but the disciples thought this man or his parents had sinned in a special manner to deserve this punishment. Very human, many feel like asking the same question when seeing such things. We are all born with the "whys."

Jesus does not preside at a scholastic debating society, threshing the empty straw of academic questions; He conducts a practical seminary. He gives the one satisfactory answer and then gives a practical illustration.

Jesus answered, "Neither hath this man sinned nor his parents, but that the works of God should be made manifest in him." What a blessed word!

Mr. Moon of Brighton told a meeting of the blind at Manchester: "When I became blind as a young boy, people condoled with my mother on the 'heavy dispensation' with which I was afflicted. They were wrong, my friends. God gave me blindness as a talent to be used for His glory. Without blindness I should never have been able to see the needs of the blind." He published the Gospel in raised type in nearly two hundred languages and dialects. What a brave speech and what a blessed work! A like story is told of Louis Braille, in whose system thousands of blind to-day read the Word of God. Another blessing in disguise.

The blinded Milton says: —

"My vision hast Thou dimmed that I may see Thyself alone."

[212]

Another blessing in disguise.

"This deafness has been of great advantage to me. I had to improve the transmitter, so I could hear it. This made the telephone commercial," says Edison. Again: "I worked over one year, twenty hours a day, to get the word 'specie' perfectly recorded and reproduced on the phonograph."

"It was this genius for hard work that fired me as a lad and made Mr. Edison my hero," says Henry Ford, also a terrible toiler.

2. THE WORKER.

"We must work the works of Him that sent Me while it is day; the night cometh, when no man can work. As long as I am in the world, I am the Light of the world."

When Christ says "We," does He mean me?

There may be a time to fiddle, but not while Rome is burning. Have you any doubts? Go to work the works of Him that sent you. Where there is need of help, give the needed help without being asked for help. When Baldwin of Philadelphia became a Christian, he quit his business of making useless jewelry and began making the very useful Baldwin locomotives. Do you see the point?

Dr. Samuel Johnson, England's greatest moralist, put on the dial of his watch "For the night cometh." Sir Walter Scott wrote: "I must home to work while it is called day; for the night cometh when no man can work. I put that text, many years ago, on my dial-stone, but it often preached in vain."

At a dinner given him at the Astor House in New York, Daniel Webster said: "The most important thought that ever occupied my mind was that of my individual responsibility to God."

When young, Dr. Chalmers spent much time on mathematical science. When older, he repented. "What, sir, is the object of mathematical science? Magnitude and the proportions of magnitude. But then, sir, I had forgotten two magnitudes. I thought not of the littleness of time; I recklessly thought not of the greatness of eternity."

Most of us must join the contrite George Macdonald: —

> When I look back upon my life nigh spent,
> Nigh spent although the stream as yet flows on, . . .
>
> With self, O Father, leave me not alone,
> Leave not with the beguiler the beguiled.
> Besmirched and ragged, Lord, take back Thine own;
> A fool I bring Thee to be made a child.

While a student at Cambridge, Edward Thring wrote out this prayer: "O God, give me work till the end of my life and life till the end of my work; for Christ's sake. Amen."

Will you pray that?

Let us join Dr. Bonar: —

Time worketh, let me work, too;	Sin worketh, let me work, too;
Time undoeth, let me do.	Sin undoeth, let me do.
Busy as time my work I ply	Busy as sin my work I ply
Till I rest in the rest of eternity.	Till I rest in the rest of eternity.

Death worketh, let me work, too;
Death undoeth, let me do.
Busy as death my work I ply
Till I rest in the rest of eternity.

3. THE WORK.

a. The Clay.

When He had thus spoken, He spat on the ground and made clay of the spittle; and He anointed the eyes of the blind man with the clay.

Tacitus tells of a blind man coming to the Emperor Vespasian to be cured by his saliva. The Rabbis and Suetonius tell of the healing virtue of saliva. In the second century the physician Severus Sammonicus prescribed clay to be applied on a bad eye.

b. The Washing.

Jesus said unto him, "Go, wash in the Pool of Siloam" (which is by interpretation, Sent). He went his way therefore and washed and came seeing.

The Pool of Siloah, or Siloam, is 52 by 18 feet, southeast of the Temple area. It is called Sent because its waters are sent through a tunnel from a spring 1,700 feet higher up the valley, made perhaps in the time of Hezekiah. The Fountain Gate was protected by the Tower of Siloah, which fell and killed eighteen people, Neh. 2, 14; 3, 15; Is. 8, 6; Luke 13, 4. In 1880 a boy found an inscription in pure Hebrew hewn in the rock by workmen when they had finished the tunnel, which they had begun at both ends. This inscription is the earliest Hebrew in existence.

Why are there orphans in the world? That you may mother them, at least in the orphanage. Why are there unfortunates in the world? That you may brother them in asylums. Why are there sick in the world? That you may nurse them in the hospitals. Why are there sinners in the world? That you may bring them forgiveness of sins. Why are there heathen in the world? That you may send them missionaries. In useful works you'll forget your useless doubts.

Helping the helpless, you make known the works of God. Do not be idly curious or harshly censorious, but practically helpful. Work while it is day; the night cometh when no man can work; then you may ask questions.

Our life is long. Not so, wise angels say
Who watch us waste it, trembling while they weigh
Against eternity one squandered day.

The neighbors therefore and they which before had seen him that he was blind said, "Is not this he that sat and begged?"

Some said, "This is he"; others, "No, but he is like him." He said, "I am he."

Therefore said they unto him, "How were thine eyes opened?"

He answered, "The man who is called Jesus made clay and anointed mine eyes and said unto me, Go to the pool of Siloam and wash; and I went and washed, and I received sight." Better than Caesar's "I came, I saw, I conquered."

POOL OF SILOAM.

Then said they unto him, "Where is He?" He said, "I know not."

They brought to the Pharisees him that aforetime was blind.

And it was the Sabbath-day when Jesus made the clay and opened his eyes.

II.
THE MIRACLE TESTED.
1. THE MAN EXAMINED.

The Pharisees also asked him how he had received his sight. He said unto them, "He put clay upon mine eyes, and I washed and do see."

Therefore said some of the Pharisees, "This man is not of God because He keepeth not the Sabbath-day." Others said, "How can a man that is a sinner do such miracles?" And there was a division among them.

They say unto the blind man again, "What sayest thou of Him because He hath opened thine eyes?"

He said, "He is a prophet."

But the Jews did not believe concerning him that he had been blind and received his sight until they called the parents of him that had received his sight.

John Hay says: —

> He stood before the Sanhedrim;
> The scowling Rabbis gazed at him;
> He recked not of their praise or blame;
> There was no fear, there was no shame,
> For one upon whose dazzled eyes
> The whole world poured its vast surprise.

2. THE PARENTS EXAMINED.

"Is this your son who, ye say, was born blind? How, then, doth he now see?"

"We know that this is our son and that he was born blind; but by what means he now seeth we know not, or who hath opened his eyes we know not. He is of age; ask him; he shall speak for himself."

These words spake his parents because they feared the Jews; for the Jews had agreed already that, if any man did confess that He was Christ, he should be put out of the synagog. Therefore said his parents, "He is of age; ask him."

The Jews put out of the synagog those that confessed Christ. The Roman emperors put to death those that confessed Christ. The Roman Pope put out of the Church Luther for confessing Christ. The Modernists put out of their Church those that confess Christ. Well, Christ foretold as much.

3. THE MAN REEXAMINED.

Then again called they the man that was blind and said unto him, "Give God the praise; we know that this man is a sinner."

When Jesus had challenged them, "Which of you convicteth Me of sin?" they were all abashed and silent. Now, behind His back, they call Him a sinner, and they urge the healed man to call Him a sinner. And this they call "giving God praise"! These hypocrites!

He answered, "Whether He be a sinner, I know not. One thing I know, that, whereas I was blind, now I see."

All the waves of their arguments dashed in vain against the rock fact of his experience.

John Hay says: —

> Their threats and fury all went wide;
> They could not touch his Hebrew pride;
> Their sneers at Jesus and His band,
> Nameless and homeless in the land,
> Their boasts of Moses and his Lord,
> All could not change him by one word.

> I know not what this man may be,
> Sinner or saint; but as for me,
> One thing I know, that I am he
> Who once was blind, but now I see.

When doctors could not heal the dislocated shoulder of George Moore, he went to Mr. Hutton, who set the bone in a few minutes. Blamed for going to a quack, Moore retorted, "Quack or no quack, he cured me, and that was what I wanted." Millions have testified Christ cured them, and facts are stubborn things.

Then said they to him again, "What did He to thee? How opened He thine eyes?"

He answered, "I told you already, and ye did not heed; wherefore would ye hear it again? Would ye also become His disciples?"

A nimble wit, a ready tongue, a bold and independent spirit. A surprising and refreshing bit of irony.

The taunt stung the bullies, and they reviled him. Poor losers.

"Thou art a disciple of that fellow, but we are Moses' disciples. We know that God spake to Moses; we know not from whence this fellow is" — has His knowledge.

The man jeered, "Why, herein is the marvel that ye know not whence He is, and yet He opened mine eyes. Now, we know that God heareth not sinners; but if any man be a worshiper of God and doeth His will, him He heareth. Since the world began, never was it heard that any man opened the eyes of one born blind. If this man were not from God, He could do nothing" — of this wonderful nature.

Delicious mockery and sound sense; a manly defense of his absent Friend.   Truth, like a torch, the more 'tis shook, it shines.

Goaded into fury, they could only make use of personal abuse.

"Thou wast altogether born in sins." How did they know? They just before had to ask the parents to identify him. Even if true, could the poor man help it? Contemptible abuse of a helpless unfortunate. Even if true, what had that to do with the fact that Jesus had healed him? A supremely silly insult.

"Thou wast altogether born in sins, and dost *thou* teach *us?*" A sinner teach the saintly Pharisees? Shades of Hillel and Shammai! An ignoramus teach the scholarly scribes? They knew it all; nobody could tell them anything. Their hearts were stone, their heads were solid ivory. And they cast him out. And he was willing to be excommunicated rather than deny his Benefactor.

What an interesting duel of wits between one poor beggar and a crowd of powerful and learned rulers! And the beggar comes off victor! Can you match it?

John Hay, Secretary of State, says: —

> They were all doctors of renown,
> The great men of a famous town,
> With deep brows, wrinkled, broad, and wise,
> Beneath their wide phylacteries;
> The wisdom of the East was theirs,
> And honor crowned their silver hairs.
> The man they jeered and laughed to scorn
> Was unlearned, poor, and humbly born;
> But he knew better far than they
> What came to him that Sabbath-day;
> And what the Christ had done for him
> He knew, and not the Sanhedrim.

"They cast him out." That little sentence is really a very big sentence, big with world-historic interest. That excommunication marks the first official breach between Judaism and Christianity. So at the Reformation. The Pope's excommunication of Luther marks the first official breach between Romanism and all Protestantism.

III.

THE MIRACLE CROWNED.

1. FAITH.

Jesus heard that they had cast him out; and finding him, — so Jesus had gone out to seek the outcast, — He asked him, "Dost thou believe on the Son of God?"

"And who is He, Lord, in order that I might believe on Him?"

"Thou hast both seen Him, and it is He that talketh with thee."

"Lord, I believe."

How swift, and with all his heart and soul!

2. WORSHIP.

And he worshiped Him.

And he did it in the presence of his fierce enemies. He confessed the Son of God before men. "I believed, therefore have I spoken," Ps. 116, 10. "With the heart man believeth unto righteousness, and with the mouth confession is made unto salvation," Rom. 10, 10.

"Wife, I have been converted; let us put up the family altar."

"Husband, there are three lawyers in the parlor; perhaps we had better go into the kitchen to have prayer."

"Wife, I never invited the Lord Jesus into my house before, and I shall not take Him into the kitchen." And in the parlor Christ was thanked and worshiped by John McLean, for many years Chief Justice of the Supreme Court of the United States.

The man had been outrageously cast out by the rulers of the visible Church; he is graciously received by the Ruler of the invisible Church. Christ made up to him for his earthly loss by giving him greater heavenly gifts.

The Pope put Luther out of the Pope's Church for confessing Christ before men, and Christ received him into His Church and confessed him before His heavenly Father.

"When my father and my mother forsake me, then the Lord will take me up," Ps. 27, 10.

IV.

THE MIRACLE A SYMBOL.

1. A STARTLING STATEMENT.

For judgment I am come into this world that they which see not might see and that they which see might be made blind.

2. AN UNEASY QUESTION.

Some of the Pharisees who were with Him heard these words and said unto Him, Are we blind also?

3. A SEVERE REPLY.

Jesus said unto them, "If ye were blind, ye should have no sin; but now ye say, We see; therefore your sin remaineth."

All men are born blind in spiritual things.

Jesus is the Light of the world to make the blind see.

He uses the means of grace.

He is the true Siloam, Sent.

He is the Godsend.

They that obey Him are healed.

The Pharisees boast of their sight and so reject the Light. They boasted, "We know," and so they would not learn.

Jesus came for judgment, testing, sifting, separating, dividing. Why, to be sure, we all know that. Why, to be sure; but do we all know just on which side of the Great Divide we shall stand?

Lord, heal my blindness, and keep me seeing.

> Just as I am, poor, wretched, blind;
> Sight, riches, healing of the mind,
> Yea, all I need, in Thee to find,
>   O Lamb of God, I come, I come.

CHAPTER XV.

JESUS THE TRUE SHEPHERD.

John 10, 1—21.

THE heads of the Church had brutally cast out a man for stoutly holding Christ to be the Savior. That was a case of bad, very bad, shepherding. Jesus denounces that malpractise and in contrast gives His own practise.

I.

THE DOOR.

1. THE PARABLE.

Verily, verily, I say unto you, He that entereth not the door into the sheepfold, but climbeth up some other way, the same is a thief and a robber. But he that entereth in the door is a shepherd of the sheep. To him the porter openeth; and the sheep heed his voice. And he calleth his own sheep each by its own name and leadeth them out. And when he hath put forth all his own, he goeth before them, and the sheep follow him, because they know his voice. But a stranger they will not follow, but will flee from him; because they know not the voice of strangers.

This parable Jesus spoke to them; but they understood not what things they were which He spoke to them.

2. THE EXPLANATION.

a. Christ Is the Door to the Sheep.

Therefore Jesus said to them again, "Verily, verily, I say to you, I am the Door to the sheep. All that came before Me are thieves and robbers; but the sheep did not heed them."

Christ is the Door to the sheep; not the misleading Jewish rulers, who had just put out an innocent man. Thus Jesus puts Himself in direct opposition to His nation's highest tribunal. He Himself is the supreme authority; all others are false Christs, Antichrists. "I have not sent these prophets, yet they ran; I have not spoken to them, yet they prophesied," Jer. 23, 21; 14, 14; 27, 15; 29, 9.

In the cathedral of Brandenburg, over the pulpit, you read, "I am the Door." A good reminder for all pulpits.

b. Christ Is the Door for the Sheep.

I am the Door; by Me, if any man enter in, he shall be saved and shall go in and go out and shall find pasture.

The thief cometh not, but that he may steal and kill and destroy; I came that they may have life and may have an abundance of true food. Num. 27, 16. 17.

Christ is the Proprietor and also the Provider.

The old city of Troy had but one gate, and you went in through that gate, or you did not go in at all. The City of God has but one gate — "I am the Door." Either you go in through Christ, or you do not go in at all.

> Other refuge have I none,
> Hangs my helpless soul on Thee.

The door of the Roman tribune was open day and night, so that the oppressed *plebs,* the common people, could run in for help at all times. Christ is the open Door at all times for the oppressed, for any one, for every one, all and sundry, each and every — "He shall be saved."

> Jesus, Lover of my soul,
> Let me to Thy bosom fly.
>
> Rock of Ages, cleft for me,
> Let me hide myself in Thee.

You cannot go into the kingdom of God through the door of your good works, for you have none to begin with. A legend tells of magic gates that could not be forced; they flew open at a single drop of blood. The door of heaven cannot be forced by all our good works; it flies open at the drop of Jesus' blood.

Christ is the Door to free service. We are not in prison, but at home. In the home we are not slaves, but children. We have the run of the place. "He shall go in and out." That also means to serve, as we may see from Moses, Joshua, Solomon, Jeremiah, and Christ, Deut. 31, 2; Num. 27, 17—23; 1 Kings 3, 7; Jer. 37, 4; Acts 21, 22. We go in for justification by faith, and then we go out for sanctification by good works.

Christ is the Door of Life. The greatest thing in all the world is life — "All that a man hath will he give for his life." But all that a man hath will not buy life. What cannot be bought Christ gives. "I am come that they may have life," even the life eternal.

Christ is the Door for pasture. He Himself is the Bread of Life and the Water of Salvation. In the Lord's Supper He gives us His body and blood for the remission of sins and also in remembrance of Him, to get strength to follow Him and grow like Him. Heathenism at its best, in the Greek tragedy, wails: "Not to be born is the best thing in the world and, failing that, to die as quickly as possible." In utter contrast with that despair comes the shout of holy joy, "I am come that they may have life and that they may have abundance." Hugh Price Hughes wrote in his last will: "Put on my tombstone, 'Thou, O Christ, art all I want.'"

> In Him the tribes of Adam boast
> More blessings than their father lost.

Over the portal in the abbey of Alpirsbach, in the Black Forest, there is carved a Hohenzollern couple kneeling and praying, and over them you read the verse: "I am the Door; if any one enter in through Me, he will be saved and will go in and out and find pasture." A good motto for all married couples. Christ is the keystone of every arch of every door by which the wonderful St. Mark's of Venice is entered. The Church cannot be entered but by Him, the Redeemer, Restorer, Creator, Teacher, Savior, and Master. Ruskin says: "It is the cross that is first seen, and always burning in the temple."

Donald A. Fraser says: —

> One only Door leads up to God;
>   'Tis Christ, His Son;
> Faith is the key that swings it broad;
>   And every one
> Who takes the key may upward plod.

And Christ says: —

> I am the Door, O waiting heart,
>   I am the Door, this day, this hour;
> Enter and learn how dear thou art
>   To Him who saved thee by His power.

II.

THE TRUE SHEPHERD.

> Jesus my Shepherd is.
>   'Twas He that loved my soul,
> 'Twas He that washed me in His blood,
>   'Twas He that made me whole;
> 'Twas He that sought the lost,
>   That found the wandering sheep;
> 'Twas He that brought me to the fold,
>   'Tis He that still doth keep.

1. SAVES HIS FLOCK.

I am the true Shepherd: the true Shepherd giveth His life for the sheep — in their behalf and stead. Is. 31, 4; 40, 11; 53, 10; Ezek. 34, 23; 37, 24; 1 Sam. 17, 35; Ps. 23; Matt. 20, 28; Mark 10, 45.

Many pastors have done the same during the persecution under the Roman emperors, during the Reformation, on Foreign Mission fields, and in our own day many Lutheran pastors in Russia.   Where did they get the strength?

> When my love for Christ grows weak,
> When for stronger faith I seek,
> Hill of Calvary, I go
> To the scenes of fear and woe;
> Then to life I turn again,
> Learning all the worth of pain,
> Learning all the might that lies
> In a full self-sacrifice.

But he that is a hireling and not a shepherd nor the owner of the sheep seeth the wolf coming and leaveth the sheep and fleeth; and the wolf teareth the sheep and scattereth the flock.   The hireling fleeth because he is a hireling and careth not for the sheep.   I am the Good Shepherd and know My own, and they know Me, even as the Father knoweth Me and I know the Father; and I give My life for the sheep.

"My own" — what a world of love!   What a fountain of happiness!

> Happy are we, God's own little flock,
> Sheltered so close in the cleft of the Rock,
> Far above tempest or danger or shock,
>   Happy are we in Jesus.

By calling Himself the true Shepherd, Christ calls Himself the true King and Messiah; the hirelings are false Messiahs.   Yes, that we are His sheep is God's doing, His alone.   "He hath made us, and not we ourselves; we are His people and the sheep of His pasture," Ps. 100, 3.

Carlyle says: "We are a flock such as there is no other.   Nay, have we not also a Shepherd if we will but hear His voice?"

A faithful pastor will also say: —

> I do not want the lambs for me,
> But, Lamb of God, alone for Thee.

The beauty of the sacrifice is that it is a willing and loving sacrifice. For this reason doth the Father love Me, because I lay down My life that I may take it again.   No one taketh it from Me, but I lay it down of Myself. I have power to lay it down, and I have power to take it again. This commandment have I received of My Father.

Dr. Bigg writes in the preface to *The Task of the Church under the Roman Empire:* "Christianity is a religion; this is its *genus,* this it has in common with all other religions. It is the religion of vicarious sacrifice, or of the cross; this is its *differentia;* in this addition lies the peculiar nature which makes it what it is and distinguishes it from every other member of the same class."

2. ENLARGES HIS FLOCK.

And other sheep I have which are not of this fold; them also I must bring, and they will hear My voice and will become one flock, one Shepherd. Eph. 2, 11—22.

He even leaves the ninety and nine in the wilderness to seek the one that is lost.

> But none of the ransomed ever knew
> How deep were the waters crossed
> Nor how dark was the night the Lord passed through
> Ere He found His sheep that was lost.
>
> "Lord, whence are those blood-drops all the way
> That mark out the mountain's track?"
> "They were shed for one who had gone astray
> Ere the Shepherd could bring him back."

The Great Shepherd works through His undershepherds, the pastors of the churches.

Christ is the Head, all Christians are the members of His body. The Head must work through His members.

> Many He has who are not of this fold,
> Out in the storm and the pitiless cold;
> These we will win by our prayers and our gold,
> Win them to love our Jesus.

III.

THE REACTION.

There was a division therefore again among the Jews for these sayings. John 9, 16.

1. UNFRIENDLY.

Many of them said, "He hath a devil and is mad; why heed ye Him?"

As then, so now; as there, so here. Do not many still curse Christ and His glorious Gospel? Read what Russia is doing to Christ's Church. In America there are societies of atheists to crush Christ — "He is mad."

DALLMANN, JOHN. 15

2. FRIENDLY.

Others said, "These are not the works of one that hath a devil. Can a devil open the eyes of the blind?"

As then, so now; as there, so here. Many are His friends and defend Him and His Gospel.

Did the Good Shepherd lay down His life for you? Were you as sheep going astray, but are now returned to the Shepherd and Bishop of your souls? 1 Pet. 21, 25. Do you heed His voice and follow Him? Do you help the Chief Shepherd in bringing other sheep into His fold? We say with John Taylor: —

> Shepherd, with joy we hear Thy call
> That leads to heaven.
> Let none from that salvation fall
> So freely given;
> But, as Thy sacred records long foretold,
> Be the wide-peopled earth one happy fold.

CHAPTER XVI.

JESUS THE SON OF GOD.

John 10, 22—42.

NTIOCHUS EPIPHANES, in 170 B. C., conquered the Jews and profaned their Temple by sacrificing a sow on the altar of burnt offering and with its broth sprinkling the Temple to ridicule the sacred services. He burned the Bibles and killed those who kept their Bibles. Judas Maccabeus defeated the Syrians in the battles of Bethoron and Emmaus and Bethzur and purified the Temple by dedicating a new altar in 167. This Feast of Dedication, or Renewal, was kept yearly in winter from December 20 to 28. Josephus says the lamps on the candlestick were lighted as a mark of rejoicing, and so it was also called the Feast of Lights. 1 Macc. 4, 41; 2 Macc. 10, 1. Josephus, *Antiq.*, 12, 7—9.

I.

TEACHING IN PUBLIC.

And it was the Feast of Dedication at Jerusalem; it was winter; and Jesus was walking in the Temple, in Solomon's Portico. This was to the east, and ruins of it remained. Josephus says it was partly undestroyed, and Tacitus mentions it as one of the defenses against Titus.

II.

A PERSONAL APPLICATION.

Then came the Jews round about Him and said, "How long dost Thou keep our soul in suspense? If Thou art the Christ, tell us frankly."

III.

A SOLEMN DECLARATION.

Jesus answered them, "I told you, and yet ye believe not. The works that I do in My Father's name, these bear witness of Me."

David Hume denied miracles because "it is contrary to all experience." Even John Stuart Mill and Jean Jacques Rousseau say that does not hold if one believes in a living God. James Hinton, scientist and philosopher, says truly: "We cannot see that we walk in the midst of miracles and draw in mysteries with every breath."

[227]

IV.

A FINAL EXPLANATION.

"But ye believe not because ye are not of My sheep."

Why are some rather than others the sheep of Christ? Christ does not tell, and so we cannot tell. Let us tell what Christ does tell.

V.

A GRACIOUS DONATION.

"My sheep hear My voice, and I know them, and they follow Me; and I give unto them eternal life."

What a majestic Giver! What a magnificent gift! What more could heart desire? All that a man hath will he give for his life — here he is given eternal life!

VI.

A DIVINE PRESERVATION.

"They shall never perish, and no one shall snatch them out of My hand. My Father, who gave them to Me, is greater than all, and no one is able to snatch them out of the Father's hand. I and the Father are one," — one in nature and one in the work of salvation — a sublime statement that Christ is true God. The "One" saves us from the Charybdis of Arianism, the "are" from the Scylla of Sabellianism, remarks Augustine.

After Luther's death, Melanchthon wrote the dying Myconius: "Dearest Frederick, those sweet words of the Son of God have often comforted me in great sorrows: 'None shall snatch My sheep out of My hand.'" They were his last words, as Lucas Cranach the Younger says on his striking portrait of Luther's friend on his death-bed.

When the Jews accused the Christians of worshiping more than one God, Justin Martyr replied: "Frequent mention is made in the Old Testament of a person who is called God and is God and yet is distinguished from the God and Father of all."

VII.

A VICIOUS DEMONSTRATION.

The Jews therefore fetched stones again to stone Him. Chap. 8, 59. The Jews clearly understood the claim of Jesus to be true God. They held it blasphemy, and for that they again took up stones in order to stone Him.

VIII.
AN ARRESTING INTERROGATION.

Though His life was threatened, Jesus was quite calm, and with mingled sadness and irony He asked the quiet question, "Many noble works have I showed you from My Father; for which of those works do ye stone Me?" Micah 6, 3.

IX.
AN ANGRY RECRIMINATION.

The Jews answered Him, "For a good work we stone Thee not, but because of blasphemy and because that Thou, being a man, makest Thyself God."

All men to-day admit Christ did many good works, and yet many stone Him for making Himself God.

X.
A SCRIPTURAL JUSTIFICATION.

Jesus answered them, "Is it not written in your Law, 'I said, Ye are gods'?" Ps. 82, 6. "If He called them gods unto whom the Word of God came, — and the Scripture cannot be broken, — say ye of Him whom the Father hath sanctified [Ps. 2; Is. 61, 1] and sent into the world, Thou blasphemest, because I said I am the Son of God?"

Christ Himself testifies to the unity of the Scripture and to the inspiration of the matter and the words.

How firm a foundation, ye saints of the Lord,
Is laid for your faith in His excellent Word!

The Word of God came to the prophets, but Christ is Himself the personal Word of God and Son of God.

"If I do not the works of My Father, believe Me not; but if I do, though ye believe not Me, believe the works that ye may know and understand that the Father is in Me and I in the Father."

Whole books have been written to show "No man can do these miracles that Thou doest except God be with him," John 3, 2, to prove He is true God.

XI.
AN ATTEMPTED ARREST.

Therefore they sought again to arrest Him. Chap. 8, 30. 32.

XII.

A SUCCESSFUL ESCAPE.

But He escaped out of their hand and went away again beyond Jordan, into the place where John at first baptized; and there He abode — in Perea — till He went to Bethany.

XIII.

A FAITHFUL ACCEPTANCE.

Many resorted unto Him and said, "John did no sign, but all things that John spake of this man were true." And many believed on Him there.

Some reject, some accept; as then, so now. God grant us grace to accept Him and to hold Him in our hearts till our dying day.

CHAPTER XVII.

JESUS RAISES LAZARUS.

John 11.

I.

JESUS AND HIS DISCIPLES.

NOW, a certain man was sick, Lazarus, Eleazar, God his help, *Gotthilf,* of Bethany, the town of Mary and her sister Martha. It was that Mary who afterward anointed the Lord with ointment and wiped His feet with her hair whose brother Lazarus was sick. Therefore his sisters sent to Him, saying, "Lord, behold, he whom Thou lovest is sick."

Enough said: Take it to the Lord in prayer and leave the rest to Him. Observe that the plea is not, "he that loveth Thee," but, "he whom Thou lovest."

Jesus, hearing it, said, "This sickness is not unto death, but for the glory of God, that the Son of God might be glorified thereby."

Now, Jesus loved Martha and her sister and Lazarus. When, therefore, He heard that he was sick, He abode two days still in the same place where He was. Then, after that, saith He to His disciples, "Let us go into Judea again." His disciples say unto Him, "Master, but just now the Jews were seeking to stone Thee, and goest Thou thither again?" Jesus answered, "Are there not twelve hours in the day? If any man walk in the day, he stumbleth not because he seeth the light of this world; but if a man walk in the night, he stumbleth because the light is not in him."

In other words, Do not hurry to worry; and if danger will really come, do not dread it. Do your duty and leave your death to the Lord. Though warned of danger, Jesus went to Bethany; though warned by the death of Hus and Savonarola, Luther went to Worms.

After this He saith, "Our friend Lazarus hath fallen asleep; but I am going to wake him up."

Our friend — the great Son of God calls us His friends; how touching! Are we treating Him as a friend? Sleep — how comforting! If we sleep in the sleeping-place, the cemetery, we shall awake again. If we are sown as precious seed in God's acre, we shall grow up again. Sleep — how that one word floods our life with golden hope!

Then said the disciples, "Lord, if he is fallen asleep, he will get well."

Says Sir Thomas Browne: —

> Sleep is a death; oh, make me try
> By sleeping what it is to die
> And as gently lay my head
> On my grave as now my bed.

John Mason Neale says: —

> No longer must we mourners weep
> Nor call departed Christians dead;
> For death is hallowed into sleep,
> And every grave becomes a bed.

Howbeit, Jesus had been speaking of his death; but they thought that He had spoken of taking of rest in sleep. Then said Jesus unto them plainly, "Lazarus is dead, and I am glad for your sakes that I was not there, so that ye may believe. Nevertheless, let us go to him."

"Sleep is so like death that I dare not venture on it without prayer," said Bishop Andrewes. Do you dare?

Then said Thomas, who is called Didymus, Twin, to his fellow-disciples, "Let us also go that we may die with Him." Consider the devotion of Thomas — he sees the danger of following Christ; he is ready to die with Christ; he rallies his fellows likewise to die with Christ.

II.

JESUS AND MARTHA.

When Jesus came, He found Lazarus had lain in the tomb four days already. Now, Bethany was nigh unto Jerusalem, about fifteen furlongs off, two miles; and many of the Jews came to Martha and Mary to comfort them concerning their brother. Then Martha, when she heard Jesus was coming, went and met Him; but Mary sat in the house — a sign of mourning, also among the Romans. Then said Martha unto Jesus, "Lord, if Thou hadst been here, my brother had not died. And even now I know that whatsoever Thou mayest ask God, God will give it Thee."

What a wonderful blending of modesty and faith! Luther hurried to Melanchthon's bed and found him almost dead. "How Satan hath abused this noble instrument!" He flung himself on his knees at the open window and wrestled with God in prayer. And Melanchthon was snatched from the verge of the grave and revived.

Jesus saith unto her, "Thy brother will rise again." Martha saith unto Him, "I know that He will rise again in the resurrection at the Last Day." Jesus said unto her, words of sublimest majesty, "I am the Resurrection and the Life; he that believeth in Me, though he were dead, yet shall he live; and whosoever liveth and believeth in Me shall never die. Believest thou this?" She saith unto Him, "Yea, Lord; I have believed that Thou art the Christ, the Son of God, that cometh into the world." When she had so said, she went her way and called Mary, her sister, secretly whispering, "The Master is here and calleth thee."

And thou, believest thou this? Yea, Lord, I believe; help Thou mine unbelief. The last words of Edward the Confessor were: "Weep not; I shall not die, but live; and as I leave the land of the dying, I trust to see the blessings of the Lord in the land of the living."

> If my immortal Savior lives,
>   Then my immortal life is sure;
> His Word a firm foundation gives;
>   Here let me build and rest secure.

TOMB OF LAZARUS.

III.

JESUS AND MARY.

As soon as she heard that, she arose quickly and went to Him. Now, Jesus was not yet come into the town, but was in that place where Martha met Him. The Jews then who were with her in the house and comforting her, when they saw that Mary rose up hastily and went out, followed her, thinking she was going to the tomb to wail there. Then, when Mary was come where Jesus was and saw Him, she fell down at His feet, saying, "Lord, if Thou hadst been here, my brother had not died." When Jesus therefore saw her wailing and the Jews also wailing which came with her, He groaned in the spirit and was troubled.

The picture is that of a horse snorting and champing its bit in rebellion against its load.

"Where have ye laid him?"

"Lord, come and see."

The Jewish rule was to have the burial-place at least a mile outside the village, and on the way the Lord's emotion found relief in tears.

"Jesus wept."

The shortest verse in the Bible and one of the greatest. The great God and Savior Jesus Christ was truly human, touched with the feeling of our infirmities, a merciful High Priest; He weeps with them that weep. Heb. 2, 17. 18; 4, 15; Rom. 12, 15.

IV.

JESUS AND THE JEWS.

Then said the Jews, "Behold how He loved him!" But some of them said, "Could not this man who opened the eyes of the blind have caused that this man should not die?"

Admitting Christ's greatness, they yet dared fault Him, even at a funeral. This agitated Him again.

Jesus therefore, again groaning in Himself, cometh to the tomb.

It was a cave, and a stone lay against it.

V.

JESUS AND MARTHA.

Jesus said, "Take ye away the stone." Martha, the sister of him that was dead, saith, "Lord, by this time he stinketh; for he hath been dead four days."

Despite her confession she was hopeless and thought Christ's efforts were useless. So much like ourselves.

Jesus said unto her, "Said I not to thee that, if thou wouldest believe, thou shouldest see the glory of God?"

A gentle, but earnest rebuke.

Then they took away the stone.

Why not obey the Lord before He must rebuke us?

VI.

JESUS AND HIS FATHER.

Jesus lifted up His eyes and said, "Father, I thank Thee because Thou hast heard Me; and I knew that Thou hearest Me always, but because of the people standing around I said it that they may believe Thou hast sent Me."

VII.

JESUS AND LAZARUS.

When He thus had spoken, He cried with a loud voice, "Lazarus, come forth!" And he that was dead came forth bound hand and foot with grave-clothes; and his face was bound about with a napkin.

Jesus saith to them, "Loose him and let him go."

"When Luther received the divine call, 'Take away the stone,' the body of the Church had already lain more than four hundred years in the Romish grave, and more than one faint-hearted Martha shrank from the smell of corruption which was being wafted by the stone-removing Reformation; but Luther's faith prospered unto the seeing of the glory of the Lord. And if we would believe, we should then know by real experience that the fragrance of incorruptible life which goes forth from the Head of the Church is powerful enough to overcome the corruption which death is working in her members. Before every Lazarus grave of Jesus' beloved Church the glory of the Lord stands ready to reveal itself."

VIII.

JESUS AND THE JEWS.

1. MANY ACCEPTED HIM.

Then many of the Judeans who came to Mary and had seen the things which Jesus did believed in Him.

Tennyson says: —

> From every house the neighbors met,
> The streets were filled with joyful sound,
> A solemn gladness even crowned
> The purple brows of Olivet. — *In Memoriam.*

Bishop Gore's New Commentary of the English liberal Episcopalians accepts the raising of Lazarus "with all its implications as the climax of all the miracles of healing."

2. SOME REJECTED HIM.

But some of them went away to the Pharisees and told them what Jesus had done.

Bayle says Spinoza, the Jewish philosopher, declared he would become a Christian could he believe in the raising of Lazarus. But he rejected Christ. Death yields more readily to Christ than man's unbelief.

IX.

THE BEWILDERED COUNCIL.

Then gathered the chief priests and the Pharisees a council and said, "What do we? For this man doeth many signs. If we let Him thus alone, all will believe on Him; and the Romans will come and take away both our place and nation."

A council without counsel. The only worry, We shall lose our jobs! They cannot deny the miracles, but they will deny Christ. At the Reformation some saw the truth of the Gospel, but they refused to accept the Gospel because they would lose their places. To-day some see the evil of the Christless lodge, but they refuse to fight the Christless lodge because they would lose their places.

X.

THE CYNICAL COUNSEL OF CAIAPHAS.

But one of them, Caiaphas, being the high priest that same year, said to them, "Ye know nothing at all nor consider that it is expedient for us that one man should die for the people and not the whole nation perish." This spake he not of himself, but being high priest that year, he prophesied that Jesus should die for the nation, and not for the nation of the Jews only, but that He might also gather in one people the children of God that are scattered abroad.

He was to save Jew and Gentile and unite them into one body, of which Christ is the Head, Eph. 2, 14—18.

This cool, cruel, calculating criminal Caiaphas will soon, as the high priest, bring the great sacrifice of the atonement for the sins of the people, and he is the chief author of the sacrifice of Christ, the great High Priest, making the atonement for the sins of the world.

They showed Wilberforce a picture of the crucifixion and said, "That

MARY AND THE ALABASTER BOX

St. Matt. 26:7; St. Mark 14:3; St. John 12:3

is the end of reformers." But Wilberforce kept right on till he had freed the slaves in the British colonies. They showed him a picture of the burning of Savonarola, but Luther kept right on till he had freed the Church.

XI.

MURDER PLANNED.

Therefore from that day forth they took counsel that they might put Him to death.

The chief rulers of God's chosen people — assassins!

XII.

JESUS IN RETREAT.

Jesus therefore walked no more openly among the Judeans; but went thence unto a country near the wilderness, into a city called Ephraim, and there He tarried with His disciples.

It was twenty miles north of Jerusalem and five miles northeast of Bethel. In B. C. 145 Demetrius II granted this Samaritan town to the Maccabean high priest Jonathan and united it to Judea. It was in a wheat country, and a Jewish proverb was to "carry straw to Ephraim," like "carry coals to Newcastle," and "carry owls to Athens."

XIII.

JESUS DISCUSSED.

Now the Passover of the Jews was at hand; and many went up to Jerusalem out of the country before the Passover to purify themselves. They sought therefore for Jesus and spake one with another as they stood in the Temple, "What think ye? That He will not come to the feast?"

XIV.

A GENERAL ALARM.

Now, the chief priests and the Pharisees had given a commandment that, if any man knew where He was, he should show it that they might take Him.

Likely they put a price on His head and advertised for His capture by placing a tablet to that effect in the Temple-courts like one discovered in the ruins.

CHAPTER XVIII.

JESUS ANOINTED.

John 12, 1—11.

I.

A GRACIOUS ACT.

IX days before the Passover, Jesus came to Bethany where Lazarus was, whom Jesus raised from the dead. So they made Him a supper there, and Martha was serving; but Lazarus was one of those reclining at meat with Him. — Come to think of it, this matter is not as simple as it reads. The government had already ordered the arrest of this fugitive from justice. In face of this the Bethany friends gave Him a testimonial banquet. And at the risk of His life Jesus attends. There is personal courage. How we love a brave man!

Martha served. See the beaming, hustling, and bustling Martha. She did what she could to show her love for Christ.

Mary would do what she could do. What could she do? She thought of her pound of ointment. Her action followed, fast as a flash. She broke the jar of alabaster — without handle or hard to handle, so smooth — and poured the precious spikenard over her Friend and wiped His feet with her flowing hair. She anointed Jesus with myrrh as her King. And the house was filled with the odor of the ointment.

Albrecht von Haller kept papers perfumed with one grain of ambergris for forty years, and then the odor was as strong as ever. The perfume of Mary's act will last through all the ages. Possibly it was the pistacia terebinthus, which grows in Judea and on Cyprus and which was used only for princely persons. Pliny calls nard the chief of unguents. In Aristophanes there is a daughter that also anoints and kisses her father's feet.

> Let my full heart what it can bestow;
> Like Mary's gift let my devotion prove,
> Forgiven greatly, how I greatly love.

Tennyson says: —

Her eyes are homes of silent prayer,
  Nor other thought her mind admits
  But he was dead, and there he sits,
And He that brought him back is there.

Then one deep love doth supersede
  All other when her ardent gaze
  Roves from the living brother's face
And rests upon the Life indeed.

All subtle thought, all curious fears,
  Borne down by gladness so complete,
  She bows, she bathes the Savior's feet
With costly spikenard and with tears.

Thrice blest whose lives are faithful prayers,
  Whose loves in higher love endure;
  What souls possess themselves so pure,
Or is there blessedness like theirs?

II.

A CARPING CRITIC.

But one of His disciples, Judas Iscariot, who should betray Him, saith, "Why was not this ointment sold for three hundred denarii and given to the poor?"

This he said, not that he cared for the poor, but because he was a thief and, having the money-box, used to steal the deposits, the gifts of friends to support Christ and His cause, Luke 8, 3. A denarius was a day's wage; so Mary's gift amounts to the earnings of a whole year.

He was enraged at seeing this big sum escape his thievish fingers, and he masks this rage with his tender heart for the poor — the hypocrite!

In Christ's own little congregation a church treasurer who stole from the Savior! "Will a man rob God?" Mal. 3, 8. Are you a good steward of God's gifts? 1 Pet. 4, 10; Luke 16, 1—14.

We hear the same surly, sullen snarls to-day. If their sympathetic souls care for the poor, why do they not care for the poor? It is safe to say the poor would get help from Mary and not from Judas, from the Christian givers of money and not from the unchristian givers of advice.

III.

A TRIUMPHANT VINDICATION.

Therefore Jesus said, "Let her alone in order that she may keep it against the day of My burying. For the poor ye have with you always, but Me ye have not always."

Longfellow says truly: —

Our Lord and Master,
When He departed, left us in His will,
As our best legacy on earth, the poor.
These we have always with us; had we not,
Our hearts would grow hard as are these stones.

Not the Judases with the money-box, but the Marys with the alabaster box are the ones that care for the poor. Lucian, the sneerer, had to say: "It is unbelievable to see the ardor with which those Christians help one another in their wants. They spare nothing. Their first Legislator has put it into their heads that they are all brothers." In the Decian persecution the prefect demanded the treasures of the Church. St. Lawrence brought him the sick, the lame, and the blind of Rome. When the plague raged in Carthage in 252, the heathen threw their dead and sick into the streets and ran off in fear and cursed the Christians. St. Cyprian told his members to love those who cursed them. They never rested till the dead were buried and the sick nursed. The apostate Emperor Julian said: "These Galileans nourish not only their own poor, but ours as well." And he taxed the people "that the Christians might not have a monopoly of good works." Has Christ done anything for you? Have you proved your thanks for what Christ has done for you? Have you made Him a supper in your duplex envelope? Have you served like Martha? Have you emptied your jewelry-box on Him? Have you raised a memorial for yourself? Have you done what you could? An old soldier brought his three months' earnings to help build a chapel at Lyons. Can you spare so much? "My Savior spared not Himself, but freely gave His life for me; surely I can spare one quarter of a year's earnings to extend His kingdom on earth."

IV.

A CURIOUS CROWD.

Now a large crowd of the Jews learned that He was there, and they came, not for Jesus' sake only, but that they might see Lazarus also, whom He had raised from the dead.

And to-day the curious crowds pack the church — to see the bride.

V.

A DEVILISH DEATH PLOT.

But the chief priests took counsel that they might kill Lazarus also because that by reason of him many of the Jews were going away and believing on Jesus.

Why does not some great artist paint these two kinds of church-members? On one side the lovers of Christ with the shining figures of the serving Martha and the impulsive Mary. On the other side, in contrast, the black figure of the thievish traitor with the evil eye, the hypocrite who whines about the poor and then sells Christ Himself for a handful of money — his real god. In the background the fiendish church officers scowling and plotting to kill Christ and even His harmless friend, the innocent Lazarus — the servant is not above the Master.

Some accept Christ, some reject Christ. "Set for the fall and rising again." Luke 2, 34.

CHAPTER XIX.

JESUS ENTERS JERUSALEM.

John 12, 12—19; Matt. 21, 1—17.

I.

THE TIME — PALM SUNDAY.

N the 10th of Nisan the Passover lamb was selected, Ex. 12, 13. On the 10th of Nisan, Joshua crossed the Jordan to conquer Canaan, Josh. 4, 19. On the 10th of Nisan, Jesus crossed the Kidron to offer Himself as the true Passover Lamb of God and as the true Joshua, the King of His people, to conquer and save the world. Caesar crossed the Rubicon to destroy the liberty of Rome; Christ crossed the Kidron to procure the liberty of the world.

II.

THE ACCLAMATION OF THE PEOPLE.

The next day a great crowd that had come to the feast, having heard Jesus is coming to Jerusalem, took the branches of the palm-tree and went forth to meet Him and kept crying out, "Hosanna! Blessed is He that cometh in the name of the Lord, even the King of Israel." Ps. 118, 25. 26.

> Ride on, ride on, in majesty;
> Hark, all the tribes hosanna cry!
> O Savior meek, pursue Thy road,
> With palms and scattered garments strow'd.

To carry palms was a mark of triumphant homage to a victor or a king. Rev. 7, 9; 1 Macc. 13, 51; Lev. 23, 40. Herodotus writes that people went before Xerxes crossing the Hellespont and burned all manner of perfumes on the bridges and strewed the way with myrtles. Sometimes the road was covered for miles with rich silks over which the king rode into the city. Both by their works and by their words the crowds were acclaiming Jesus as their Messianic King. Sir Walter Raleigh spread his fine cloak over the mud, so that Queen Elizabeth might walk over it. Shall we do less for our King?

DALLMANN, JOHN.   [241]   16

III.

THE PROCLAMATION OF THE PRINCE OF PEACE.

And Jesus, having found a young ass, sat thereon; as it is written, "Fear not, daughter of Zion; behold, thy King cometh, sitting on an ass's colt," Zech. 9, 9. 10.

Jesus did not come as "the man on horseback"; He came as the Prince of Peace. His lowliness was also understood full well by the old

JESUS ENTERING JERUSALEM.

heathen Romans, who sneered at the Christians as *asinarii*. They had a crude picture showing a Christian worshiping an ass as his god. The King rode into the city of the great King — on a borrowed donkey. Do you lend your auto to Christ when He needs it for His work in His kingdom?

Fling wide the portals of your heart,
Make it a temple set apart
From earthly use for heaven's employ,
Adorned with prayer and love and joy;
So shall your Sovereign enter in
And new and nobler life begin.
To Thee, O God, be praise
For word and deed and grace.

IV.

THE WONDERING DISCIPLES.

These things understood not His disciples at the first; but when Jesus was glorified, then remembered they that these things were written of Him and that they had done these things unto Him.

Like the disciples we, too, very often do not understand the Lord's doings; but later on we shall understand. Let us possess our souls in patience; time will tell.

V.

THE PRAISING PEOPLE.

The people that was with Him when He called Lazarus out of the grave and raised him from the dead bore witness — praised the deed. For this cause the people also met Him, for that they heard that He had done this sign.

VI.

THE FEARFUL PHARISEES.

The Pharisees said among themselves, "Behold how ye prevail nothing; lo, the world is gone after Him."

What an astounding admission of the weakness of the rulers! What an astounding confession of the power of Christ! John plainly exults over the situation.

> Ride on, ride on, in majesty,
> In lowly pomp ride on to die;
> Bow Thy meek head to mortal pain,
> Then take, O Christ, Thy power and reign.

CHAPTER XX.

SOUGHT BY GREEKS.

John 12, 20—50.

"We would see Jesus," for the shadows lengthen
 Across this little landscape of our life;
"We would see Jesus" our weak faith to strengthen
 For the last weariness, the final strife.

"We would see Jesus," the great Rock Foundation,
 Whereon our feet were set by sovereign grace;
Not life nor death with all their agitation
 Can thence remove us if we see His face.

I.

THE REQUEST.

AT the rising of the Sun of Righteousness wise men from the East came to worship Him; now, at the setting of the Sun, wise men from the West came to interview Him. There were certain Greeks among those in the habit of coming up to worship at the feast. They may have been circumcised members of the synagog; they may have been interested proselytes of the gate, but not circumcised; they may have been heathen, for heathen might bring an offering to the Temple; at the Passover of A. D. 37 the Syrian governor interrupted his march to go up to Jerusalem and offer sacrifice. Yes, Caesar Augustus and his wife Livia sent costly gifts to the Temple, and he ordered a daily sacrifice for himself of two rams and a bullock.

These came to Philip, who was from Bethsaida of Galilee, and asked him, "Sir, we wish to see Jesus." Philip telleth Andrew, and both tell Jesus.

II.

THE RESPONSE.

Jesus answered them, "The hour is come that the Son of Man be glorified." He will be glorified in His crucifixion, resurrection, and ascension. He will be glorified in the coming of the Gentiles into His kingdom. This was foretold by the prophets, Micah 4, 1—5; Is. 11, 10; 19, 18—25; 42, 1—8; 49, 6; 60, 3; Zech. 8, 20—23. It was foretold by Himself, John 3, 14—17; 10, 16—18. The Son of Man will be the Savior of the sons of men.

"Verily, verily, I say unto you, Except the grain of wheat fall into the ground and die, it abideth alone; but if it die, it bringeth forth much fruit." 1 Cor. 15, 36.

This is the first illustration of the great paradox that death is the gate of life. In the death of Christ is the life of His Church. His life at death did not terminate; then it began to germinate. "From the dying of the grain of wheat sprouts the harvest of the Gentiles," says St. Bernard. Every soul in heaven is the "much fruit" of Christ's death, Is. 53, 10.

"He that loveth his life loseth it; and he that hateth his life in this world shall keep it to life eternal."

This is the second illustration of the paradox of the Cross. The apostate who denied Christ saved his life in this world and lost it in death eternal; the martyr who confessed Christ lost his life in this life and kept it to life eternal. Not pagan self-expression, but Christian self-suppression. Not high living and low thinking, but high thinking and plain living. Not "living the life of Riley," but living the life of Christ. You enjoy life when you improve life.

"If any man serve Me, let him follow Me; and where I am, there shall also My servant be. If any man serve Me, him will the Father honor."

This is the third illustration of the paradox that the Passion of Christ is His glorification. Not selfish enjoyment, but unselfish employment is the path to greatness in the kingdom of Christ, Mark 9, 35; 10, 43. 45. Christ came, not to be served, but to serve. As Christ, so the Christian. Christ's life makes a Christlike life. Have you the love of life? Then lead the life of love. Serve, and you will deserve the Distinguished Service medal. Imitation of Christ brings assimilation with Christ, and conformation to Christ, and transformation into the image of Christ, and coronation and domination and glorification with Christ.

> My knowledge of the life is small,
>   The eye of faith is dim;
> But 'tis enough that Christ knows all
>   And I shall be with Him.

And I shall be like Him. 2 Tim. 2, 11. 12; Rom. 8, 29; 6, 5; 2 Cor. 4, 10; Rev. 12, 11; Phil. 3, 21; 1 John 3, 2.

The saintly Henry Martyn labored among the heathen with great patience, but with little result. He died. His death created a revival of missionary interest. The corn of wheat fell into the ground and died and brought forth much fruit. "The blood of the martyrs is the seed of the Church."

Walter C. Smith says truly: —

> But all through life I see a Cross
> Where sons of God yield up their breath.
> There is no gain except by loss,
> There is no life except by death
> And no full vision but by faith
> Nor glory but by bearing shame
> Nor justice but by taking blame;
> And that eternal Passion saith,
> "Be emptied of glory and right and name."

Carlyle says: "Annihilation of self; *Selbsttoetung,* as Novalis calls it; casting yourself at the footstool of God's throne 'to live or to die forever; as Thou wilt, not as I will.' Brother, hadst thou never in any form such moments in thy history? Thou knowest them not even by credible rumor? Well, thy earthly path was peaceabler, I suppose. But the Highest was never in thee, the Highest will never come out of thee. Thou shalt at best abide by the stuff; as cherished house-dog guard the stuff, perhaps with enormous gold collars and provender; but the battle and the hero-death and victory's fire-chariot carrying men to the Immortals shall never be thine. I pity thee; brag not, or I shall have to despise thee."

"Now is My soul troubled." Ps. 42, 6. 7; 43, 5; Matt. 26, 38. 40; Luke 12,50. "And what shall I say? Father, save Me from this hour."

Christ was made sin for us, the propitiation for the sins of the world, which lay upon Him alone. The wages of sin is death, and death fronted Him in the most fearful form. He was human, and He dreaded death and prayed to be saved from it — if possible. 2 Cor. 5, 21; Rom. 3, 25; 8, 3; John 1, 29; 3, 14; Matt. 20, 28; 26, 39. He remembered it was not possible —

"But for this cause came I unto this hour."

His suffering as our Substitute is the ground of our salvation. He had to suffer and die so we might not die forever. And in a burst of holy and heroic resolve He cries, "Father, glorify Thy name!"

The Father is glorified through the works of the Son, for He works through the Son, and, "I and the Father are one." The Father is our Savior through the Savior.

III.

THE HEAVENLY VOICE.

Then came a voice out of heaven, "I have glorified, I will again glorify" — My name.

IV.

THE OPINION OF THE PEOPLE.

The people therefore that stood by and heard, said that it had thundered; others said, "An angel hath spoken to Him."

V.

THE EXPLANATION.

Jesus answered, "This voice hath not come for My sake, but for your sakes" — a warning to escape the Judgment.

"Now is the judgment of this world; now shall the prince of this world be cast out. And I, if I be lifted up from the earth, will draw all men to Myself." This He said, signifying by what manner of death He was about to die — lifted up on the cross. Deut. 21, 23; Is. 53, 8; Gal. 3, 13.

By His death Christ overcame the world and destroyed the works of the devil.

The Word of the Cross is the power of God unto salvation, 1 Cor. 1, 18. Christ's cross is Christ's throne. His suffering secured His sovereignty. On the cursed cross He was glorified, Gal. 6, 14. "In the Cross of Christ I glory." "We preach Christ Crucified."

The Cross is the magnet to draw men to Christ.

> Draw us to Thee
> Unceasingly,
>   Into Thy kingdom take us;
> Let us fore'er
> Thy glory share,
>   Thy saints and joint heirs make us.

VI.

THE PEOPLE'S REJOINDER.

The people answered Him, "We have heard out of the Law that the Christ abideth forever. How, then, dost Thou say, The Son of Man must be lifted up" — die? "Who is *this* Son of Man?" Dan. 7, 13.

True, He was to abide forever. Is. 9, 7; 53, 10; Ezek. 37, 25; Dan. 2, 44; 7, 14. 27; Ps. 72, 5. 7. 17. 37. 38; 89, 4; 110, 4; Micah 4, 7; 2 Sam. 7, 16. But first He was to suffer and die. Is. 53, 7; Dan. 9, 26. They overlooked the Suffering Servant and thought only of the Conquering King.

It is of the utmost importance to compare Scripture with Scripture. When people do not do so, they are in great peril of running into false teaching and clinging to it, thinking they have Scripture on their side.

VII.

THE LORD'S REJOINDER.

1. *A blessed revelation.* — Christ calls Himself the Light, and He does it four times in only two verses. He repeats it to show its importance. The word is a mine of meaning; and it is an ever-flowing spring of comfort.

2. *A great opportunity.* — "Yet a little while is the Light among you."

The sun is westering, soon it will set; then night will fall. Time flies. Yesterday is no longer yours; do not regret it, forget it. To-morrow is not yet yours; do not dream about it. To-day is yours, and only to-day, the present fleeting moment. "To-day if ye hear His voice, harden not your hearts." "Whatsoever thy hand findeth to do, do it with all thy might" — and do it now.

3. *An earnest exhortation.* —

a. "While ye have the Light, *believe* in the Light" — trust Christ, the only Savior.

b. *Walk* as ye have the Light. In the measure that ye have the Light, walk, go forward, grow more Christlike.

4. *A terrible danger.* — "That darkness may not overtake you; and he that walketh in darkness knoweth not whither he goeth." Jer. 13, 15. 16; Is. 8, 20.

Darkness, gross darkness, did overtake the Jews when Titus made the historic and savage destruction of Jerusalem, which Josephus describes. And the Jews as a people are still groping in darkness, not knowing whither they are going. Some of them cynically say, "America is our Promised Land, and Washington is our Messiah."

5. *A glorious goal.* — "That ye may become sons of light."

Can there be a greater object in human life than to become like the Light? Luke 16, 8; 1 Thess. 5, 5; Eph. 5, 8. And then the glorious

JESUS WASHING THE DISCIPLES' FEET

St. John 13:5

future — blaze forth as the sun in the kingdom of your Father. Matt. 13, 43; 1 Tim. 6, 16.

These last verses of Christ, Luther in 1545 put at the end of his last edition of the New Testament. What a deep thought!

VIII.

THE SAVIOR REJECTED.

John 12, 37—43.

Though He had done so many and various signs before them, yet they believed not on Him, that the saying of Isaiah, the prophet, might be fulfilled which he spake, Lord who hath believed our report, and to whom hath the arm of the Lord been revealed?

The arm of the Lord is Christ. Is. 53, 1; 51, 59; 52, 10; Ps. 22, 1; 78, 11. 12; Rom. 10, 16; 1, 16.

Therefore they could not believe; for Isaiah said again, He hath blinded their eyes and hardened their hearts that they should not see with their eyes nor understand with their hearts and should turn and I should heal them. Is. 6, 9. 10; Matt. 13, 14; 1 Pet. 2, 8; Acts 28, 25.

Those unwilling to believe become unable to believe, self-hardened. A solemn subject.

These things said Isaiah because he saw His glory, and he spoke of Him. Is. 6, 1. 3; Rev. 4, 8—11; 5, 12—14.

The glory of Jehovah was the glory of Christ and of the Holy Spirit — the Holy Trinity. It should set us to thinking that Isaiah foretold the unbelief of the Jews as well as the suffering of the Savior. The prophecy is still being fulfilled, the Jews are still unbelieving.

Chrysostom remarks: "It was not because Isaiah spake that they believed not, but because they were about not to believe that he spake."

IX.

THE FINAL PUBLIC APPEAL.

John 12, 44—50.

Jesus cried aloud, for emphasis, "He that believeth on Me believeth not on Me [only], but on Him that sent Me. And he that beholdeth Me beholdeth Him that sent Me. I am come a Light into the world that whosoever believeth on Me may not abide in darkness. And if a man

hear My words and keepeth them not, I judge him not; for I came not
to judge the world, but to save the world." Titus 3, 11 — self-condemned.

"He that rejecteth Me and received not My words hath one that
judgeth him: the Word that I have spoken, the same shall judge him
in the Last Day." Deut. 18, 18. 19. "For I have not spoken from Myself,
but the Father, who sent Me. He hath given Me a commandment what
I should say and what I should speak. And I know that His commandment is life everlasting; whatsoever I speak therefore, even as the Father
hath said unto Me, so I speak."

These things spoke Jesus, and He departed and hid Himself from
them.

The preacher of Christ must preach like Christ, preach the same
thing, and preach with the same boldness and conviction. These burning
words end the public preaching of Christ; they are a solemn protest that
it is not the Father's fault if any one is lost. What a self-portrait of Jesus!
In order to save the world, even the unbelievers, He perfectly, heroically,
unselfishly, obeyed the Father's will. "Let this mind be in you which
was also in Christ Jesus," Phil. 2, 5.

X.

THE SAVIOR ACCEPTED.

Yet even of the rulers many believed on Him; but because of the
Pharisees they did not confess Him lest they should be put out of the
synagog; for they loved the praise of men more than the praise of God.
John 5, 44; Prov. 29, 25.

At the time of the Reformation there were such "believers" who dared
not confess openly for fear of being put out of the Church. Are there
such "believers" to-day? Are there people who know the truth and do
not act according to it for fear of business, politics, society? Listen to
Burns: —

> An atheist's laugh is a poor exchange
> For Deity offended.

We love praise from good men. "Praise from Sir Hubert is praise
indeed." But praise from God is the supreme praise. Get this praise
from God, "Well done, good and faithful servant."

From these men we learn that "believers" may become unbelievers,
self-hardened, Beware! 2 Pet. 2, 21; Heb. 6, 4.

Hindenburg, "a still, strong man if ever there was one," loved the praise of God more than the praise of men. He wrote: "The decisive factor in my life and action was not a desire for the applause of the world. It was rather my own conviction, a sense of duty, and my own conscience which have guided me throughout my life." And the reviewer of his biography by Goldsmith and Voight concludes: "His career is a striking illustration of the meek, the strong, and the humble inheriting the earth."

CHAPTER XXI.

JESUS AT THE LORD'S SUPPER.

John 13, 1—30.

I.

SERVICE.

1. THE SLAVING LORD.

THERE had been a strife among the disciples which of them should be accounted the greatest. And this unholy quarrel was carried on even at the Passover. Matt. 18, 1—6; 20, 20—28; Mark 9, 34; Luke 9, 46; 22, 24. It seems pride kept each one of the disciples from the customary washing of the feet.

It is very plain the apostles did not know Peter was the "Prince of the Apostles," or they would not have wrangled about rank. Peter seems not to have known he was the "Prince of the Apostles," or he would soon have cut short the wrangle about rank by simply saying, "I am the Prince of the Apostles." The Lord Himself did not know He had made Peter the "Prince of the Apostles," or He would sharply have reminded them that He had made Peter the "Prince of the Apostles." This rank wrangle about rank brought on the following astounding action of Christ.

Now, before the feast of the Passover, Jesus, knowing that His hour was coming that He should depart out of this world unto the Father, having loved His own who were in the world, loved them unto the end — or uttermost, in a remarkable manner.

Are not our cold hearts thrilled on hearing that we are "His own"? The soldier is proud to be in the "King's Own" regiment.

And during supper, the devil having already put into the heart of Judas Iscariot, Simon's son, to betray Him, Jesus, knowing that the Father had given all things into His hands and that He came forth from God, He riseth from supper and layeth aside His outer garment; and took a towel and girded Himself. Then He poureth water into the pitcher and began to wash the disciples' feet and to wipe them with the towel wherewith He was girded.

Suetonius writes Caligula insulted senators by making them wait at table, girded with a towel like slaves. Which shows how deeply Christ humbled Himself in this act. Imagine the looks on the twelve faces!

[252]

So He cometh to Simon Peter, who saith, "Lord, dost *Thou* wash *my* feet?"

Peter's fine sense of the fitness of things simply could not tolerate the intolerable. And our heart goes out to the rough, but noble fisherman. Jesus answered, "What I do thou knowest not now; but thou shalt know hereafter."

That should have satisfied Peter. And that gentle word should satisfy us when we are also bewildered by the doings of the Lord. But the impulsive Peter now even more positively blurts out, "Never shalt Thou wash my feet!"

Same old Peter; he knows better than his Lord, and he tries to master his Master. How human!

Now Jesus threatens him sternly, "If I wash thee not, thou hast no part with Me" — no share in Me and My blessings.

Peter is overwhelmed and now eagerly says, "Lord, not my feet only, but also the hands and the head." Again he knows better than his Lord. Queer Peter! So much like ourselves.

Jesus saith, "He that is bathed needeth not save to wash his feet," — dusty from walking, — "but is clean every whit."

Bathed in the full bath of Holy Baptism, we are clean every whit, and yet we need a daily washing of the feet, soiled from walking in the sinful world.

Jesus adds an ominous word, "And ye are clean, but not all." For He knew who was betraying Him; therefore said He, "Ye are not all clean."

What a remarkable duel of words! It is Peter all over, running true to form, his reverence almost irreverence, taking away our breath. And Christ — how patient with His "terrible infant." Are we any better?

Could we bear from one another
  What He daily bears from us?
Yet this glorious Friend and Brother
  Loves us though we treat Him thus;
Though for good we render ill,
He accounts us brethren still.

O blessed Jesus, when I see Thee bending
  Girt as a servant at Thy servants' feet,
Love, lowliness, might, in zeal all blending,
  To wash their dust away and make them meet
To share Thy feast — I know not to adore
Whether Thy humbleness or glory more.

2. THE SLAVES OF THE LORD.

So, after He had washed their feet and had taken His garments and had sat down again, He said unto them, "Understand ye what I have done to you? Ye call Me the Master and the Lord, and ye say well, for so I am. If I, then, the Lord and the Master, have washed your feet, ye also ought to wash one another's feet. For I have given you an example that ye also should do as I have done to you. Verily, verily, I say unto you, A slave is not greater than his lord, neither one that is sent greater than he that sent him. If ye know these things, blessed are ye if ye do them."

THE BEATITUDE OF SERVICE.

Jesus joins knowing and doing; what Jesus hath joined together let no man put asunder. Peter never forgot this. He says: "Be clothed with the slave's costume of humility" to wash His disciples' feet, 1 Pet. 5, 5. The great God and Savior Jesus Christ washes feet. Christ's "Vicar on earth," the Pope, has his feet — kissed!

On Green Thursday "the Servant of the servants of God," the Pope, goes through a theatrical foot-washing. So also did the courts of Austria, Bavaria, Russia, and Spain. In 1530 England's proudest cardinal, Wolsey, washed, wiped, and kissed the feet of fifty-nine poor men at Peterborough. The practise was kept up by English kings till the times of James II. Holy George Herbert never mentioned the name of Christ without adding "my Master."

> How sweetly doth "My Master" sound,
>   "My Master"!
> As ambergris leaves a rich scent
>   Unto the taster,
> So do these words a sweet content,
>   An oriental fragrancy —
> "My Master"!

How may I obey my Master? One simple way is to give, and give till it hurts, in my duplex envelope — support students, and missionaries, and deaconesses, and orphanages, and hospitals, and homes for the aged, the epileptics, and the blind. The Christian is not above Christ. If I really believe Christ has cleansed me every whit, I will try to cleanse others, soul and body. Let us live up to the motto of the Prince of Wales, *"Ich dien',"* "I serve." Let us live up to the motto of Frederick the Great, "I am the first servant of the State."

> Wouldst thou the holy hill ascend
>   And see the Father's face?
> To all His children lovely bend
>   And seek the humblest place.
>
> Thus humbly doing on the earth
>   What things the lofty scorn,
> Thou shalt assert the noble birth
>   Of all the lowly born.

The infidel John Stuart Mill says "not even now would it be easy even for an unbeliever to find a better translation of the rule of virtue from the abstract into the concrete than the endeavor so to live that Christ would approve our life."

Would Christ approve my life? If not, is it not high time to reform? Whittier says: —

> O Lord and Master of us all,
> Whate'er our name or sign,
> We own Thy sway, we hear Thy call,
> We test our lives by Thine.

Robert Morrison wrote for another missionary to help him in China. A country lad, poorly clad and rough of manner, offered to go. He was told he was not fit for a missionary, but he could go as a servant to the missionary. "Very well, sir; I will go as a servant. I am willing to be a hewer of wood and a drawer of water or to do anything to help the cause of my heavenly Master." That servant became the great and famous Dr. Milne.

II.

TREASON.

"I speak not of you all, — I know whom I chose, — but that the Scripture may be fulfilled, He that eateth My bread lifteth up his heel against Me" — to kick Me. Ps. 41, 9. 10.

Eating bread with a superior was a pledge of loyalty, and to betray a messmate was a heinous breach of sacred hospitality.

"From now I tell you before it come to pass that, when it is come to pass, ye may believe that I am He" — Jehovah. It was His prerogative to foretell the future. Is. 41, 26; 48, 5; Ezek. 24, 24.

"Verily, verily, I say to you, He that receiveth whomsoever I send receiveth Me; but he that receiveth Me receiveth Him that sent Me."

How do you receive your pastor, whom Christ has sent to you? A man said, "When our lodge elects an officer, we treat him with the greatest honor and respect; church-members tear their pastors to pieces."

A STARTLING ANNOUNCEMENT.

When Jesus had said this, He was troubled in spirit — quivering with emotion — and testified, "Verily, verily, I say to you, One of you shall betray Me."

Certainly an astounding announcement. This is the moment shown in the great picture of Leonardo da Vinci. A disciple beloved by Christ, yet a traitor to Christ.

THE STARTLED DISCIPLES.

The disciples looked one on another, being uncertain of whom He spake. They were scared and embarrassed. The silence was oppressive. The suspense was intolerable. Peter comes to the rescue; he relieves the tension.

Now, there was leaning on Jesus' bosom one of His disciples, whom Jesus loved. Simon Peter therefore maketh a sign to him and saith to him, "Tell who it is of whom He speaketh." He, leaning back, as he was, on Jesus' breast, saith unto Him, "Lord, who is it?"

"The disciple whom Jesus loved" — what immortality! Proud of his friendship with Sir Philip Sidney, Lord Brooks put on his gravestone,

"Here lies Sir Philip Sidney's friend."

May we put on your grave,

"Here lies Christ's friend"?

Jesus therefore answereth, "He it is for whom I shall dip the sop and give it him."

The sop was a morsel of unleavened bread; it was dipped into the common dish of charoseth — figs, nuts, almonds, and other fruits stewed in wine. To give such a sop was a mark of special honor.

JUDAS.

So when Jesus had dipped the sop, He taketh it and giveth it to Judas, the son of Simon Iscariot.

Christ's last appeal, so tender and touching, did not touch Judas; he had hardened himself.

And after the sop, then Satan entered into him.

That horrible short statement should make one shudder. Solemnly ask, Who is in my heart? It is either Christ or Satan.

JUDAS DISMISSED.

Therefore saith Jesus unto him, "What thou doest, do quickly."

At last the love of Jesus gave up and let the soul of Judas commit suicide. The long-suffering of God waited one hundred and twenty years in the days of Noah, but at last His patience gave out. "My Spirit shall not always strive with man," Gen. 6, 3. Then came the Flood.

EXIT JUDAS.

Now, no man at the table knew for what intent He spoke thus to him. For some thought, because Judas had the purse, that Jesus had said unto him, Buy what we need for the feast, or that he should give something to the poor — to help keep the feast. Deut. 16, 14.

The Passover night was the liveliest night of all the year, as lively as the day. Is. 30, 29.

So, having received the sop, that one went out at once; and it was night.

It was night outside, and it was night in the soul of Judas. Of his own free will he went from the Light into the night. John Bunyan says long after he loved Christ, the Tempter "would intermix in such sort with all I did that I could not eat my food nor stoop to pick up a pin nor chop a stick without hearing this whisper, 'Sell Christ — sell Him for this — sell Him for that. Sell Him! Sell Him!'"

And we are tempted to sell and betray.

CHAPTER XXII.

JESUS' FAREWELL WORDS.

I.

FELLOWSHIP.

John 13, 31—38.

1. BETWEEN THE FATHER AND THE SON.

THEREFORE, when Judas was gone out, Jesus said, "Now is the Son of Man glorified, and God is glorified in Him, and God shall glorify Him in Himself and shall glorify Him at once."

The Cross glorifies Christ because it shows His love as nothing else can. The Cross glorifies Christ because it is the power which draws men to Christ as nothing else does. The Cross glorifies God because it shows the love of God for the world which gave His Only-begotten to the world as a sacrifice. The Cross glorifies God because God was in Christ, reconciling the world unto Himself. God glorified Christ in Himself with His own eternal glory. God did it straightway when Christ descended into hell, rose from the dead, ascended into heaven, and sat on the right hand of God the Father Almighty, from thence He shall come to judge the quick and the dead.

"Little children, yet a little while I am with you. Ye will seek Me, and as I said unto the Jews, Whither I go, ye cannot come, so now I say to you."

They cannot follow Him into death and into heaven — now; but soon.

2. BETWEEN THE CHRISTIANS.

"A new commandment I give unto you, That ye love one another; as I have loved you, that ye also love one another."

The love of Christ for us is the motive for us to love one another; it also shows the measure in which we are to love one another: as Christ, so the Christian. From this great command Maundy Thursday is named.

"By this will all know that ye are My disciples, if ye have love one to another."

Only by God's love we know that He is our Father and Savior, and only by our love the world will know we are God's children. The world will not understand our creeds, but it will understand our deeds. Jerome writes that John in his old age ever repeated, "Little children, love one another." Why no more? "That is enough." Tertullian says the heathen cried in surprise, "See how these Christians love one another!" Why did they? Lucian says, "Their Master put it into their heads they are brothers." And Minucius Felix says, "They love before they know one another." Has your love grown cold?

RASHNESS REVEALED.

Simon Peter could not get it through his head what Jesus had said a few moments ago about going away, and so up and asked, "Lord, whither goest Thou?"

Jesus answered, "Whither I go thou canst not follow Me now; thou shalt follow afterwards."

That gentle word would have been enough for any ordinary person, but Peter was not an ordinary person; he was, in fact, a very extraordinary person, and in the most extraordinary manner he talks up against his Master.

"Why cannot I follow Thee now? I will lay down my life for Thee."

Christ did not want him to die *now;* but Peter wanted to die *now.* Same old Peter, blind, blunt, blundering, blurting out nearly a flat contradiction of Christ. Christ had to repress the irrepressible.

RASHNESS REBUKED.

Jesus answered him, "Wilt thou lay down thy life for Me? Verily, verily, I say unto thee, The cock shall not crow till thou hast denied Me thrice."

Die? Lie! Was ever irony so sad and so severe? "God resisteth the proud," says Peter, and Peter knew, 1 Pet. 5, 5. It was enough to silence even Peter. The others were also depressed, and Christ had to comfort their troubled hearts.

II.

CHRIST THE COMFORTER.

John 14.

"This is the best and most comforting sermon Christ made on earth — a treasure and gem that cannot be paid with the wealth of the world. Here He has richly poured out the high, hearty comfort that all Christendom has and that a man in all troubles and sufferings should desire," says Luther of this and the two following chapters.

1. THE HEAVENLY HOME.

A. THE CURE FOR HEART TROUBLE.

"Let not your heart be troubled."

Very good advice; but how can I help being troubled?

"Believe in God and in Me believe."

Mr. Fujimoto believed in God, but farther he could not go. He prayed two hours and then seemed to hear a voice, "Believe also in Me."

CHRIST THE CONSOLER.

He read John 14—16 and became a believer in the Lord Jesus Christ. Without Christ, men are without God and without hope. Eph. 2, 12.

Trust in Christ is Christianity; nothing else is. In Christ we see God, and God is for us. If God be for us, who can be against us? "A mighty Fortress is our God. . . .   The Kingdom ours remaineth." Rom. 8, 31; Ps. 27, 13; 46; 141,8. Cromwell said: "As for the pleasures of this life and outward business, let that be upon the bye. Be above all these things by faith in Christ, and then you will have the true use and comfort of them — and not otherwise." Carlyle adds: "How true is this! — equal in its obsolete dialect to the highest that man has yet attained to in any dialect, old or new." Sherman said: "I am not afraid of dangers that I can see; but Grant is not afraid of dangers he cannot see." True Christians are like Grant.

> The heart that trusts forever sings
> And feels as light as it had wings;
> A well of peace within it springs.
>   Come good or ill
> Whate'er to-day, to-morrow, brings,
>   It is His will.

B. THE PLACE.

"In My Father's house are many dwellings."

It is the house of the Father and therefore a home — no place like home. "Children, the milk and honey are beyond this wilderness." That dwelling is an abode where we abide. Here we rove and roam; there is the real Alabama, where we rest. Lord Tennyson said, "I want to live forever and ever. And God gives me my desire."

> Since Christ has gone to heaven, His home,
>   I, too, that home one day must share,
> And in this hope I overcome
>   All doubt, all anguish, and despair;
> For where the Head is, well we know,
> The members He has left below
>   In time He surely gathers.

"If not, I would have told you."

This is Christ's signature to the deed to my heavenly home. "He said it." I trust *Him*. Christianity is the only religion of a well-founded, firmly grounded, joyous hope. "And hope maketh not ashamed."

C. THE PREPARATION.

"I go to prepare a place for you." Heb. 11, 16.

On earth the Lord and Master washed His disciples' feet; in heaven the great God and Savior is preparing a room for us. No wonder His name is called "Wonderful."

> Christ is our place preparing;
>   To heaven we, too, shall rise
> And, joys angelic sharing,
>   Be where our Treasure lies.

> There may each heart be found,
>   Where Jesus Christ has entered;
>   There let our hopes be centered,
> Our course still heavenward bound.

> I long to see the place my Lord
> In love prepares for me.

D. The Reception.

"Even though I prepare a place for you, I come again and will receive you unto Myself, that, where I am, ye may be also."

What a reception! What a home-coming! What a reunion! Forever with the Lord! 1 Thess. 4, 14—17. Said the dying Mrs. Oliphant: "I have no thoughts, not even of my boys, but only of my Savior's waiting to receive me, and of my Father."

> When I'm to die,
> "Receive me," I'll cry;
> For Jesus has loved me, I cannot tell why.
> But this I can find —
> We two are so joined
> He'll not be in glory and leave me behind.

Do you own a house in the heavenly Father's house?

> Jerusalem, my happy home,
> Name ever dear to me,
> When shall my labors have an end
> In joy and peace and thee?

Are you homesick for your real "real estate"?

> I am far frae my hame, an' I'm weary aftenwhiles,
> For the langed-for hame-bringing, an' my Father's welcome smiles;
> I'll ne'er be fu' content until my een do see
> The gowden gates o' heaven an' my ain countrie.
>
> The earth is flecked wi' flowers, mony-tinted, fresh, and gay;
> The birdies warble blithely, for my Father made them sae;
> But these sichts an' these soun's will as naething be to me
> When I hear the angels singing in my ain countrie.
>
> I've His gude word o' promise that some gladsome day the King
> To His ain royal palace His banished hame will bring;
> Wi' een an' wi' heart running ower we shall see
> The King in His beauty an' oor ain countrie.
>
> He's faithfu' that hath promised, He'll surely come again,
> He'll keep His tryst wi' me, at what hour I dinna ken;
> But He bids me still to wait an' ready aye to be
> To gang at ony moment to my ain countrie.

E. The Perfect Way.

"Whither I go ye know, and the way ye know."

"Lord, we know not whither Thou goest; and how should we know the way?" said Thomas.

Peter was bad enough, in all conscience; but Thomas is much worse.

He flatly contradicts his Master on both points. If he did not know, it was because he had not paid attention to the Teacher or because he was a very dull pupil. He makes the insulting suggestion that the fault lies with the Teacher. Christ had to endure the contradiction of sinners, also the contradiction of saints, Peter and Thomas.

H. ZATZKA.

"I AM THE WAY, THE TRUTH, AND THE LIFE."

They say the secret of teaching is patience. Well, gentle patience is shown by Christ; He has not a word of rebuke. He says, —

"I am the Way, the Truth, the Life; no one cometh to the Father but by Me."

Rejoice! Christ is the open Way for all. Through His death both Jews and Gentiles have access to the Father; yea, boldness and access with confidence, Eph. 2, 18; 3, 12.

Beware! Christ is the only Way to the Father. Through Christ to the Father. Without Christ to the devil. These are the two terminals; there is no half-way station, no purgatory. Every other way leads astray. No compromise with any other religion. Christianity is exclusive.

> Thou art the Life!
> All ways without Thee paths that end in death;
> All life without Thee with death-harvest ripe;
> All truths dry bones, disjoined, and void of breath —
> Thou art the Life!

Are you at present traveling on the only way to the Father?

John Arnd puts it this way: Without the way no man goeth on; without the truth nothing is known; and without life no man liveth. Therefore look unto Me, who am the Way in which you ought to walk; the Truth in which you ought to believe; and the Life in which you ought to live and hope. I am the Way that endureth to all ages, the infallible Truth, and the Life everlasting. The royal way to immortal life is through My merit; the truth itself is My Word; and life is through the power of My death; and therefore, if ye continue in this way, the truth will carry you on to eternal life. If ye will not err, come and follow Me; and if ye will possess life eternal, put your whole trust in Me, who for you endured the death of the cross. And what is that royal way, that infallible truth, and that endless life — the best and most noble way and truth and life of all others? Truly, other ways there can be none than the most holy and precious merit of Christ; nor other truth than the Word of God; not other life than love on earth and immortality of life in heaven.

> No more the way is hidden
>   Since Christ, our Head, arose;
> No more to man forbidden
>   The road that heav'nward goes.
> Our Lord is gone before;
>   But here He will not leave us,
>   In heaven He'll soon receive us;
> He opens wide the door.

> May we, His servants, thither
>   In heart and mind ascend;
> And let us sing together:
>   "We seek Thee, Christ, our Friend,
> Thee, God's anointed Son,
>   Our Life, and Way to heaven,
>   To whom all power is given,
> Our Joy, and Hope, and Crown!"

2. THE REVELATION OF THE FATHER IN CHRIST.

"If ye had known Me, ye would have known My Father also; from henceforth ye know Him and have seen Him."

Philip saith to Him, "Lord, show us the Father, and it will satisfy us."

Jesus saith, "Have I been so long time with you, and yet dost thou not know Me, Philip? He that hath seen Me hath seen the Father; how sayest thou, Show us the Father? Believest thou not that I am in the Father and the Father is in Me? The words that I speak unto you I speak not of Myself, but the Father, abiding in Me, doeth His works. Believe ye Me" — My words — "that I am in the Father and the Father in Me; or else, if ye believe not My words, believe Me because of the very works."

I am a spirit, and I make known my love, my anger, my wisdom, my folly, through the deeds of my body. God is a spirit, and He makes Himself known through the deeds of His body in Christ Jesus. In Christ, God is embodied, Col. 1, 15; Heb. 1, 3.

Luther says: "I cannot think of God but there arises in me the picture of a Man who hangs on the cross." There the Father reveals Himself as nowhere else. The learned Baron von Bunsen said: "I see Christ, and through Christ I see God." Christianity is not hazy and misty, but very sharply outlined in Christ.

3. PRECIOUS PROMISES.

A. As to Power.

"Verily, verily, I say unto you, He that believeth on Me, the works that I do shall he do also; and greater than these shall he do because I go unto the Father."

By Christ's going away the disciples were discouraged, but just by that they were to be encouraged. After Christ's going away Peter on Pentecost converted three thousand. Paul planted the Cross in the great cities of the Roman Empire, and in a little over two hundred years the Christian cross displaced the pagan eagle. Luther with his Justification by Faith in a short time created the whole Protestant world and even drove some corruptions out of the Papacy. Dr. Walther came into the wilds of Missouri, and in a short time the Missouri Synod was sending the Gospel into many parts of the world.

B. As to Prayer.

"And whatsoever ye shall ask in My name, that will I do that the Father may be glorified in the Son. If ye shall ask anything in My name, I will do it."

"Raleigh, when will you leave off begging?" thundered Queen Elizabeth. "When Your Majesty will leave off giving." Our royal Majesty will never thunder at us; He is only too glad to grant our requests; in fact, He invites them. From words to works, from prayer to performances.

"If ye love Me, ye will keep My commandments."

Astounding words! This Man claims the right to give commandments binding all men and in all their conduct. And obedience flows from love to Him. And if we love Him, His commandments are not grievous. It can be done. Paul says: "I can do all things through Christ, strengthening me." And Christ promises a special Strengthener, Comforter, Paraclete, Advocate, Pleader, Convincer, Persuader.

4. THE COMFORTER.

A. GIVEN.

"I shall pray the Father, and He will give another Comforter that He may abide with you forever, the Spirit of Truth."

Observe the Holy Trinity — Christ prays; the Father gives; the Comforter abides.

"You are called Theophorus, God-bearer; what mean you by this?" asked the pagan judge. Ignatius replied, "God dwells in me." Charged with blasphemy, Ignatius replied, "The Holy Spirit dwells in me." And he proved it by suffering a cruel death.

Are you a Theophorus, a God-bearer? Do you prove it by a holy life?

B. REJECTED.

"Whom the world cannot receive because it seeth Him not, neither knoweth Him."

The worldly world is worldly-wise, yet totally blind and utterly foolish in all spiritual things; it therefore cannot and will not see and receive the Holy Spirit, the Spirit of Truth, the gift of God Himself, 1 Cor. 2, 14. As the world treated Christ, though sent by the Father, so the world treats the Spirit, though sent by the Father.

C. RECEIVED.

"But ye know Him; for He abideth with you and is in you." Rom. 8, 9; 1 John 2, 27; 2 John 2; 2 Cor. 13, 14. The gift of the Father, asked for by Christ, the Holy Ghost, is our blessed possession. How do I know? "The Holy Ghost has called me by the Gospel, enlightened me with His gifts, sanctified and kept me in the true faith." Here I have the living Witness within me.

5. THE WONDERFUL SAVIOR.

A. ABSENT, YET PRESENT.

"I shall not leave you orphans — I am coming to you."

Absent bodily, present really. This was one of Melanchthon's favorite texts, quoted with deep feeling after the death of Luther in letters of February 19 and March 1, 1546, to Justus Jonas: "On this journey, when I was alone and my grief broke forth anew, I thought of our miseries, of the guidance of the Church and the university, and of our orphaned state. Amid these thoughts I support myself with the words of the Son of God, 'I will not leave you orphans.'"

B. UNSEEN, YET SEEN.

"Yet a little while and the world seeth Me no more; but ye see Me."

Unseen to the sight of the senses; seen by faith, the sight of the soul. My eyes deceive me often; my faith deceives me never, built up on the truth.

C. DYING, YET LIVING AND LIFE-GIVING.

"Because I live, ye also shall live." Cf. Rev. 1, 18.

During the dark days of the Augsburg Confession in 1530, Luther on the Coburg wrote these words: "I shall not die, but live and declare the works of the Lord," Ps. 118, 17. And he wrote the notes and sang the triumphant words. *"Vivit,* He lives," Luther wrote on the wall of his study. A friend asked the meaning. Luther answered, "Jesus lives; and if He did not live, I would not care to live an hour."

> Jesus, my Redeemer, lives!
>   I, too, unto life must waken;
> Endless joy my Savior gives;
>   Shall my courage, then, be shaken?
> Shall I fear, or could the Head
> Rise and leave His members dead?

This beautiful hymn some credit to the Great Elector's wife, Louise Henrietta of Orange, on whose coffin under the cathedral are inscribed Gal. 2, 20; Ps. 118, 21; Job 13, 15; 1 Cor. 15, 57.

6. THE WONDERFUL GIFT OF THE WONDERFUL SAVIOR.

"At that day ye shall know that I am in My Father and ye in Me and I in you." What a blissful union!

> So near, so very near, to God,
>   I cannot nearer be;
> For in the person of His Son
>   I am as near as He.

"He that hath My commandments and keepeth them, he it is that loveth Me; and he that loveth Me shall be loved of My Father, and I will love him, and I will manifest Myself to him."

Judas, not Iscariot, answered, "Lord, what has happened that Thou wilt manifest Thyself unto us and not unto the world?"

Jesus answered, "If a man love Me, he will keep My Word; and My Father will love him, and We will come unto him and make Our abode with him. He that loveth Me not keepeth not My words; and the word which ye hear is not Mine, but the Father's who sent Me."

7. THE TEACHING SPIRIT.

"These things have I spoken to you while yet abiding with you. But the Comforter, the Holy Ghost, whom the Father will send in My name, He shall teach you all things and bring to your remembrance all that I said to you."

Here Godet sees the inspiration of the gospels. Again observe the Holy Trinity — the Father, in the name of Christ, will send the Holy Ghost. The Son comes "in the name" of the Father to reveal the Father, and so the Holy Ghost comes "in the name" of the Son to reveal the Son. The glorious prophecy was gloriously fulfilled in the glorious gospels and epistles, in which the Holy Ghost reveals to us who the Son is and what He has done for our salvation. As we study more and more, we get to know Him better and better. Are you an eager pupil of the Holy Ghost? Are you studying His text-book? "What is written in the Law? How readest thou?" "Ye do err, not knowing the Scriptures." Luke 10, 26; Matt. 21, 42; 22; 29; Mark 12, 10, 24.

8. THE SAVIOR'S LEGACY OF PEACE.

"Peace I leave with you, My peace I give to you; not as the world giveth, give I to you. Let not your heart be troubled, neither let it be afraid."

All that the world could give it did give to Goethe. Did he have peace? He sadly bewails the world's turmoil and then piteously wails out: "Sweet peace, come, O come, into my breast!" He never had a moment to which he could say, "Tarry." Mark Twain at seventy-one said, "Well, I don't know what you think of it, but I think I have had enough of this world, and I wish I were out of it." "I don't say much about it, but that expresses my view," replied his multimillionaire American friend, nearly as old.

The world cannot give peace, for it has no peace. "There is no peace, saith the Lord, unto the wicked," Is. 48, 22. On the other hand, the Christian exults: —

Through Jesus' bloody merit	My courage shall not fail me,
I am at peace with God;	For God is on my side;
What, then, can daunt my spirit,	Though hell itself assail me,
However dark my road?	Its rage I may deride.

"Being justified by faith, we have peace with God through our Lord Jesus Christ," the Prince of Peace, who is our Peace, who gives us the peace of God which passeth all understanding. Rom. 5, 1; Is. 9, 6; Eph. 2, 14.

A man visited Bengel to hear how that great Lutheran theologian would pray. Bengel worked at his books till midnight, and yet the visitor lingered. At last Bengel put his books by, kneeled, and said, "Lord Jesus, matters between us are still the same," and went to bed. Peace, perfect peace.

Theodore Cuyler says, as New York's greatest railroad magnate lay dying, he asked for a hymn. They sang "Come, Ye Sinners, Poor and Needy." "Sing that again; I am poor and needy." Worth fifty millions — poor and needy. He found peace in Christ. The poor soldier dying at Waterloo was rich. "I die happy. I possess the peace of God, which passeth all understanding."

Peace, peace, I leave with you,
My peace I give to you,
    Perfect and pure;
Not as the world doth give,
Words that the soul deceive;
Ye who in Me believe
    Shall rest secure.

The world can neither give nor take,
    Nor can they comprehend
The peace of God which Christ has brought,
    The peace which knows no end.

At the word of the Prince of Peace we bring this peace to the world by the Gospel of Peace and are rewarded with the beatitude, "Blessed are the peacemakers." Phil. 4, 7; Matt. 5, 9.

9. CHRIST'S GOING.

A. A GROUND FOR JOY.

"Ye have heard that I said unto you, 'I go away and come unto you.' If ye loved Me, ye would have rejoiced that I go to the Father; for the Father is greater than I" — in My present state of a slave and obedience to the death on the cursed tree of the cross.

They ought to have rejoiced unselfishly at His promotion to glory with His Father in heaven. They ought to have rejoiced because in the Head the members, too, are glorified.

B. A GROUND OF FAITH.

"And now I have told you before it come to pass, that, when it is come to pass, ye may believe."

Forewarned — forearmed. Fulfilled prophecies prove the truth of the Bible and confirm faith and enlarge the joy.

10. THE FORESEEN VICTORY.

"I will no more speak much with you, for the Prince of the World cometh and hath nothing in Me" — absolutely sinless. "But that the world may know that I love the Father, and as the Father gave Me commandment, thus I do."

"Thus I do" — salvation is the work of Christ.

"Thus I do" — because I love the Father, to carry out the Father's love of the world to save the world, John 3, 16.

"Thus I do" — because I obey the Father: obedient unto death, even the death of the cross. By His obedience He atoned for our disobedience.

"Thus I do" — that the world may know.

"Arise, let us go hence!" Forward! March! On to victory!

> Thy saints in all this glorious war   They see the triumph from afar
> Shall conquer though they die;   With faith's discerning eye.

"In this chapter we have the great articles of Christian teaching in the most impressive form and fundamentally established as in hardly another place of Scripture," says Luther.

"Read to me," said the dying Sir Walter Scott, a man of many books. "From which book?" asked the son-in-law. "Need you ask? There is but one." Lockhart took the Bible and read John 14. "He listened with mild devotion and said when I had done, 'Well, this is a great comfort.'" Yes, it has been "a great comfort" to millions.

CHAPTER XXIII.

JESUS THE TRUE VINE.

John 15.

BOVE the door of the Temple, Herod had placed a wreath of golden vines with clusters a man's stature in length, Josephus tells us. It was a world's wonder, and Plutarch and Tacitus tell us the pagans thought the Jews were worshipers of Bacchus. It was to show that Israel was the vine planted by God in Palestine. Ps. 80, 8—19; Jer. 2, 21; Is. 5, 1; Ezek. 19, 10. It was a type of the New Testament Church, of Christ and His disciples.

I.

THE CHRISTIAN'S RELATION TO CHRIST.

John 15, 1—11.

I AM THE TRUE VINE, YE ARE THE BRANCHES.

Here is a union, not of beads strung together on a string, not of boards nailed or glued together, but of the parts of a living body. It is the same life from the deepest root to the farthest shoot.

What a glorious honor for the Christian to be thus in living union with the glorious Christ! But at what a price! Our war for the Union cost millions of lives and billions of dollars; but to bring about the union between Christ and His branches cost the sacrifice of the Son of God. Ponder and wonder.

"My Father is the Husbandman," the Vintner, the Owner and Dresser. At Christmas He planted the Vine, and in time believers were grafted upon it as branches, especially at Pentecost.

If our heavenly Father is the Owner and Dresser, why worry? · Would He harm the Vine or the branches?

"Every branch in Me that beareth not fruit He taketh away. If a man abide not in Me, he is cast forth as a branch and is withered; and men gather them and cast them into the fire, and they burn." It is good for nothing. Either in Christ or in the fire. Christ says this to church-members. This thing has happened; it can happen to us. Beware!

"Every branch in Me that beareth fruit He cleanseth, pruneth, that it may bear more fruit."

[271]

Mr. Cecil wondered why a fine pomegranate-tree in the Botanical Gardens at Oxford was cut almost through the stem near the root. "It bore nothing but leaves; after it was almost cut through, it began to bear plenty of fruit."

Good is not good enough; we must do better and better and still better. Good, better, best! Did you do better this year than last year?

Luther says: "This life is not holiness, but a becoming holy; not health, but a becoming healthy; not a being, but a becoming; not a rest, but an exercise; it is not the end, but it is the way; all does not yet glow and sparkle, but all is polishing."

Michelangelo says: "The more the marble wastes, the more the statue grows."

Mentone has sunshine and is sheltered by rocks, and the citron harvest lasts from January 1 to December 31. We have the Sun of Righteousness, and we are sheltered under the Rock of Ages; so let us bear fruit at all times, from January 1 to December 31.

"Now ye are clean," or pruned, "through the Word which I have spoken to you."

The Word of Christ grafts us into Christ and justifies us; it also keeps us fruitful in Christ and sanctifies us. The Word of Christ is the means of grace. Do you gladly hear the preached Word in church? Do you eagerly study the written Word at home with your family? If not, why not?

"Abide in Me and I in you. As the branch cannot bear fruit of itself, except it abide in the vine, so neither can ye except ye abide in Me. He that abideth in Me and I in him, the same beareth much fruit; for apart from Me ye can do nothing. If ye abide in Me and My words abide in you, ask whatsoever ye will, and it will be done unto you."

"*Iesu, Iuva!*" — "Jesus, help!" is at the top of every work of Johann Sebastian Bach. The world's mightiest master of music thereby declares apart from Jesus he could do nothing.

> Jesus immutably the same,
> The true and living Vine,
> Around Thy all-supporting stem
> My feeble arms I twine.
>
> Quickened by Thee and kept alive,
> I flourish and bear fruit;
> My life I from Thy sap derive,
> My vigor from Thy root.

Whittier says: —

> No pride of self Thy service hath,
>   No place for me and mine;
> Our human strength is weakness, death
>   Our life, apart from Thine.

Harriet Beecher Stowe prays: —

> Abide in me; there have been moments pure
>   When I have seen Thy face and felt its power;
> Then evil lost its grasp, and passion hushed,
>   Around the divine enchantment of the hour.

> These were but seasons beautiful and rare;
>   Abide in me, and they shall ever be;
> I pray Thee now fulfil my earnest prayer,
>   Come and abide in me and I in Thee.

"Herein is My Father glorified that ye bear much fruit and become My disciples" — better and better disciples, more like Christ.

You sing the doxology "Glory be to the Father." Very well; still better, work the doxology of good works — and more good works. What a glorious goal to glorify the Father by good works!

> A charge to keep I have,
> A God to glorify.

"The chief end of man is to glorify God."

"As the Father hath loved Me, I also have loved you."

No wonder the Father loved His perfect Son; but wonder of wonders that the Son should love lost sinners.

"Abide in My love" — to you. How do we remain objects of Christ's love?

"If ye keep My commandments, ye will abide in My love" — to you; "even as I have kept My Father's commandments and abide in His love" — to Me.

The more we obey, the more we enjoy the love of Christ; then His commandments are not grievous, but pleasant.

Like Christ, like Christian. How practical Christ and the Christian!

> O Love, who formedst me to wear
>   The image of Thy Godhead here,
> Who soughtest me with tender care
>   Through all my wand'rings wild and drear, —
> O Love, I give myself to Thee,
> Thine ever, only Thine, to be.

DALLMANN, JOHN.   18

Why did Christ say these things? "These things have I spoken unto you (1) that My joy may be in you."

Christ is human and has a heart. His heart is hungry for happiness. We are to give Him this happiness by doing many good works. We are to be His joy and pride. Will you buy Christ a Christmas present to fill His hungry heart with gladness?

"These things have I spoken to you . . . (2) that your joy over Me may be made full."

Is your heart made full of joy over Christ? Rejoice and sing your joyous Christmas and Easter hymns.

> Joy to the world! the Lord is come.

> O rejoice, ye Christians, loudly,
> For your joy has now begun. . . .
> Joy, O joy, beyond all gladness!
> Christ hath done away with sadness!

II.
THE CHRISTIAN'S RELATION TO CHRISTIANS —
LOVE AND FELLOWSHIP.
John 15, 12—17.

1. LOVE COMMANDED.

"This is My commandment, That ye love one another as I have loved you" — in quality and in quantity. Can you think of anything nobler for yourself?

2. LOVE PROVED.

"Greater love hath no man than this, that a man lay down his life for his friends."

Christ laid down His life for His — enemies! Friend in need, Friend indeed.

> What a Friend we have in Jesus!

> O Friend of souls, how blest am I
> When'er Thy love my spirit calms!

> In Thee alone will I rejoice;
> Thou art the Friend, Lord, of my choice.

> Hence, world, with all thy flattering toys!
> In God alone lie all my joys;
>   O rich delight, my Friend is mine!

Jonathan Edwards bade farewell to his relatives and then said, "Now, where is Jesus of Nazareth, my true and never-failing Friend?" And so saying, he passed away to his Friend.

Seneca told a courtier he had no right to mourn the death of a son because Caesar was his friend. What right have you to mourn anything if Christ is your Friend?

"Ye are My friends if ye do the things which I command you." What kind of friend have you been to Christ? Abraham was called the friend of God — he obeyed God. Jas. 2, 23.

> Blest be Thy love, dear Lord,
>   That taught us this sweet way,
> Only to love Thee for Thyself,
>   And for that love obey.

M. D. Babcock says: —

> And hast Thou said, "My friend
>   Is he who keeps My Word"?
> This I can do e'en to the end;
>   I can be faithful, Lord.

3. LOVE INSPIRED.

"No longer do I call you slaves, for the slave knoweth not what his lord doeth; but I have called you friends, for all things that I heard of My Father I have made known to you." Gen. 18, 17.

"Ye did not choose Me, but I chose you and appointed you that ye should go and bring forth fruit and that your fruit should remain, that, whatsoever ye shall ask of the Father in My name, He may give it you.

"These things I command you that ye love one another."

Parmenio had great fame as a general, still greater fame as the friend of Alexander the Great. Let your greatest fame be that you are the friend of Christ and of Christ's brethren.

CHAPTER XXIV.

JESUS' FAREWELL COUNSELS.

John 15, 18—16, 33.

I.

THE CHRISTIANS WILL BE HATED.

John 15, 18—25.

1. EXPECTATION.

"IF the world hateth you, know that it hath hated Me before you. If ye were of the world, the world would love his own; but because ye are not of the world, but I chose you out of the world, therefore the world hateth you."

They cast out of the synagog the blind man merely for being the friend of Christ. They set about to kill the innocent Lazarus merely for being the friend of Christ. They stoned Stephen merely for being the friend of Christ. "Yea, and all that would live godly in Christ Jesus shall suffer persecution," 2 Tim. 3, 12. Remember the fine saying of old Ignatius: "Christianity is not talk, but power, when it is hated by the world." General Bragg of Wisconsin's famous Iron Brigade said of President Cleveland: "We love him for the enemies he has made." A fine tribute of a fine man to a fine man. Have you made the world your enemy? Thank God, He will love you.

2. EXPLANATION.

"Remember the word that I said to you, 'The slave is not greater than his lord.' If they persecute Me, they will persecute you also; if they kept My Word, they will keep yours also."

How human! A choice bit of irony crops out of all of Christ's seriousness and solemnity. We can easily see the sad smile on His sad face. No doubt He means what the Lord said to Ezekiel, 3, 7: "They will not hearken to thee because they will not hearken to Me."

"But all these things will they do to you for My name's sake, because they know not Him that sent Me.

"If I had not come and spoken to them, they would have no sin; but now they have no excuse for their sin.

"He that hateth Me hateth My Father also" — because He is revealed in the words and works of the Son. Without Christ, without God — idolatry, atheism. Paul repeats this in Eph. 2, 12. We must repeat this to the world and expect the hate of the world.

Long ago old Tertullian boldly and bitterly told the Roman pagans: "Among all the malefactors you condemn there is not a Christian to be found chargeable with any crime but His name. So much is the hatred of our name above all the advantages of virtue flowing from it. Setting aside all inquiry into the principle of our religion and its Founder and all knowledge of them, the mere name is laid hold of, the name is attacked, and a word alone prejudges a sect unknown, and its Author also unknown, because they have a name, not because they are convicted."

As then, so now. Russia is ferociously persecuting Christians "for His name's sake." Here we have the A. A. A. A. — American Association for the Advancement of Atheism.

"If I had not done among them the works which none other did, they would have no sin; but now have they both seen and hated both Me and My Father.

"But *this cometh to pass* that the word may be fulfilled that is written in their Law, They hated Me without cause." Ps. 35, 19; 69, 4.

Is there in all the world a word more awful and sorrowful, terrible and horrible?

When President Taft was elected to stay home, he went about the country lecturing against Christianity. "They hated Me without cause." A Rabbi invited some ministers to the dedication of his synagog, and they came. The next Saturday he sneered at Christianity. "They hated Me without cause."

II.

THE COMFORTER.

John 15, 26—16, 15.

1. INFORMATION.

"When the Comforter is come, whom I will send to you from the Father, the Spirit of Truth, who proceedeth from the Father, He shall bear witness of Me."

Once again observe the Holy Trinity. The Holy Spirit proceedeth from the Father, proceedeth by the Son and from the Son. John 20, 22.

So we confess in the Nicene Creed; and some Greek Fathers say the same. And the whole blessed Trinity is active in our salvation. The Holy Spirit beareth witness of Christ in the hearts of the believers through the Gospel. Dr. Walther declares the best way to become sure of the truth of the Bible is to make a reverent study of the Bible.

2. OBLIGATION.

"Ye also bear witness, for ye are with Me from the beginning." The Holy Ghost bore witness through the apostles. Acts 5, 32; 1 Cor. 15, 8. The apostles bore witness unto death. Though dead, they yet speak to us through their writings, also inspired by the Holy Ghost.

From the inspired Bible we witness to all the world, witness of Christ's person and work.

"God will not deal with us men but through His external Word and Sacrament. All that is praised as of the Spirit outside this Word and Sacrament is of the devil," says Luther in the Smalcald Articles, P. III, Art. VIII.

And Christians witness by their lives. Henry M. Stanley was not a Christian when he searched for Livingstone in Africa, but after living with Livingstone, Stanley said: "Here is a man who is manifestly sustained as well as guided from Heaven. The Holy Spirit dwells in him. God speaks through him. The heroism, the nobility, the pure and stainless enthusiasm at the root of his life, come, beyond a question, from Christ. There must therefore be a Christ; and it is worth while to have such a Helper and Redeemer as this Christ undoubtedly is and as He here reveals Himself in this wonderful disciple." And Stanley became a Christian, lived a Christian, died a Christian.

3. PERSECUTION PROPHESIED.

"These things have I spoken to you that ye should not be made to stumble. They will put you out of the synagogs; yea, a time is coming when whosoever killeth you will think he is offering service to God.

"And these things will they do to you because they have not known the Father nor Me.

"But these things have I told you that, when their hour is come, ye may remember that I told you them. And these things I said not to you at the beginning because I was with you."

When Saul was persecuting the Christians, he thought he was worshiping God with sacrifice. Acts 26, 9; Gal. 1, 13. 14. The heathen thought they were worshiping God when they killed Christians for atheists. The poor woman thought she was worshiping God when bringing her sticks to burn John Hus, who cried out, "Holy simplicity!" He thought he was worshiping God, did young Kaiser Karl, when he banned the damned Luther at Worms in 1521. On July 1, 1523, they thought they were worshiping God when on the market-place of Brussels they burned young Henry Voes and John Esch for Lutherans, the first-fruits of a vast army of Protestant martyrs. Charles IX massacred thousands of Protestants in France on St. Bartholomew's Day, and Pope Gregory XIII held a solemn thanksgiving service and struck a medal in memory of this victory over the "heretics."

In 1562 the town of Orange was taken, and the Protestants were hacked to pieces, burned at slow fires, or left, infamously mutilated, to bleed to death. Noble ladies, first sacrificed to the lust of the soldiers, were exposed in the streets to die either naked or pasted over in devilish mockery with torn leaves of their Bibles.

In the land of Luther, Lutherans were persecuted, and many fled to America, South America, and Australia. Some fled to the wilds of Missouri and organized the Synod of Missouri, Ohio, and Other States.

4. THE COMFORTER PROMISED.

"But now I go My way to Him that sent Me, and none of you asketh Me, Whither goest Thou?" What a sad complaint!

"But because I have said these things to you, sorrow hath filled your heart." Thinking only selfishly of themselves.

"Nevertheless I tell you the truth, It is expedient for you that I go away; for if I go not away, the Comforter will not come to you; but if I depart, I will send Him to you." Lose to gain — how often we fail to see it! And yet again, observe the Holy Trinity — the Father, the Savior, the Comforter.

5. THE COMFORTER WILL CONVICT THE WORLD.

"And when He is come, He will convict the world of sin and of righteousness and of judgment.

(1) "Of sin, because they believe not on Me."

According to Christ, sin is unbelief. No one is lost for his *sins* because

Christ died for our sins. He is lost for his *sin* of not believing that Christ died for our sins. He is lost for spurning the pardon. Unbelief reveals the sinfulness of man, which will not endure the truth of Christ.

> Come, Holy Spirit, come!
>   Let Thy bright beams arise;
> Dispel the sorrow from our minds,
>   The darkness from our eyes.
>
> Convict us of our sin;
>   Then lead to Jesus' blood
> And to our wondering view reveal
>   The mercies of our God.

The Comforter will convict the world —

(2) "Of righteousness, because I go to My Father and ye behold Me no more."

Christ is the Righteous One. 1 John 2, 1; 1 Pet. 3, 18; Acts 3, 14; 7, 52.

But the Jews treated the Righteous One most unrighteously. But the righteous God will not leave Him in the lurch, with His character besmirched. God rescued Him from infamy and glorified Him in the ascension and by seating Him at His own right hand to rule the world and to judge the world. Righteousness is no idle dream at which to scoff; there is a righteous God in heaven. His vindication of Christ is a proof. Furthermore, Christ on the cross earned righteousness for the unrighteous sinner. The Father made Him who knew no sin to be Righteousness unto us. The Jews were "ignorant of God's righteousness," Rom. 10, 3. We no longer try to establish our own righteousness, but by the work of the Holy Ghost we in faith accept Christ, who of God was made unto us Righteousness. And so we rejoice: —

> Jesus' blood and righteousness
> My jewels are, my glorious dress,
> In these 'fore God I'll victor stand
> When I shall reach the heavenly land.

The Comforter will convict the world —

(3) "Of judgment, because the prince of this world hath been judged."

By His death, Christ destroyed him that had the power of death, that is, the devil, and delivered them who through fear of death were all their lifetime subject to bondage. Heb. 2, 14. 15; John 12, 31. 32. Men may no longer sneer, "Might makes right." By raising Christ in glory to heaven, God proclaims that Right makes might. Satan is dethroned, and Christ is enthroned. Right overcomes wrong. At the Judg-

ment all wrongs will be righted.   In this glorious and victorious faith
the Christians will go into the world and preach Christ.

> This world's prince may still
> Scowl fierce as he will,
> He can harm us none,
> He's judged, the deed is done;
> One little word can fell him.

6. THE COMFORTER WILL TEACH.

"I have yet many things to say to you, but ye cannot bear them
now" — a heavy burden.

"But when He, the Spirit of Truth, is come, He will guide you into
truth in all its parts; for He shall not speak of Himself, but whatsoever
He shall hear, *that* will He speak, and He will declare to you the things
to come."   Here Godet sees the inspiration of the epistles.

"He shall glorify Me; for He shall receive of mine and shall declare
it to you.   All things whatsoever the Father hath are Mine; therefore said
I that He shall take of Mine and shall declare it unto you."

And yet once more, observe the Holy Trinity — what the Father hath
is Christ's, and the Holy Ghost will declare it to us.   As Christ spoke not
of Himself, so the Holy Ghost will not speak of Himself; as Christ
glorified the Father, so the Holy Ghost will glorify Christ — by setting
Him in the right light.

On Melanchthon's desk was found a note telling why he was glad
to die — "because I will then know fully the blessed mystery of the Most
Holy Trinity."   And when dying, he had read to him John 14—17.

Irenaeus says all that the apostles learned from the Holy Ghost they
first preached with their living voice and then at God's behest wrote it in
the Scriptures to be the pillar and ground of our faith. 1 Tim. 3, 15.

Milton says: —

> He to His own a Comforter shall send,
> The promise of the Father, who shall dwell
> His Spirit within them and the law of faith
> Working through love upon their hearts shall write
> To guide them in all truth.

By the invention of John Hays Hammond, Jr., an operator on shore
can by radio control the direction and the speed of a boat on the ocean.
By His Holy Spirit God in heaven directs the hearts of His children
on earth.

III.

COMFORT AT PARTING.

John 16, 16—33.

1. THE PARTING WILL BE SHORT.

(1) The Statement.

"A little while, and ye behold Me no more; and again a little while, and ye shall see Me, because I go to the Father."

(2) The Bewilderment.

Then said some of His disciples among themselves, What is this that He saith unto us, A little while, and ye behold Me not; and again a little while, and ye shall see Me: and, Because I go to the Father? They said therefore, What is this that He saith, This little while? We know not what He saith."

(3) The Explanation.

Jesus knew that they were desirous to ask Him and said, "Do ye inquire among yourselves of that I said, A little while, and ye behold Me not; and again a little while, and ye shall see Me?

"Verily, verily, I say unto you, That ye shall weep and lament, but the world shall rejoice; and ye shall be sorrowful, but your sorrow shall be turned into joy.

"A woman when she is in travail hath sorrow because her hour is come; but as soon as she is delivered of the child, she remembereth no more the anguish, for joy that a man is born into the world. And ye now therefore have sorrow; but I will see you again," — and visit with you, — "and your heart shall rejoice, and your joy no one taketh away from you."

Jesus is the man born into the world, the First-born of the dead, the other Adam, the Beginner of a new mankind. Rev. 1, 5; Acts 26, 23; 1 Cor. 15, 20. 23; 45—49; Rom. 5, 14.

Not many days after, these fearsome disciples joyfully saw the risen Redeemer and joyfully preached Jesus and the resurrection and joyfully went into prison for preaching Jesus and the resurrection, joyful they were counted worthy to suffer shame for His name. Acts 4, 23—31; 5, 41.

Paul the aged was in Rome and in chains. Did he repine? "I rejoice, yea, and will rejoice. Yea, and if I be offered upon the sacrifice and ser-

KAULBACH.

NERO.

vice of your faith, I joy and rejoice with you all. For the same cause also do ye joy and rejoice with me." Phil. 1, 18; 2, 17. 18; 3, 1. No, our joy no one taketh from us.

> Death itself cannot us deaden,
> But relief
> From all grief
> To us then is given;
> It but ends life's mournful story,
> Clears the way
> That we may
> Pass to heavenly glory.

Thus triumphantly died Paul Gerhardt, praying his own hymn. And these words of rejoicing we read over his statue in the cemetery at Graefen-hainichen.

> "A little while, and ye again shall see Me."
> Surely Thou tarriest long,
> Bridegroom beloved! When shall this night of weeping
> Be turned to song?
> With heaven so far beyond us
> And earth so near to lure us and beguile,
> How long? Oh, Thou didst promise but to tarry
> "A little while."
>
> "A little while," the whole creation waits Thee
> In hopes and fear.
> Surely the sound of that swift-driven chariot
> At length I hear.
> O earth! earth! earth! arouse thee!
> Wake from thy tears, put on thy glory-smile!
> Surely He cometh, and He will but tarry
> "A little while."

2. PROMISE OF ANSWERED PRAYER.

"And in that day ye will entreat Me for nothing. Verily, verily, I say unto you, If ye ask anything of the Father, He will give it you in My name. Hitherto have ye asked nothing in My name; ask, and ye shall receive that your joy may be fulfilled."

> O wondrous love, to bleed and die,
> To bear the cross and shame,
> That guilty sinners such as I
> Might plead Thy gracious name!

"These things have I spoken unto you in proverbs; but the time cometh when I shall no more speak to you in proverbs, but I shall show you plainly of the Father. In that day ye shall ask in My name; and I say not to you that I will pray the Father for you, for the Father Himself

MAR SABA, VALLEY OF THE KEDRON.

loveth you because ye have loved Me and have believed that I came out from God.

"I came forth from the Father and am come into the world; again, I leave the world and go to the Father."

A brief autobiography, comprehensive and majestic — Preexistence, Incarnation, Crucifixion, Ascension.

3. A CONFIDENT CONFESSION.

His disciples say, "Lo, now speakest Thou plainly and speakest no proverb. Now know we that Thou knowest all things and needest not that any man should ask Thee; by this we believe that Thou camest forth from God."

4. AN EARNEST WARNING.

Jesus answered, "Do ye now believe? Behold, an hour cometh, yea, is now come, that ye shall be scattered, every man to his own home, and shall leave Me alone; and yet I am not alone, because the Father is with Me."

What soldier would run away and leave his general alone? Jesus foresaw and foretold that His disciples would run away in Gethsemane and leave Him alone. Alone, and yet not alone — "the Father is with Me."

Paul was alone in prison, and yet not alone — the Lord cheered him. And at his first trial all forsook him; yet he was not alone, the Lord strengthened him. Acts 23, 11; 2 Tim. 4, 16. 17. At Worms Luther stood alone before the world, and yet not alone, the Lord strengthened him. So we; "when my father and my mother forsake me, then the Lord will take me up," Ps. 27, 10; 23, 4.

Beaten by the lone Luther, Kaiser Karl V wearily laid aside the crown of his world empire to hide in the convent of San Geronimo on the Yuste to do penance for his sins of unchastity, and he wrote: "I have tasted more satisfaction in my solitude in one day than in all the triumphs of my former reign. The sincere study, profession, and practise of the Christian religion have in them such joy as is seldom found in courts and grandeur." And he died in the faith he had all his life persecuted — "relying alone on the merits of Christ."

From his Aberdeen prison the saintly Samuel Rutherford wrote: "The Lord is with me; I care not what man can do. I burden no man, and I want nothing. No being is better provided for than I am. My chains are overgilded with gold.   No pen, no words, no engine, can express to you the loveliness of my only, only Lord Jesus."

Verily, for the Christian —

> Stone walls do not a prison make
> Nor iron bars a cage.

5. COURAGE IN TROUBLE.

"These things I have spoken unto you that in Me ye might have peace.   In the world ye shall have tribulation; but be of good cheer; I have overcome the world."

The Christian has a twofold life — (1) in the world, (2) in Christ. And he has a twofold experience — (1) in the world, tribulation; (2) in Christ, peace.   Why peace?   Because Christ has overcome the world, vanquished it.

And because of Christ's victory the Christian, too, has a victory over the world.   "Our faith is the victory that overcometh the world."   "Thanks be to God, which giveth us the victory through our Lord Jesus Christ." 1 John 5, 4; 1 Cor. 15, 57.

All the other writers in the New Testament have the word to "overcome" only five times; John uses it twenty-three times.   John is the apostle of love indeed, but also the apostle of war and of victory.

During the critical days of the historic *Reichstag* at Augsburg in 1530, when the Lutherans made their glorious confession of faith before Kaiser Karl V, Luther in June, from the Coburg, cheered the timid Melanchthon: " 'Be of good cheer, I have overcome the world.'   That will not prove false; of this I am certain, that Christ is the Victor of the world.   Why, then, should we fear a conquered world as if it were the conqueror?   Such a saying a man might fetch from Rome and Jerusalem on his knees."

"Invictus!"

CHAPTER XXV.

JESUS' PRIESTLY PRAYER.

John 17.

THUS this prayer was first called by David Chytraeus of Rostock, "the last of the fathers of the Lutheran Church," who died in 1600.

Luther says: "Of all works of our Lord Christ we should specially wish to hear how He bore Himself when praying and talking with His dear Father; for much has been written how He preached and wrought wonders, but little how He prayed. . . . Had it not been written, we would run after it to the end of the world. And it is indeed an immeasurably fervent and hearty prayer, in which He opens and pours out all the bottom of His heart both toward us and His Father."

Here we are in the Holy of Holies, listening to our High Priest dedicating Himself for His sacrifice for us and our salvation.

Herder says poetically John wrote his gospel with a pen dropped from the wing of an angel; one may be forgiven for adding he wrote this prayer with a pen dropped from the wing of an archangel.

"Plain and artless as is the language, it is nevertheless so deep, rich, and wide that no one can find its bottom or extent," says Luther of the most remarkable prayer of our Priest after His most remarkable sermon. And Melanchthon in his last lecture shortly before his death said: "There is no voice ever heard, either in heaven or on earth, more exalted, more holy, more fruitful, more sublime, than this prayer offered up by the Son of God Himself."

During his last illness John Knox had this chapter read to him daily. On the last day, November 24, 1572, he said to his wife, "Go, read where I cast my first anchor." And so she read this chapter.

The dying Bossuet had this prayer read to him sixty times; Spener, three times, though he had never preached from it, thinking it beyond his powers. And this is no attempt to preach from it, simply an attempt to give a setting to the flashing brilliants. "Put off thy shoes from off thy feet, for the place whereon thou standest is holy ground," Ex. 3, 5.

I.

THE HIGH PRIEST PRAYS FOR HIMSELF.

John 17, 1—5.

After having spoken these things, Jesus lifted up His eyes to heaven and said, —

1. THE INTRODUCTION.

"Father, the hour is come." *The* hour, the greatest hour in the life of the Savior and the history of mankind, the hour in which everything in time and eternity came to a head.

2. THE PETITION.

"Glorify Thy Son."

3. THE PURPOSE.

"That Thy Son may glorify Thee."

4. THE PLEA.

"Even as Thou gavest Him authority over all flesh, that whatsoever Thou hast given Him, to them He should give eternal life."

"It would be terrible to believe in a future life. Conscience is an evil beast, which arms man against himself," said Pope Leo X. Only too true if one is such a vile villain — and has no Savior. But what unspeakable joy if one has a Savior!

"Now, this is the eternal life, that they know Thee the only true God and Him whom Thou hast sent, Jesus Christ." Without Christ no God and no eternal life. Eph. 2, 12.

God *and* Christ equals God *in* Christ, equals God known *through* Christ and Christ on the cross. There is the saving knowledge of God in the bright light of a noonday sun burst.

That God I can know, and trust, and love, and follow, and copy. This is the life, the eternal life. Begun now, it will go on forever.

"Praised be the Lord! This is enough both for me and for eternity," cried Bishop John Fisher of Rochester as he read these words on the way to execution under Henry VIII.

Hear Luther: "In deep spiritual temptations nothing has helped me better, with nothing have I heartened myself and driven away the devil better, than with this, that Christ, the true eternal Son of God, is 'bone of our bone and flesh of our flesh' and that He sits on the right hand of God and pleads for us. When I can grasp this shield of faith, I have already chased away the Evil One with his fiery darts."

"I can only comprehend God as God is seen in Christ," confessed Arnold of Rugby, and Charles Kingsley, and Robert Browning, and many others. Benjamin Jowett, the Master of Balliol at Oxford, said in a sermon: "The search for truth is one thing; fluttering after it is another." He did not flutter; he was plainly an earnest and honest searcher for truth, and he found the truth in the Word made flesh. He came *unto* Him, and he came *after* Him.

Says Macaulay: "It was before Deity embodied in a human form, walking among men, partaking of their infirmities, leaning on their bosoms, weeping over their graves, slumbering in the manger, bleeding on the cross, that the prejudices of the synagog, and the doubts of the Academy, and the fasces of the lictor, and the swords of thirty legions were humbled in the dust."

5. THE FOUNDATION OF THE PLEA.

"I glorified Thee on the earth, having accomplished the work which Thou hast given Me to do."

Here Christ gave an account of His stewardship on earth. He made a report of the work entrusted to Him. So did His great apostle — The good fight I have fought, the course I have finished, the faith I have kept; henceforth there is laid up for me the crown of righteousness. 2 Tim. 4, 7. 8.

We must all appear before the judgment-seat and give an account of our stewardship. What kind of report can we make? We glorify God by doing His work. If we glorify Him, He will glorify us.

"I have accomplished the work" — who can repeat that?

Kaiser William I worked hard every day though feeble with age. "I have no time to be tired." Cecil Rhodes, "So little done, so much to do!"

"My book, my book! I shall never finish my book!" wailed H. T. Buckle, dying at Damascus. So G. J. Romanes and millions more.

"I have accomplished the work," said Christ at the end of His life, looking His Father in the eye. What majesty!

6. THE REQUEST REPEATED.

"And now glorify Me, Thou, Father, with Thyself with the glory which I had with Thee before the world was."

Christ was with the Father in glory from eternity; the same Christ was in the flesh on earth; the same Christ is now again at the side of the Father in glory.

> The Head that once was crowned with thorns
> Is crowned with glory now;
> A royal diadem adorns
> The mighty Victor's brow.

II.

THE HIGH PRIEST PRAYS FOR HIS APOSTLES.

John 17, 6—19.

1. THAT THEY MAY BE GUARDED.

"I made known Thy name to the men whom Thou gavest Me out of the world." Ps. 22, 22; Heb. 2, 12. Christ is Jehovah. "Thine they were, and to Me Thou gavest them, and Thy Word they have kept. Now they know that all things whatsoever Thou hast given Me are from Thee. For I have given them the sayings which Thou gavest Me; and they received them and knew surely that I came forth from Thee and believed that Thou didst send Me." That is the purpose of God's Word, to beget saving faith in Christ as the Savior.

"I pray for them. I pray not for the world, but for those whom Thou hast given Me; for they are Thine. All things that are Mine are Thine, and Thine are Mine [Rev. 5, 12; 7, 12], and I have been glorified in them." No creature can say to God, "All Thine are mine." Christ said it — Christ is God. Will you say to God, "All things that are mine are Thine"?

> Naught that I have my own I call,
> I hold it for the Giver;
> My heart, my strength, my life, my all,
> Are His, and His forever.

Do you prove it by your offerings? The Jews crucified Christ, the disciples glorified the Crucified. Is Christ being glorified in you?

"And I am no longer in the world, and these are in the world, and I am coming to Thee. Holy Father, guard them in Thy name" — in the knowledge of Thee — "which Thou hast given to Me that they may be one even as We" — one community, separated from the world and devoted to God. "While I was with them, I guarded them in Thy name" — in the knowledge of Thee — "which Thou hast given Me, and I kept them; and not one of them perished but the son of perdition, that the Scripture might be fulfilled." John 13, 18; Is. 57, 12. 13; Ps. 41, 9; 109, 8; 69, 25.

Swinburne says: —

> Who shall keep Thy sheep,
>   Lord, and lose not one?
> Who save One shall keep
> Lest the shepherd sleep?
>   Who beside the Son?

2. THAT THEY MAY HAVE JOY.

"But now I am coming to Thee; and these things I speak that in the world they may have My joy made full in themselves.

"I have given them Thy Word; and the world hated them because they are not of the world, even as I am not of the world. I pray not that Thou shouldest take them out of the world, but that Thou shouldest keep them from the evil" which surrounds them and tempts them. "They are not of the world, even as I am not of the world."

3. THAT THEY BE SANCTIFIED.

"Sanctify them in the truth: Thy Word is truth." Ps. 119, 142; 2 Sam. 7, 28.

Electric light and power come to me through the wire; so Christ comes into my heart through the Gospel. The Word of Grace is the means of grace, "able to build you up," Acts 20, 32. It separates from the unholy world and consecrates for the holy work. "The end of the truth is not wisdom, but holiness," says Westcott.

Do you know in order to do?

The court of Henry VIII was worldly, but Thomas More tried to keep himself unworldly. He entertained the great of the kingdom, he also dined and supped the poor at his table; he built a library, he also built a home for the aged poor; when most involved in the king's business, he built himself a chapel; when most in the king's palace, he was most among the cottages; he never took the seat of the Lord Chancellor without first on bended knee asking a blessing from his aged father; he never undertook a new public work without first receiving the Lord's Supper, trusting more to the grace than to his own wit; he obeyed his conscience rather than the king and had his head chopped off by the king.

"As Thou didst send Me into the world, even so I sent them into the world."

What for? To carry on the same work for which I came into the world. I saved the world by My work; they are to save the world by preaching My work.

"And in their behalf I sanctify Myself," consecrate Myself for self-sacrificing service — Himself the Victim and Himself the Priest. "That they also may be sanctified in truth," — truly consecrated for self-sacrificing service — themselves the victims and themselves the priests. Titus 2, 14; Heb. 2, 11.

Are you sanctified wholly? 1 Thess. 5, 23; 2 Thess. 2, 13.

III.

THE HIGH PRIEST PRAYS FOR HIS WHOLE CHURCH.
John 17, 20—26.

1. TO BE LIKE CHRIST.

"Yet not for these alone do I pray, but also for those who believe in Me through their word" — for you and me!

Their word was preached and also written in the New Testament. Through that word all believers come to be believers. Faith cometh by hearing, hearing by the Word of God.

Here the Church is thrown open to the Gentiles, over which Luther is justly joyful and jubilant. "We may justly write this comfortable text in letters of gold, as it relates to us all. For it is our glory and comfort, our treasure and pearl, so that for us Gentiles the whole Scriptures do not afford a more comfortable saying than this."

"That they all may be one, as Thou, Father, art in Me and I in Thee, that they also may be in Us." What a union! Through union with Christ we are in union with the Father and partakers of the divine nature, 2 Pet. 1, 4. Through union with Christ, Christians are in union with one another, one heart and one soul, one will and one work, all ruled by the Spirit of Christ. The only Christian union is the union in the truth.

> Blest be the tie that binds
> Our hearts in Christian love;
> The fellowship of kindred minds
> Is like to that above.

Why this union? "That the world may believe that Thou didst send Me." In union there is strength. What a heavy responsibility rests upon those who break or hinder this union by disloyalty to the plain Word of Christ!

"And the glory which Thou hast given Me I have given them, that they may be one, even as We are one, I in them and Thou in Me, that they may be perfected into one." Again, why this union? "That the world may know that Thou didst send Me and didst love them as Thou didst love Me."

The loving life of the Christians is not indeed a means of grace, but it is indeed a means of attracting the world to the means of grace.

2. TO BE WITH CHRIST.

"Father, I will" — what divine authority and assurance! No creature can speak thus to the Creator. Only the eternal Son can speak thus to the eternal Father.

"Father, I will that what Thou hast given Me be with Me where I am that they may behold My glory which Thou hast given Me; for Thou lovedst Me before the foundation of the world."

To be with Christ — what heaven! No wonder Paul had a desire to depart and to be with Christ. Phil. 1, 23.

> "Forever with the Lord!"
>   Amen! so let it be;
> Life from the dead is in that word,
>   'Tis immortality.

To behold His glory — what heaven! That is the Vision Splendid, the Beatific Vision. What a feast for our wondering eyes!

> I know not, O I know not,
>   What joys await us there,
> What radiancy of glory,
>   What bliss beyond compare.

We shall see and also share. We shall be like Him, for we shall see Him as He is, 1 John 3, 2.

"O righteous — or gracious — Father, the world knew Thee not" — one can almost hear the Savior sigh and sob as He speaks this solemn sentence, so simple and so severe. Amid the gloom a gleam of joy, "But I knew Thee, and these knew that Thou didst send Me."

Because Christ knew God, He was fitted to go on: "And I made known to them Thy name and will make it known." And that name is Love. And why does Christ make known that name of Love? "That the love wherewith Thou didst love Me may be in them and I in them." Wonderful words of love, love too wonderful for words!

All we know of God comes through Christ. The more we study the Word of Christ, the more we know God, and the more Christ dwells in our hearts by faith. And so we rejoice with M. D. Babcock: —

No distant Lord have I
  Loving afar to be;
Made flesh for me, He cannot rest
  Until He rests in me.

Brother in joy and pain,
  Bone of my bone was He;
Now, intimacy closer still,
  He dwells Himself in me.

I need not journey far
  This dearest Friend to see;
Companionship is always mine,
  He makes His home with me.

While our High Priest prays for us, we also pray: —

Look, Father, look on His anointed face
  And only look on us as found in Him;
Look not on our misusing of Thy grace,
  Our prayer so languid, and our faith so dim.
For, lo! between our sins and their reward
We set the Passion of Thy Son, our Lord.

CHAPTER XXVI.

JESUS IN GETHSEMANE.

John 18, 1—11.

Toward the Garden called Gethsemane
We turn our faces and our steps to-day
And wait in hushed and pitying grief apart
While Christ the world's sins takes upon His heart.
For this He came — the Child of Bethlehem!
    To meet this hour, He trod strange, toilsome roads,
Misunderstood, hated, despised, and feared.
    He takes at last the heaviest of all loads —
To bear for others punishment and pain
And so redeem the world for God again.

I.

ON TO GETHSEMANE!

HAVING spoken these words, — of prayer, — Jesus went forth with His disciples over the brook Cedron — as David before Him, 2 Sam. 15, 23. This was a winter torrent, black from the blood of the sacrificed animals which was drained into the ravine. There was a garden, rather an orchard, Gethsemane, press for oil, on the Mount of Olives, into which He entered and His disciples.

Caesar crossed the Rubicon to destroy the liberty of Rome; Christ crossed the Cedron to bring liberty to the world.

II.

HERE COMES THE TRAITOR!

But Judas also, who was betraying Him, knew the place; for Jesus ofttimes resorted thither with His disciples. Judas then, having received the cohort of Roman soldiers from Fort Antonia and Levitic Temple officers from the chief priests and Pharisees, cometh thither with lanterns and torches and weapons.

Two went to the same place — Jesus to pray, Judas to betray.

III.

JESUS MEETS HIS ENEMIES.

1. THE BETRAYAL.

Jesus therefore, knowing all things that were coming upon Him, went forth and saith unto them,

"Whom seek ye?"

GARDEN OF GETHSEMANE ON THE MOUNT OF OLIVES.

JUDAS GUIDES THE SOLDIERS.   BIDA.

"Jesus the Nazarene."

"I am He."

Now, Judas also, who was betraying Him, stood with them and kissed Him.

"Kisses hell at the lips of Redemption," says S. T. Coleridge.

> Judas, dost thou betray Me with a kiss?
> Canst thou find hell about My lips and miss
> Of life just at the gates of life and bliss? — *George Herbert.*

"Why did Christ bear with Judas for three years?" J. Stuart Holden replied: "My friend, I have never had time to think about the case of Judas because for the last fifteen years or more I have been pondering the mystery of Christ's choice of me and why He bears with me." We reverently say, Amen.

2. THE OVERPOWERING MAJESTY.

As soon as Jesus said, "I am He," they went backward and fell to the ground.

Again therefore He asked them, "Whom seek ye?" And they said, "Jesus the Nazarene."

3. THE WILLING SUBSTITUTE.

Jesus answered, "I told you that I am He; if, therefore, ye are seeking Me, let these go their way," — He talks like a prince, not like a prisoner, — that the word might be fulfilled which He spake, "Of those whom Thou hast given Me, I lost not a single one of them." 17, 12.

It certainly is passing strange that the disciples were not arrested.

IV.

PETER'S WILD DEVOTION.

Then Simon Peter, having a sword, Luke 22, 38, drew it and smote the high priest's slave and cut off his right ear. The slave's name was Malchus.

The Popes have often been the successors of Peter in shedding the blood of "heretics" against the will of the Savior.

Peter was asked to watch one hour with Christ — Peter slept. He was not asked to take the sword, but he took the sword. And what did he gain? He cut off a slave's ear! Rash, reckless, ridiculous Peter! Christ's word will fell, Peter's sword will not quell.

THE KISS OF JUDAS.   BIDA.

V.

THE SAVIOR'S MILD REBUKE.

1. Then said Jesus unto Peter, "Cast the sword into its sheath."

And Paul says: "We do not war after the flesh, for the weapons of our warfare are not carnal," 2 Cor. 10, 3. 4.

And Luther says: "A spirit you cannot strike — with a sword — or pierce — with a spear. It is against the Holy Ghost to burn heretics." This was one of the reasons for which the Pope excommunicated him.

> Armies Thou hast in heaven which fight
> And follow Thee, all clothed in white;
> But here on earth, though Thou hadst need,
> Thou wouldst no legions, but wouldst bleed.
> The sword with which Thou wouldst command
> Is in Thy mouth, not in Thy hand;
> And all Thy saints do overcome
> By Thy blood and their martyrdom.
> HENRY VAUGHAN, *The Men of War.*

2. Jesus adds, "The cup which the Father hath given Me, shall I not drink it?"

If it is the Father that gives you the cup, will you not drink it?

> Whatever God ordains is good!
> His loving thought attends me;
> No poisoned draught the cup can be
> That my Physician sends me,
> But medicine due;
> For God is true.
> Of doubt, then, I'll divest me
> And on His goodness rest me.

CHAPTER XXVII.

JESUS BEFORE THE HIGH PRIEST.

John 18, 12—27.

I.

JESUS LED TO ANNAS.

ANNAS, or Hanan, or Ananus, of Alexandria was invited to Jerusalem by Herod the Great and made high priest under Caesar Augustus by Governor Quirinius in the thirty-seventh year after the Battle of Actium, 7 A. D., in the place of Joazar, who had made himself impossible. When Tiberius, in the year 14, sent Valerius Gratus to govern Syria, Annas was deposed, and Ishmael was imposed; two years after he was deposed, and Eleazar was imposed; after a year he was deposed, and Simon was imposed; in the year 18 he was deposed, and Joseph was imposed. He is called Caiaphas, better Kajaphas, son-in-law of Annas, and he managed to hold down his job till 36. Later four other sons and one grandson of Annas became high priests, for which he was called the happiest of men. Former high priests retained the title of high priest and many rights and duties of the office.

Josephus says there were three million Jews at the Passover and 255,600 lambs were slain. It seems the family of Annas had a sort of monopoly of the sale of the lambs, and it can readily be seen they made enormous private profits. Of course, they bitterly hated Christ for clearing the Temple-court.

They were Sadducees, and the Talmud curses "the family of Hanan and their serpent-hissings." Hanan means "Merciful," but his nickname was "Viper."

It is likely Annas and Caiaphas had apartments in different wings of one palace, the courtyard being the same.

The Roman cohort and the Temple officers of the Jews took Jesus and bound Him and lead Him to Annas first; for he was father-in-law of Caiaphas, who was high priest that year. What a year!

Now, it was Caiaphas who advised the Jews it was expedient one man should die for the people. Chap. 11, 50. 51.

Cold comfort for Christ from such cruel criminals. It was a sort of preliminary hearing.

II.

PETER DENIES CHRIST.

When Jesus was bound in Gethsemane, all His disciples fled, as He had foretold. Simon Peter, however, rallied from his panic and stole after Jesus from afar. And so did another disciple. Now, that disciple was known to the high priest and went in with Jesus into the courtyard of the high priest.

But Peter was standing outside at the door. Then went out the other disciple, who was known to the high priest, and spoke to the janitress and brought in Peter.

Strange? Nonnus of Panopolis in Upper Egypt says John had been delivering the choice fish of Lake Galilee to the house of Annas and so was known to the janitress. Easy.

Then said the slave girl, the janitress, to Peter, "Art thou not also one of this man's disciples?"

He saith, "I am not."

Die? Lie!

Now, the slaves and the officers were standing there, having made a fire of coals, for it was cold; and they were warming themselves; and Peter was standing with them and warming himself.

Why, to be sure — "When in Rome, do as the Romans do."

III.

JESUS BEFORE THE HIGH PRIEST.

1. THE EXAMINATION.

The high priest then asked Jesus about His disciples and about His doctrine.

He had no accusation and no witnesses. Then why arrest Him? The priest craftily tried to worm out of the prisoner some admission which would incriminate Him, show Him up as a dangerous revolutionist. Jesus saw the snare.

2. THE REPLY.

"I have spoken frankly to the world; I always taught in synagog and in the Temple, where all the Jews come together; and in secret I spoke nothing. Why askest thou Me? Ask those who have heard what I spoke to them; behold, these know what I said."

There are fifteen distinct references to Christ's habit of teaching in the synagog. Is it your habit to go to church regularly? Frances Ridley Havergal said: "An avoidable absence from the house of God is an infallible sign of spiritual decay. Disciples first follow Christ at a distance and then, like Peter, do not know Him."

"In secret I spoke nothing."

His good news was for the whole world. Why join a secret society? The Christian's good news is for the whole world.

3. THE OUTRAGE.

When Jesus had said this, one of the officers standing by gave Him a blow, with his hand or with his stick, saying,

"Answerest Thou the high priest thus?"

Copying these words, a Persian boy asked Missionary Henry Martyn, "Sir, did not his hand wither?"

4. THE CHALLENGE.

Jesus answered him, "If I spoke evil, bear witness of the evil; but if well, why smitest thou Me?"

Keenly feeling the insult, Jesus yet reviled not again. With meek majesty and majestic meekness He manfully protested against the outrage.

The world still abuses Christ. Why? What evil hath He done?

5. THE DISMISSAL.

Jesus avoided the trap to incriminate Himself.

Annas therefore sent Him bound to Caiaphas, the high priest.

IV.

PETER DENIES CHRIST THE SECOND TIME.

While Christ was standing before the priest, Simon Peter was still standing and warming himself. They said therefore unto him, "Art thou also one of His disciples?" He denied and said, "I am not."

V.

PETER DENIES CHRIST THE THIRD TIME.

One of the slaves of the high priest, being kinsman of him whose ear Peter cut off, saith, "Did not I see thee in the Garden with Him?" Of course, now Peter could deny no longer, could he? You do not know Peter!

PETER'S DENIAL.

H. TOLD.

Again then Peter denied. And at once a cock crowed.

Don't lie; you'll have to tell twenty lies to support one lie. Froude shows Queen Elizabeth stooped to "a deliberate lie." At times "she seemed to struggle with her ignominy, but it was only to flounder deeper into distraction and dishonor."

Speak every man truth with his neighbor.

To Christ before the priest, Peter before the slaves and soldiers is a side-piece. But what a contrast! There — Christ the noble Confessor; here — Peter the base denier. Loudly protesting he would die with Christ, yet so quick to deny Christ! Better stand alone out in the cold than warm yourself at the fire of Christ's enemies. "Blessed is the man that walketh not in the counsel of the ungodly nor standeth in the way of sinners nor sitteth in the seat of the scornful," Ps. 1. "Thou shalt not tempt the Lord, thy God." Rush not into temptation. "Lead us not into temptation."

> Beware of Peter's word
> Nor confidently say,
> "I never will deny Thee, Lord,"
> But, "Grant I never may!"

Many warmed themselves at the world's fire and denied Christ, denied Him for a position, a promotion, an office, a husband, a wife. How do we know? We have experienced it in our own Church.

Let us pray, each and every one: —

> In the hour of trial,
> Jesus, plead for me
> Lest by base denial
> I depart from Thee;
> When Thou seest me waver,
> With a look recall
> Nor from fear or favor
> Suffer me to fall.
>
> With forbidden pleasures
> Would this vain world charm
> Or its sordid treasures
> Spread to work me harm;
> Bring to my remembrance
> Sad Gethsemane
> Or, in darker semblance,
> Cross-crowned Calvary.

CHAPTER XXVIII.

"JESUS SUFFERED UNDER PONTIUS PILATE."

John 18, 28—19, 15.

PONTIUS PILATE, in all Roman history the man most named, named every time millions of Christians — for nineteen centuries — recite the Apostles' Creed. — In the year 14 Augustus died at the age of seventy-seven, on beautiful Capri. He was followed by his stepson Tiberius, when fifty-six, who had taken Augsburg in Germany fifteen years before the birth of Christ. He sent golden vessels to the Temple at Jerusalem. When complaints were lodged against the cruelty of Valerius Gratus, the governor of Judea, Tiberius sent Germanicus to investigate, but he died at Antioch, perhaps of poison.

In 26 Sejanus, the powerful freedman of Tiberius, sent the Roman knight Pontius Pilate to be fifth procurator, or governor, of Judea, the others having been Coponius, Marcus Ambivius, Annius Rufus, Valerius Gratus.

Pilate had trouble from the very beginning. His soldiers entered Jerusalem by night and planted their standards with the little silver figures of the emperor on Fort Antonia. In the morning the Jews were horrified, and they hurried to Caesarea and for five days and nights lay on the ground pleading for the removal of this idolatry. On the sixth day Pilate gathered them in the race-course, and soldiers sprang forward with drawn swords threatening instant death if they ceased not their clamor and would not quietly return home. The Jews flung themselves on their faces and bared their necks, ready to die rather than have their religion violated. Pilate was baffled; he ordered the removal of the images from Jerusalem to Caesarea.

Pilate built a much-needed aqueduct of brick, twenty-five miles long, but paid for it out of the Temple treasury. An abusive mob surrounded Pilate, but his soldiers beat many to death and trampled upon many more.

Putting down a revolt, he massacred Galilean worshipers and mingled their blood with the blood of their sacrifices in the Temple, which sent a shudder through the land. Luke 13, 1.

Pilate hung votive shields with the emperor's name in Herod's palace. A company of nobles with the four sons of Herod protested. Pilate ignored the protest. They complained to Rome. Tiberius rebuked Pilate and ordered the shields removed. Luke 23, 12 may refer to this. By such a man Jesus was judged.

I.

PILATE AND THE JEWS.

WITHOUT THE PRETORIUM.

They led Jesus from Caiaphas to the Pretorium; and it was early; but they themselves went not into the Pretorium that they might not be defiled, but might eat the passover. The feast lasted seven days.

Going into the house of a heathen made a Jew "unclean" till sunset, so the Rabbis ruled. They would murder an innocent man, they would not enter the house of a Gentile. In the striking phrase of Christ, they "strained out the gnat and swallowed the camel," Matt. 23, 24.

Sir Fowell Buxton at Civitavecchia found a very religious prisoner by the name of Gasparoni. He thought nothing of murdering many men, but he never murdered or ate meat on a Friday!

Are there such "Jews" and such "Catholics" among us? Do people break plain laws of God to keep the rules of men?

Pilate therefore went out to them and saith, "What accusation bring ye against this man?"

"If this fellow were not a malefactor, we should not have delivered Him up to thee."

A rather insolent demand. They refused to bring an accusation and the proofs; all they demanded was for him blindly to do their bidding.

This looked like an opening to get rid of the case. Pilate therefore said, "Take Him yourselves and judge Him according to your law."

"It is not lawful for us to put any one to death." In other words, we have tried the prisoner in due form and sentenced Him to death. All we want is to have the sentence confirmed and a death-warrant granted. They had the law on their side, and Pilate had to review the case.

The proud Jews pocketed their pride and publicly owned their degrading subjection. A bitter pill, but they swallowed it. Why was this?

That the saying of Jesus might be fulfilled, which He spake, signifying what kind of death He should die. John 12, 32. Roman crucifixion, not Jewish stoning.

From the following it seems Pilate must have known something of Christ's claim to be a king. Luke 23, 2. They had condemned Him to death for blasphemy, now they accuse Him as a rebel.

II.

PILATE AND CHRIST.

WITHIN THE PRETORIUM.

"I Am a King."

Pilate therefore entered again into the Pretorium and called Jesus and asked, "Art Thou the King of the Jews?"

Jesus answered, "Sayest thou this thing of thyself, or did others tell thee of Me?"

Pilate answered, "Am I a Jew? Thy nation and the chief priests delivered Thee to me; what hast Thou done?"

Jesus answered, "My kingdom is not of this world. If My kingdom were of this world, then would My servants fight that I should not be delivered to the Jews; but now is My kingdom not from hence." Here again Christ pronounces the great principle of the separation of Church and State. Matt. 22, 21.

Pilate therefore said, "So, then, Thou *art* a king?"

Jesus answered, "Thou sayest that I am a king. [Luke 22, 70.] To this end have I been born, and to this end am I come into the world, that I should bear witness unto the truth. Every one that is of the truth heareth My voice," obeys it as the supreme authority. No such claim on man's allegiance was ever made by any other master. As Christ, so the Christian. For what have you been born into this world? Are you of the truth, and do you obey Christ's voice?

Christ's kingdom is not of this world; the Pope's kingdom has been of this world till September, 1870, and again since February 11, 1929. Again the Pope boasts that his kingdom is of this world, that he is an earthly, a temporal ruler, the political prince of the Vatican City.

Christ's kingdom is not of this world, but it will endure beyond this world.

> Crowns and thrones may perish,
>   Kingdoms rise and wane,
> But the Church of Jesus
>   Constant will remain.

> Gates of hell can never
>   'Gainst that Church prevail;
> We have Christ's own promise,
>   And that cannot fail.

> Onward, Christian soldiers,
>   Marching as to war,
> With the Cross of Jesus
>   Going on before.

In the Second Article of our Creed we confess two violent contrasts: "His only Son, our Lord — suffered under Pontius Pilate." Again: "Suffered under Pontius Pilate — sitteth on the right hand of God the Father Almighty, from thence He shall come to judge the quick and the dead."

Pilate said, "What is truth?" He knew that line of talk. The Stoics preached only the wise man is a king; Plato said the world would never be happy till kings were philosophers or philosophers kings. He may have jested, as Bacon suggested. He may have been a sad agnostic like Pliny the Elder, who said, "There is only one thing certain, *viz.*, that there is nothing certain." He may have been a practical politician, who simply had no time for such impractical philosophers. Be that as it may, certain it is he did not know the Truth when he saw Him, and he did not want to learn.

III.

PILATE AND THE JEWS.
WITHOUT THE PRETORIUM.
"NOT GUILTY."

And when he had said this, he went out again to the Jews and said, "I find no crime in Him." Pilate said this after he had examined Christ and convinced himself. Pilate said this as an impartial man, without any bias for or against Christ. Pilate said this of his own free will. Pilate said this officially and judicially, as the governor sent by Tiberius Caesar to mete out justice. Pilate said this and thus reversed the judgment of the Jews. Pilate said this and — dismissed the case? No! Pilate said this and then practically resigned his office and left the innocent prisoner to the tender mercies of His deadly enemies.

Pilate said, "But it is a custom of yours that I should release unto you one at the Passover; will ye therefore that I release unto you the King of the Jews?"

Then they yelled again, "Not this man, but Barabbas!" Now, Barabbas was a robber.

George Herbert warns you: —

Thou who condemnest Jewish hate
For choosing Barabbas, a murderer,
Before the Lord of Glory,
Look back upon thine own estate,
Call home thine eye (that busy wanderer) —
That choice may be *thy* story.

That has been the story of many, that they chose Barabbas rather than Christ.

Said the dying converted Jewish scholar Tremellius, "Not Barabbas, but Jesus."

IV.

PILATE AND CHRIST.

WITHIN THE PRETORIUM.

A. Scourged.

Then Pilate therefore took Jesus and scourged Him.

Jesus was tied to a pillar, such as Sir C. Warren found in a cavern on the site of what Ferguson calls the Tower of Antonia. On the tense, bent, bare back the strong arms of the Roman soldiers laid the lash, straps with leaden balls or sharply pointed bones. The first stroke usually drew blood, and soon the whole back was a mass of raw and quivering flesh. Even strong men often died under this flagellation. "We are healed by His stripes" — blue, livid weals, wales, welts. 1 Pet. 2, 24.

B. Barrack-Room Sport.

And the soldiers plaited a crown of thorns and put it on His head, and they put on Him a purple robe, and they kept on coming to Him and saying to Him, "Hail, King of the Jews!" And they kept on slapping Him in the face.

Bara, the dying converted Tahitian, had a real understanding of the crown of thorns: "Jesus gives me for my head a pillow without thorns."

While the world still mocks Christ, let us reverently worship Him as our King: —

> All hail the power of Jesus' name!
> Let angels prostrate fall!
> Bring forth the royal diadem
> And crown Him Lord of all!

On the way to burn John Hus, the Council of Constance — Pope, priests, and professors — placed on his head a paper cap with three painted devils and the title "Heresiarch."

Downhearted? He rejoiced, "My Lord Jesus Christ for my sake wore a crown of thorns; why therefore should not I for His sake wear this shameful crown?" Yes, why not? The slave is not above his Master.

V.

PILATE AND THE JEWS.

WITHOUT THE PRETORIUM.

"ECCE HOMO!"

And Pilate went out again and saith to them, "Behold, I bring Him out to you that ye may know that I find no crime in Him."

Jesus therefore came out wearing the crown of thorns and the purple robe. And Pilate saith unto them, —

"Behold the man!"

DUERER.

BEHOLD THE MAN!

Ridiculous and harmless, let Him off.

We worship in the words of Paul Gerhardt: —

> O bleeding Head, and wounded,
>   And full of pain and scorn,
> In mockery surrounded
>   With cruel crown of thorn!
> O Head, once crowned with glory
>   And heavenly majesty,
> But now despised and gory,
>   Yet here I welcome Thee!
>
> *My* burden in Thy Passion,
>   Lord, Thou hast borne for me,
> For it was *my* transgression
>   Which brought this woe on Thee.
> I cast me down before Thee,
>   Wrath were my rightful lot;
> Have mercy, I implore Thee,
>   Redeemer, spurn me not.

When the chief priests therefore and the police officers saw Him, they yelled, "Crucify! crucify!"

Pilate saith to them, "Take Him yourselves and crucify, for I find no crime in Him."

A good preacher, this Pilate — I find no crime in Christ. A responsive congregation — "Crucify!"

A joke of a judge — "Take Him yourselves and crucify; for I find no crime in Him!"

The Jews answered, "We have a Law, and by our Law He ought to die, because He made Himself the Son of God." Lev. 24, 16.

Roman practise respected the laws of the provinces, and the Jews meant to warn Pilate not to ignore their Law.

VI.

PILATE AND CHRIST.

WITHIN THE PRETORIUM.

PILATE AFRAID.

When Pilate heard this word, he was more afraid and went again into the Pretorium and saith to Jesus, "Whence art Thou?"

But Jesus gave Him no answer.

Therefore saith Pilate, "Speakest Thou not to *me?*   Knowest Thou not that I have authority to release Thee and have authority to crucify Thee?"

Jesus answered, "Thou hast no authority whatever against Me except it had been given thee from above; therefore he that delivereth Me to thee hath greater sin." Caiaphas and his Sanhedrin.

Upon this Pilate was seeking the more to release Him; but the Jews fell a-howling, "If thou release this fellow, thou art not Caesar's friend; every one that maketh himself a king is a rebel against Caesar."

A broad hint they would accuse him of treason — the greatest offense for a Roman. Sejanus, the all-powerful favorite freedman, had already been killed by the terrible Tiberius, and the same fate would befall Pilate if the ugly story reached Tiberius his procurator had sided with a ringleader of sedition.

TIBERIUS.

The same threat was made another time, and Philo says: "He was afraid that, if a Jewish embassy were sent to Rome, they might discuss the many maladministrations of his government, his extortions, his unjust decrees, his inhuman punishments."

As a matter of fact the Jews did complain to Rome when he put down the Samaritans, and the Legate Vitellius ordered him to report to Tiberius,

who died March 16, 37, before Pilate arrived.   That is all we know of the widest-known and the ignoblest Roman of them all.

Legend has him commit suicide, and in Switzerland they named for him Mount Pilatus.

VII.

PILATE AND THE JEWS.

WITHOUT THE PRETORIUM.

"ECCE REX!"

When Pilate felt the force of these words, he brought Jesus out and sat down in the judgment-seat in a place that is called the Pavement, but in the Hebrew, Gabbatha, a broad, raised platform.   Such a pavement Julius Caesar carried about with him and from it gave judgment.

Now it was the preparation of the Passover, Friday, about the sixth hour; and he saith to the Jews, "Behold your King!"

What contemptuous words of this contemptible judge!

But they yelled, "Away with! Away with! Crucify Him!"

Pilate saith to them, "Shall I crucify your King?"

Insulting sarcasm to them, clothed in tender concern for them.

The chief priests answered, "We have no king but Caesar!"

The scepter had departed from Judah.

They rejected the King of Glory — 1 Sam. 12, 12 — and accepted the lecherous and treacherous Tiberius; they rejected their Savior and accepted their destroyer; they rejected the Perfect Man and accepted a moron.   Josephus, the Jew, says no nation under heaven was more wicked than the Jews.

Jesus was sentenced as a rebel and at once hustled off to execution.

"Christ, our Passover, is sacrificed for us."

REJECTED!

Rejected, neglected, reproached, and despised,
By all in whose stead Thou wast sorely chastised:
   Have mercy, Lord Jesus!
Encompassed by sinners and poured out like water,
The Sinless for sinners was led to the slaughter:
   Have mercy, Lord Jesus!
Lord, grant us repentance and faith in Thy death,
Strength, courage, to serve Thee to our dying breath:
   Have mercy, Lord Jesus! — W. G. Polack.

Then therefore Pilate delivered Him to them that He might be crucified.

"Thou wilt go to the cross. Go, soldier, prepare the cross," were the words of the awful order. The ruled ruling the ruler! The Governor governed by the governed!

About seven years before, Tiberius had ordered no one should be excuted until ten days after being sentenced, murderers and rebels excepted.

"WAS CRUCIFIED, DEAD, AND BURIED."

John 19, 17—42.

FOOTPRINTS.

Who is it treads this cobbled road
 With labored, panting breath
And struggles underneath the load
 That holds a gruesome death?
Whose scarlet footprints on the street
 Are tracks of sweat and blood?
Who is this Man that goes to meet
 His death upon the rood?

Footprints they are of One who came
 From heaven to earth below
To take on Him the sinners' shame,
 Sin, guilt, wrath, death, and woe;
Footprints of One who bore our grief
 And all our sorrows, too,
That we from sin might have relief
 And come to God anew.

Oh, mark it well to-day, my soul,
 Thy blessed Savior trod
This awful path to make thee whole,
 To bring thee back to God.
Upon these prints repentant gaze
 And count all else but loss,
By faith to serve Him all thy days
 Who, willing, bore thy cross. — *W. G. Polack.*

I.

THE DEAD MARCH ON THE VIA DOLOROSA.

THEY received Jesus — He came into His own, and His own received Him not — and led Him away to hang Him on a cross.

II.

JESUS BEARS THE CROSS.

And bearing His cross for Himself, He went out to a place called Skull, which is in Hebrew Golgotha.

Roman law made felons bear their own gibbet, and *Furcifer!* "Gallows-bearer!" was hissed at them.

Golgotha, or Calvary, looked like a skull, or it was strewn with the skulls of criminals executed there. Outside the gate the bodies of sacrificed victims were burned, outside the gate the body of Christ, the Victim, was sacrificed. Lev. 24, 14; Heb. 13, 11—13.

Under an Eastern sky,
Amid a rabble cry,
A man went forth to die —
 For me.

Thorn-crowned His blessed head,
Blood stained His every tread,
Cross-laden on He sped —
 For me.

On the way Christ broke down under the heavy load, and so they forced Simon of Cyrene, a city in North Africa with a large Jewish colony, to bear His cross, and we pray with H. R. Mackintosh: —

Thou must have looked on Simon;   Till I shall see and follow
Turn, Lord, and look on me   And bear Thy cross for Thee."

Unless you take up your cross and follow Christ, you cannot be His disciple. Matt. 10, 38; 16, 24.

III.

JESUS IS CRUCIFIED.

There they crucified Him. Cicero calls crucifixion "the most cruel and the most terrible punishment." The Jews did not crucify Christ. Why, no, to be sure; they forced Pilate to do their dirty work. The Popes never burned heretics. Why, no, to be sure; they forced "the secular arm" of the kings to do that dirty work.

Jesus was obedient unto death, even the death of the cross, and thus became a curse for us. Phil. 2, 8; Deut. 21, 23. There is humiliation. Also glorification. He became a curse for us to remove the curse from us and bestow a blessing upon us. Gal. 3, 13. 14.

THE NEW CALVARY.

Here He made reconciliation between God and man by taking away the handwriting that was against us. Eph. 2, 16; Col. 1, 20; 2, 14.

The cross is the tree of knowledge and the tree of life. I am crucified with Christ. If we suffer with Him, we shall also reign with Him. We preach Christ Crucified. 1 Cor. 1, 23; Gal. 2, 20; 6, 14; 2 Tim. 2, 11.

The wicked Colonel Gardiner dreamed Christ on the cross said to him, "I have suffered this for thee, and is this thy return?" He became a devoted Christian.

Tacitus tells us the emperor began to wear an amber ring, which was worthless, but then soon it became all the rage among the Romans. Christ, our King, hung upon the cursed cross, and now we sing, "In the Cross of Christ I glory."

We say with old Venantius Fortunatus: —

> Faithful cross, above all other,
> One and only noble tree!
> None in foliage, none in blossom,
> None in fruit thy peer may be;
> Sweetest wood and sweetest iron,
> Sweetest Weight is hung on thee.

IV.

JESUS IN THE MIDST.

And two others with Him, on either side one, and Jesus in the midst. The Holy One was numbered with the transgressors. Is. 53, 12.

Three hung upon their crosses. One died *for* sin; another died *to* sin; the other died *in* sin. One accepted Christ, the other rejected Christ.

THE CROSS-BEARER.   FROM PAINTING BY L. THIERSCH.

What think ye of Christ? What shall I do with Jesus? Matt. 22, 42; 27, 22. What Ittai said to David I will say to Christ: "As the Lord liveth, surely in what place my Lord the King shall be, whether in death or life, even there also will Thy servant be," 2 Sam. 15, 21.

V.

THE TITLE.

Pilate wrote a title also and put it on the cross — to publish the crime; so was the Roman law. And the writing was: —
JESUS THE NAZARENE
THE KING OF THE JEWS.

VI.

THE LANGUAGES.

This title then read many of the Jews, for the place where Jesus was crucified was nigh to the city; and it was written in Hebrew, Latin, Greek — the national, the official, the common tongue, the most important languages of that time and likely of all time.

The Hebrew was consecrated by enshrining the Old Testament, the Greek was consecrated by enshrining the New Testament, the Latin was also consecrated by enshrining the theology drawn from the Old and the New Testament.

Luther said: "As we love the Gospel, so let us study the languages." Thereby he has consecrated philology; he has done more for that science than any other man, as President Eliot of Harvard testifies. And Lutheran theologians above others have been famous for their knowledge of these languages. Bishop Pearson and also King of Lincoln say a good theologian ought to know them. That is why we spend so many years in their study at our colleges and seminaries. That is why we translate directly from Hebrew and Greek into English, German, and almost all the languages and dialects in the world. That work was begun in the time of Luther, and it has been carried on to the present time and will be carried on, please God, to the end of time. The Christian Church is the world's greatest philological society.

The British and Foreign Bible Society has hung in the place of honor a fine painting of Luther translating the Bible. The greatest Bible society pays homage to the greatest Bible translator.

VII.

THE PETULANT PROTEST.

Then said the chief priests of the Jews to Pilate, "Write not, 'The King of the Jews,' but that He said, 'I am King of the Jews.'"

VIII.

THE ROUGH REFUSAL.

Pilate answered, "What I have written I have written."

IX.

GAMBLING AT THE CROSS.

Then the four soldiers, when they had crucified Jesus, took His garments, according to Roman custom, and made four parts, to every soldier a part; and also His tunic. Now, the tunic was without seam, woven from top throughout. They said therefore to one another, "Let us not rend it, but cast lots for it whose it shall be," "that the scripture might be fulfilled which saith, They parted My raiment among them, and for My vesture they did cast lots," Ps. 22, 18. These things therefore the soldiers did.

The papists claim Queen Helena, the mother of Constantine, found this robe and took it to Treves (Trier). Leo X, in 1512, ordered it to be shown every seven years. In 1810 it was viewed by 227,000 people, in 1844 by still more. Johann Ronge and many others quit the Pope's church in disgust.

Gambling at the cross! Well, they were hardened Roman soldiers; killing was their business; what did they care about just one more criminal crucified? Especially a Jew.

Gambling at the cross — in church, for the benefit of Christ! Well, they are hardened church-members, much more hardened than the hardened Roman soldiers.

I will do as did the soldiers. I will take Christ's robe of righteousness and wear it to cover my unrighteousness. Is. 61, 10.

> With my Savior's garments on,
> Holy as the Holy One.

Thus I put on the Lord Jesus as my perfect righteousness. Rom. 13, 14; Gal. 3, 27.

And then I will also put on the "new man" of my holiness. Eph. 4, 24; Col. 3, 12; 1 Cor. 1, 30.

Philip II of Spain cried, "Oh, would God I had never reigned! Oh, that I had lived alone with God! What does all my glory profit but that I have so much the more torment in death?" The learned Salmasius declared, "I have lost a world of time. Oh, sirs, mind the world less and God more!" Baron von Bunsen said, "My riches and experience is having known Jesus Christ. All the rest is nothing."

"You are dying as you lived, great to the last." Archbishop Whately replied, "I am dying as I lived, in the faith of Jesus. . . . Do not call intellect glorious; there is nothing glorious out of Christ. . . . It is not my fortitude that supports me, but my faith in Christ."

X.
THE GROUP AT THE CROSS.

Now, there stood by the cross of Jesus His mother and His mother's sister (Salome, the wife of Zebedee and mother of James and John, maternal cousins of Jesus), Mary, the wife of Cleopas (and mother of Joseph and James the Little), and Mary the Magdalene — and the disciple whom Jesus loved.

XI.
THE LEGACY FROM THE CROSS.

1. THE LEGACY TO HIS MOTHER.

Jesus, now, seeing the mother and the disciple whom He loved standing by, saith to the mother, "Woman, behold thy son!"

2. THE LEGACY TO HIS DISCIPLE.

Then saith He to the disciple, "Behold thy mother!" And from that hour that disciple took her unto his own home.

As in death He hung,
His mantle soft on thee He flung
Of filial love and named thee son;
When now that earthly tie was done,
To thy tried faith and spotless years
Consigned His Virgin Mother's tears.
Latin Hymn; *Isaac Williams*, tr.

The grace of our Lord Jesus Christ! Even in the pains of the cross Christ was thoughtful of the welfare of His mother.

DALLMANN, JOHN.   21

This grace of our Lord Jesus Christ was with John. As a brother of Christ he cared for the mother of Christ. This grace of our Lord Jesus Christ be in you all. Are you looking for the social gospel? Learn it from the Cross of Christ — and practise it. Every Christian is a social-welfare worker.

Christ says, "Whosoever shall do the will of My Father who is in heaven, the same is My brother, and sister, and mother," Matt. 12, 50. Those in need of care He puts into your care. Do you care? Are you His brother, His sister?

XII.

"I THIRST!"

After this, Jesus, knowing that all things were now finished, that the Scripture might be fulfilled, saith, "I thirst!" Ps. 22, 15; 69, 21.

Down with a fever in Spain, the mighty Caesar with "the tongue that bade the Romans mark him, cried as a sick girl, 'Give me some drink, Titinius!'" The pains of a wounded soldier are all swallowed up in the fierce pain of thirst, and his only wail is, "Water! Water!" Jesus suffered the unspeakable agony in Gethsemane, He was marched to Annas, from Annas to Caiaphas, from Caiaphas to Pilate, from Pilate to Herod, from Herod to Pilate, He endured the cruel scourging of the Roman soldiers, He dragged His cross till He broke down, He hung upon the cross for six long hours! With all this great suffering and loss of blood, no wonder He cried, "I thirst!"

That cry shows Christ was truly human, with all our human pains and needs.

Now, there was set a vessel full of vinegar; and they filled a sponge with vinegar and put it upon hyssop and put it to His mouth. Ex. 12, 22; Ps. 51, 7.

Christ thirsted in my stead that I might never, like Dives, beg for a drop of water to quench my thirst, "for I am tormented in this flame."

"I thirst!" is still the cry of Christ in His needy members in orphanages, homes for the aged, hospitals, asylums, colleges, seminaries. May He say to us, "I was thirsty, and ye gave Me drink. Inasmuch as ye have done it unto one of the least of these My brethren, ye have done it unto Me"! Matt. 25, 35. 40. The rough Romans had pity and gave Him drink; shall we do less?

Melanchthon's friend and biographer, Joachim Camerarius, thought "hyssop" should be "hysso," the soldier's *pilum,* or javelin. And sure enough, an ancient manuscript has that reading.

XIII.

"IT IS FINISHED!"

When Jesus therefore had received the vinegar, He said, "It is finished!"

"It is finished!" — His life on earth, of course; but more.

"It is finished!" — Symbol, type, prophecy, fulfilled and become history. Luke 18, 31.

"It is finished!" — The work His Father gave Him to finish. John 4, 34; 17, 4.

"It is finished!" — All righteousness fulfilled; He was made unto us righteousness. He loved me and gave Himself for me. Matt. 3, 15; Rom. 10, 4; 1 Cor. 1, 30; Gal. 2, 20; Eph. 5, 2. 25; 1 Pet. 2, 24.

Now the soul can trust and rest in the finished work of Christ.

> Thy work, not mine, O Christ,
>   Speak gladness to my heart;
> They tell me all is done,
>   They bid my fear depart.
> To whom save Thee,
>   Who canst alone
>   For sin atone,
> Lord, shall I flee?

XIV.

THE VOLUNTARY DEATH.

And having bowed the head, He of His own free will gave up the spirit.

The writer here uses the words of Is. 53, 12 and thus identifies the Servant of Jehovah with Christ.

Mr. Charles of Balas labored all his life to translate the Bible into Welsh and prayed to live long enough to finish the work; then "I shall willingly lay down my head and die." The Lord granted him life till he could say, "It is finished."

XV.

THE CERTAINTY OF DEATH.

The Jews therefore, because it was preparation, that the bodies might not remain upon the cross on the Sabbath (for the day of that Sabbath was a great day), besought Pilate that their legs might be broken and that they might be taken away.   Deut. 21, 22 fulfilled.

The soldiers therefore came and broke the legs of the first and of the other who was crucified with Him — a Roman custom.

But when they came to Jesus and saw that He was dead already, they broke not His legs.   Their cruel mercy was not needed.   But one of the soldiers with a spear pierced His side, to make sure He was dead, and forthwith came out blood and water.

> Let the water and the blood
> From Thy riven side which flowed
> Be of sin the double cure,
> Cleanse me from its guilt and power.

So we pray with Toplady, and we rejoice with Watts: —

> My Savior's piercèd side
>   Poured out a double flood:
> By water we are purified
>   And pardoned by the blood.

Yes, now were the wells of salvation digged; now was the fountain opened; now was the Rock smitten. Is. 12, 3; Zech. 13, 1; 1 Cor. 10, 4.

Prof. J. V. Simpson, to whom we are thankful for introducing the anesthetic use of chloroform, agrees with other physicians that Christ died literally of a broken heart.

XVI.

THE TRUTHFUL EYE-WITNESS.

He that hath seen it, hath borne witness, and his witness is true; and he knoweth that he speaketh truth that ye also may believe.

XVII.

THE SCRIPTURE FULFILLED.

For these things came to pass that the scripture might be fulfilled, "A bone of Him shall not be broken." Ex. 12, 46; Num. 9, 12; Ps. 34, 20.

John here connects the Passover lamb with Christ, the true Lamb of

JESUS REDEEMS THE WORLD

St. Matt. 27:50; St. Mark 15:37; St. Luke 23:46; St. John 19:30

God, and points out what Paul says outright, "Christ, our Passover, is sacrificed for us; therefore let us keep the feast." 1 Cor. 5, 7. 8.

And, again, another scripture saith, "They shall look upon Him whom they pierced." Zech. 12, 8—14. This was fulfilled in Christ; Zechariah foretold it of the Messiah.

Now, you also look upon Him whom they pierced; look and repent of your sins; look and also be saved through faith in Him.

XVIII.

JOSEPH GETS THE BODY.

After these things, Joseph of Arimathea, being a disciple of Jesus, but secretly, for fear of the Jews, besought Pilate that he might take away the body of Jesus; and Pilate gave leave. He came therefore and took away His body.

Cicero against Verres says: "The bodies of the beheaded shall be thrown to the beasts. If this is grievous to parents, they may buy the liberty of burial." Later Augustus ordered such favors be granted, especially on the Emperor's birthday.

Taking bribes was one of the charges against Pilate; yet in this case he seems to have given the body as a free gift. Mark 15, 45.

XIX.

NICODEMUS BRINGS SPICES.

There came also Nicodemus (who at the first came to Jesus by night), bringing a mixture of myrrh and aloes, about a hundred pounds — a vast amount of costly spicery, aromatic and antiseptic. 2 Chron. 16, 14 mentions like honor at the burial of King Asa.

XX.

THE WINDING-SHEET.

Then took they the body of Jesus and wound it in linen cloths with the spices, as is the custom of the Jews to bury.

In other words, Jesus was buried with the honors given to a great Rabbi. This action was a public protest against the action of the rulers; for the cursed crucified were not even buried like the stoned, they were covered up at any place.

THE HOLY SEPULCHER.

XXI.
THE ENTOMBMENT.

Now, in the place where He was crucified there was a garden and in the garden a new tomb, in which no one had ever been buried. There, then, because of the Jews' preparation, for the tomb was near, they laid Jesus.

He bears Him to his new-hewn tomb,
  Jesus, to whom he did not bow;
He leaves Him in its sacred gloom,
  His Lord and Savior now.

O darkest woe!
Ye tears, forth flow!
  Has earth so sad a wonder?
God the Father's only Son
  Now is buried yonder!

O sorrow dread!
Our God is dead!
  But by His expiation
Of our guilt upon the cross
  Gained for us salvation.

THE EMPEROR HADRIAN AND HIS ARCH AT JERUSALEM.

In an Eastern monastery there is a crucifix with the words: *Tot pro te: quot pro me?* "Thus much for thee; how much for Me?"

Zinzendorf, in a church, saw a painting of the crucifixion with the words: —

> All this I did for thee;
> What hast thou done for Me?"

He started the world-wide Moravian Missions.

Let us pray with Harriet Appleton Sprague: —

> The way of sorrows Thou for me hast trod;
> My feet are loath to follow Thee, O God!
> Thy sacred hands were pierced for love of me;
> My hands, O Jesus, labor not for Thee.
> The cruel cross Thou, Lord, for me didst bear;
> Would I — a craven — fail Thy load to share?
> The thief who cried to Thee Thou didst not spurn;
> With penitence and love to Thee I turn;
> Unstable, weak, yet would I follow Thee.
> Lord Jesus, guide and strengthen even me.

A spot was pointed out to Helena, the mother of Constantine the Great, as the burial-place of Christ, and he displaced a Venus temple with the Church of the Holy Sepulcher, and here millions have worshiped.   In 1842 the German Pastor Otto Thenius pointed out a spot north of the Damascus Gate as a more likely place, and in 1883 "Chinese" Gordon agreed, also Major Conder, and many more.

We may never be sure of the exact spot — what of it?   Christ suffered without the gate and was buried in a near-by garden.

CHAPTER XXX.

"THE THIRD DAY HE ROSE AGAIN FROM THE DEAD."

John 20.

He who on Calvary died indeed,
As from eternity decreed, —
O sinful world, give heed, give heed:
    He is not here!

He trod the wine-press all alone,
For all men's sins He did atone;
Though laid in death behind this stone:
    He is not here!

He lives! Now Death need not affright;
He hath abolished Death's dread might,
Brought immortality to light:
    He is not here! — *W. G. Polack.*

I.

MARY MAGDALENE.

NOW, on the first day of the week cometh Mary Magdalene early, while it was yet dark, to the tomb and seeth the stone taken away from the tomb. Therefore she runneth and cometh to Simon Peter and to the other disciple, whom Jesus loved, and tells them, "They have taken away the Lord out of the tomb, and we know not where they have laid Him."

II.

PETER AND JOHN.

Peter therefore went forth and that other disciple and set out for the tomb. And the two were running both together, and the other disciple ran in front, more quickly than Peter, and came first to the tomb — simply because he could run faster. Stooping down, he seeth the linen cloths lying; yet he did not go in. Why not? We are not told, and so we do not know. Now Simon Peter also cometh, following him, and went into the tomb and beholdeth the linen cloths lying and the napkin that was upon His head, not lying with the linen cloths, but rolled up in a place by itself.

Careful order, no confusion; so the tomb had not been rifled by enemies.

Finding one of his children greatly shocked by the first sight of death,

[328]

EUGENE BURNAND.

JOHN AND PETER HASTENING TO THE SEPULCHER ON EASTER MORNING.

Arnold of Rugby opened his Bible at this verse and said, "Nothing, to my mind, affords such comfort as the thought that all these had been round our Lord Himself, who died and is now alive forevermore."

Then, therefore, went in also the other disciple who came first to the tomb, and he saw and believed — that the Lord was risen.

For even yet they understood not the Scripture, which had foretold that He must rise again from the dead. Ps. 16, 10.

So the disciples went away again to their own homes. The first to believe that Christ rose from the dead.

III.

THE ANGELS AND MARY.

But Mary was standing by the tomb outside, weeping. While she was weeping, she stooped down into the tomb and beholdeth two angels in white sitting, one at the head and one at the feet, where the body of Jesus had lain. They say, "Woman, why weepest thou?" She saith, "Because they have taken away my Lord, and I know not where they have laid Him."

IV.

JESUS AND MARY.

Having said this, she turned herself back and beholdeth Jesus standing and knew not that it was Jesus. Jesus said, "Woman, why weepest thou? Whom seekest thou?"

The first words of the risen Redeemer. What comfort! No need for weeping if we have a risen Redeemer.

Supposing that it was the gardener, she saith, "Sir, if Thou hast borne Him hence, tell me where Thou hast laid Him, and I will take Him away."

Jesus saith to her, "Mary!"

She turned herself and saith to Him in Hebrew, "Rabboni!" which means more than Teacher; it really means divine Lord.

Jesus saith, "Grasp Me not; for I have not yet ascended to the Father. But go to My brethren and say to them, I ascend to My Father and your Father and to My God and your God."

Do not grasp — go and tell! How practical! Say it, not with Easter flowers, but with Easter collections.

"My brethren" — even after the glorious resurrection! Do you value that title?

V.

MARY AND THE DISCIPLES.

Cometh Mary the Magdalene telling the disciples, "I have seen the Lord!" and that He had said these things to her.

The blessed messenger of the Easter-message. Are you celebrating Easter by telling His brethren?

Say with Hardenberg: —

I say to all men, far and near,   And what I say let each this morn
   That He is risen again,   Go tell it to his friend
That He is with us now and here   That soon in every place shall dawn
   And ever will remain.   His kingdom without end.

VI.

JESUS AND THE DISCIPLES.

Luke 24, 33.

THE RISEN REDEEMER'S GREETINGS AND GIFTS.

When now it was evening on that day, the first of the week, and the doors had been locked where the disciples were for fear of the Jews, came Jesus and stood in the midst — Ps. 22, 22 — and saith to them, "Peace to you!"

I can only wish you a good morning, I cannot give you a good morning; but when Jesus wishes you peace, He gives peace. And He even gives you the reason for it — He showed them both His hands and His side.

Enough said without a word said. A sermon without words, a sermon in action.

Of course we now read, The disciples *therefore* were glad when they saw the Lord. Yes, *therefore.*

Before the resurrection — sad; after the resurrection — glad.

Says Paul Gerhardt: —

This is a sight that gladdens   My trust or fortitude
   And fills my heart with glee;   Or any precious good
Now naughtsoever saddens   Which by His victory
   My soul nor takes from me   My Savior gained for me.

Then saith He to them again, "Peace to you!"

Remember it is the risen Redeemer that speaks with divine authority when He gives three things.

1. THE SACRED MISSION.

"As the Father hath sent Me, even so send I you."

This has been called "the charter of the Christian Church."

Christ is the Father's Apostle, Heb. 3, 1, and the Christians are Christ's apostles. The Father sent Christ to save the world, and Christ sends us to save the world by the saving Gospel. And we are to do so in the same spirit of love and sacrifice.

God had but one Son, and He made Him a minister, — what honor in that calling! Missionary Carey's son Eustace was also a missionary, but took a government position, which many thought a promotion. But Carey said, "Eustace has shriveled into an ambassador."

2. THE HEAVENLY PREPARATION.

When He had said this, He breathed upon them and saith to them, "Receive ye the Holy Ghost."

He breathes on us and gives us the Holy Ghost as we carefully and prayerfully study the Holy Book. Then the Holy Ghost teaches us what to believe and how to live. Then we know we have the Holy Ghost; then we are fitted out to do the work Christ gives us to do.

3. THE OFFICE OF THE KEYS.

"Whosesoever sins ye forgive, they are forgiven to them; whosesoever sins ye retain, they are retained."

In these words Christ instituted the Office of the Keys, the Key of Absolution and the Key of Excommunication. He gives to His Church the power to forgive sins and to retain sins. That is the work of the Church.

WHO HAS THESE KEYS?

1. In Matt. 16, 19 the Keys were given to Peter. The Pope claims to be the successor of Peter and as such to have the Keys and the power to rule the Church.

Ministers have the power of the keys, says the Anglican Dean Alford, "not by *successive delegation* from the apostles, *of which fiction I find in the New Testament no trace,* but by their mission from Christ, the Bestower of the Spirit." (Italics his own.)

2. In our text the Keys were given to the apostles — "and them that were with them," Luke 24, 33.

The episcopal bishops claim to be the successors of the apostles and as such to have the Keys and the right to rule the Church.

3. In Matt. 18, 17—20 the Keys were given to the Church, to all Christians. The congregation is to rule itself and to use the Key of Absolution and the Key of Excommunication, to take in members and to put out members.

The congregation exercises this office through its called pastor, to whom it transfers or delegates this power. And so we confess in our Small Catechism: "I believe that, when the called ministers of Christ deal with us by His divine command, especially when they exclude manifest and impenitent sinners from the Christian congregation, and, again, when they absolve those who repent of their sins and are willing to amend, this is as valid and certain, in heaven also, as if Christ, our dear Lord, dealt with us Himself."

They that deny the preacher has power to forgive sins contradict the clearest words of Christ, deny the complete redemption of Christ, and rob men of the most needful comfort.

VII.

THOMAS AND THE OTHER DISCIPLES.

1. THOMAS ABSENT.

But Thomas, one of the Twelve, called Didymus, or Twin, was not with them when Jesus came. Why not? We are not told, and so we do not know, and so no one has a right to blame him. Yet, whatever the reason, think of what Thomas missed.

> Oh, what peace we often forfeit,   All because we do not frequent
> Oh, what needless pain we bear,   Meetings when the Lord is there!

Let us not forsake the assembling of ourselves together, as the custom of some is, Heb. 10, 25.

2. THOMAS NOT COMFORTED.

The other disciples therefore said to him, "We have seen the Lord."

Do you try to cheer your mourning friends with the comfort of the risen Redeemer? It is the only true comfort.

3. THOMAS MAKES HIS OWN DEMANDS.

But he said to them, "Except I see in His hands the print of the nails and put my finger into the print of the nails and put my hand into His side, I will not believe." As if that were faith!

The king of Burma, a very hot country, interrupted an Englishman —

"You have told me many wonderful things, and I believe them. But I never will nor can believe water gets so hard you can walk on it. If the whole world told me so, I would not believe it." A Burmese Thomas. A farmer at a circus saw a giraffe and yet said, "There ain't no sich animal." No, the Thomases have not died out.

Many men feel like this: —

My name, it is Henry Jowett;	If there's any knowledge, I know it;
I'm the Master of Balliol College.	What I don't know isn't knowledge.

VIII.

JESUS AND THOMAS.

1. JESUS' GRACIOUS INVITATION.

And after eight days again His disciples were within and Thomas with them. Jesus cometh, the doors being shut, and stood in the midst and said, "Peace to you!"

After greeting them all, Jesus leaves the ninety and nine and goes right for the one sheep that was lost and meets the unreasonable conditions of the dogged disbeliever.

Then said He to Thomas, "Reach hither thy finger and see My hands, and reach hither thy hand and put it into My side, and be not faithless, but believing." What a loving, gracious, and stooping Savior!

2. THOMAS'S TRIUMPHANT FAITH.

Thomas answered, "My Lord and my God!"

The glorious climax of the Gospel. From the deepest depths of pessimistic skepticism rises the shout of spontaneous and exultant faith. The abrupt and dramatic end of the Gospel. The most obstinate Thomas was forced by infallible proofs to accept the risen Redeemer as his Lord and God. What excuse can you have for not believing? Thomas did the work of unbelieving so thoroughly that we need not do it over again. We thank him for his work and for his confession.

The *New Commentary on the Holy Scripture,* edited by Bishop Charles Gore, the leader of the liberal English Episcopalians, accepts as overwhelming the evidence for Christ's resurrection.

The story of Thomas, too, was written aforetime for our learning that through patience and through comfort of the Scriptures we might have hope. Rom. 15, 4.

3. JESUS' LAST BEATITUDE.

Jesus saith to him, "Because thou hast seen Me, thou hast believed; blessed are they that have not seen and yet have believed."

Dr. Arnold firmly and earnestly repeated these words and thus died a blessed death, with the Lord's last beatitude on his lips. "We walk by faith, not by sight," 2 Cor. 5, 7.

In his *Religio Medici* Sir Thomas Browne says: "I believe He was dead and buried and rose again; and desire to see Him in His glory rather than to contemplate Him in His cenotaph, or sepulcher."

Thomas Scott was a preacher who denied Christ. Convicted of sin when sick, he came to faith in the Savior, and his famous commentary rings with the praises of the Redeemer. Thomas Chalmers was a preacher who did not preach Christ crucified. On a sick-bed he faced death and found the Savior. He became a most powerful preacher of the Cross of Christ. Richard Holt Hutton of the *Spectator* did not believe in Christ. By the needs of his soul he was driven to Christ and spent a long life in commending his crucified and risen Savior. They learned to say, "My Lord and my God!"

David Hume sighed: "There were moments when, amidst all the pleasures of philosophical discovery and the pride of literary fame, he wished he had never doubted." Said the physician of the infidel Voltaire, "He died under the torment of furies."

IX.

THE PURPOSE OF "THIS BOOK."

Many other signs did Jesus in the presence of the disciples which are not written in this book; but these have been written that 1. ye may believe that Jesus is the Christ, the Son of God; and 2., believing, ye may have life in His name.

Gladstone calls it "the impregnable Rock of Holy Scriptures," and Roosevelt's favorite hymn was: —

> How firm a foundation, ye saints of the Lord,
> Is laid for your faith in His excellent Word.

Christ is the Life, and He gives us life in His name.

> His name the sinner hears
>   And is from sin set free;
> 'Tis music in his ears,
>   'Tis life and victory.
> New songs shall now his lips employ,
> And dances his glad heart for joy.

CHAPTER XXXI.

THE EPILOG.

John 21.

AT LAKE TIBERIAS.

1. JESUS BLESSES COMMON LABOR.

AFTER these things Jesus manifested Himself again to the disciples at the Lake of Tiberias; and He manifested Himself on this wise. There were together Simon Peter, and Thomas, called Didymus, Twin, and Nathanael of Cana in Galilee, and the sons of Zebedee, and two others of His disciples.

"I go a-fishing," Simon Peter saith unto them. "We also go with thee," said John and the others. They went forth and entered into the boat; and that night they caught nothing.

But when dawn was now breaking, Jesus stood on the shore; but the disciples knew not that it was Jesus.

Then Jesus saith to them, "Boys, you haven't caught any fish?"
"No."

And He said unto them, "Cast the net on the right side of the boat, and ye will find." They cast therefore, and now they were not able to draw it for the multitude of the fishes.

2. THE LOVED DISCIPLE RECOGNIZES THE LORD.

Therefore that disciple whom Jesus loved saith to Peter, "It is the Lord." He was the first to recognize his Master's voice.

3. PETER WORSHIPS THE LORD.

Now, when Simon Peter heard that it was the Lord, he girded on his outer garment (for he was naked) and threw himself into the lake — to go and worship the Lord. It was wrong to appear naked before God, and so this girding himself was an act of confessing Christ as God.

[336]

"IT IS THE LORD!"

4. LANDING THE CATCH.

But the other disciples came in the small boat, for they were not far from land, only about two hundred cubits off, hundred yards, towing the net of fishes.

Now, when they got out upon the land, they see a fire of coals there and a dried fish lying thereon and a loaf.

Jesus saith to them, "Bring of the fishes which ye have now caught."

Simon Peter went aboard and drew the net to land full of great fishes, a hundred and fifty and three; and for all there were so many, the net was not torn.

Unseen by us, the Lord watches us at our daily labor. Unless He bless the labor, they labor in vain that fish or build or do any other work. When the Lord blesses our labor, do we, like Peter, rush to worship Him?

5. JESUS FEEDS HIS DISCIPLES.

Jesus saith unto them, "Come, breakfast."

And none of the disciples durst ask Him, Who art Thou? knowing that it was the Lord.

Jesus then cometh and taketh the bread and giveth them, and the fish likewise.

The great God and Savior had washed His disciples' feet; here He, with His own pierced hands, starts a fire, roasts the fish, toasts the bread, serves the breakfast, and waits on the table for His tired and hungry friends. Wonderful? Well, no; not if you know that His name shall be called "Wonderful."

This is now the third time that Jesus was manifested to the disciples after that He was risen from the dead.

If this is not enough for you, nothing will be enough for you.

6. JESUS RESTORES PETER.

Now, when they had breakfasted, Jesus saith to Simon Peter, "Simon, son of John, lovest thou Me more than these?" He saith unto Him, "Yea, Lord; Thou knowest that I love Thee." He saith unto Him, "Feed My lambkins."

He saith to him again a second time, "Simon, son of John, lovest thou Me?" He saith unto Him, "Yea, Lord; Thou knowest that I love Thee." He saith unto him, "Shepherd my sheeplings."

He saith unto him the third time, "Simon, son of John, lovest thou Me?" Peter was grieved because He said unto him the third time, "Lovest thou Me?" And he said unto Him, "Lord, Thou knowest all things; Thou knowest that I love Thee." Jesus saith unto him, "Feed My sheep."

A triple question, a triple answer, a triple command. They show the supreme thing is love. He that most loves Christ will be most like Christ.

> Which of all our friends to save us
> Could or would have shed his blood?
> But Immanuel died to have us
> Reconciled in Him to God.
> This was boundless love indeed:
> Jesus is a Friend indeed.

Do you love Him? Obey Him.

> More love, O Christ, to Thee,
> More love to Thee.

As Christ was willing to restore Peter, He will be glad to restore you.

> This hath He done, and shall we not adore Him?
> This shall He do, and can we still despair?
> Come, let us quickly fling ourselves before Him,
> Cast at His feet the burthen of our care.

General Harrison taught in a Sunday-school even on the Sunday before leaving for Washington to be inaugurated as President of the United States. When his Washington gardener advised him to keep a dog to protect his fruit, he replied, "Rather set a Sunday-school teacher to take care of the boys." Postmaster-General John Wanamaker left Washington every week-end to teach his class in Philadelphia on Sundays.

7. JESUS TEACHES PETER.

"Verily, verily, I say unto thee, 'When thou wast young, thou girdedst thyself and walkedst whither thou wouldest; but when thou shalt be old, thou shalt stretch forth thy hands, and another shall gird thee and bring thee whither thou wouldest not.' "

Now, this He spoke, signifying by what kind of death he should glorify God. 2 Pet. 1, 14. And when He had spoken this, He saith unto him, "Follow Me."

8. PETER ASKS ABOUT JOHN.

Turning around, Peter seeth the disciple whom Jesus loved following, who also leaned on His breast at Supper, and said, "Lord, who is he that betrayeth Thee?" Peter seeing this man saith to Jesus, "Lord, but this man, what?" What about him? What shall he do?

Christ might have answered, "Glad you mentioned it, Peter; I might have forgotten that very important matter. What shall John do? Why, Peter, don't you know I made you the prince of the apostles, My representative on earth? John must simply obey you." Christ might have said that, but He did not say that. On the contrary.

9. JESUS REBUKES PETER.

"If I will that he tarry till I come, what is that to thee? Follow thou Me."

No, Peter was no Pope, no prince over John or any other of the apostles.

It is a sort of sacrilege to break into God's temple and try to pry into His secret sanctuary and find out more than He would have us know. Be content to know what God wants *you* to know and do what He wants *you* to do.

Keble says: —

"Lord, and what shall this man do?"
　　Ask'st thou, Christian, for thy friend?
If his love for Christ be true,
　　Christ hath told thee of his end:
This is he whom God approves,
This is he whom Jesus loves.

Ask not of Him more than this,
　　Leave it in his Savior's breast
Whether, early called to bliss,
　　He in youth shall find his rest,
Or, armed in his station, wait
Till his Lord be at the gate.

Sick or healthful, slave or free,
　　Wealthy or despised and poor —
What is that to him or thee,
　　So his love to Christ endure?
When the shore is won at last,
Who will count the billows past?

Only, since our souls will shrink
　　At the touch of natural grief,
When our earthly loved ones sink,
　　Lend us, Lord, Thy sure relief,
Patient hearts their pain to see
And Thy grace to follow Thee.

"Follow thou Me." Doing that, we'll have our heads and hands quite full. Do not worry — work!

Again, no matter what others may do, "follow thou Me." Christ is our Leader, others are misleaders.

Say as said brave Joshua, "Choose you this day whom ye will serve; . . . but as for me and my house, we will serve the Lord," Josh. 24, 15. Do as did Paul; when called by Christ, he conferred not with flesh and blood, but obeyed at once and obeyed unto the glorious and victorious end. Gal. 1, 16.

In John's gospel the last word of Christ — "Follow thou Me."

Come, follow Me, the Savior spake,
　　All in My way abiding;
Deny yourselves, the world forsake,
　　Obey My call and guiding;
O bear the cross, whate'er betide,
Take My example for your guide.

Then let us follow our dear Lord,
　　Bearing the cross appointed,
And, bravely cleaving to His Word,
　　In suffering be undaunted.
Who has not stood the battle's strain
The crown of life shall ne'er obtain.

10. A FALSE REPORT.

This saying therefore went forth among the brethren, "That disciple dieth not"; yet Jesus said not, "He dieth not," but, "If I will that he tarry till I come, what is that to thee?"

How did the false report start? They said Jesus said what Jesus hadn't said. How did false doctrines arise? They said Jesus said what Jesus hadn't said. Be sure you know just what the Bible says and then say just what it says — no more, no less: quote, do not misquote.

11. THE TRUSTWORTHY WITNESS.

This is the disciple who testifieth of these things and wrote these things; and we know that his testimony is true.

12. MANY THINGS NOT WRITTEN.

And there are also many other things which Jesus did, the which, if they should be written every one, I suppose that even the world itself could not contain the books that should be written.

What Rabbi Elieser said of the Law we may surely say of the Gospel:

> Could we with ink the ocean fill
>   And were the skies of parchment made;
> Were every stalk on earth a quill
>   And every man a scribe by trade,
>   To write the love
>   Of God above
> Would drain the ocean dry;
>   Nor could the scroll
>   Contain the whole
> Though stretched from sky to sky.

Henry W. Frost truly calls

THE BIBLE

> The Book of books, holy, sublime, and true,
>   Spirit-inspired in every thought and word,
>   Revealing God, and Christ as Savior-Lord,
> Teacher of all that men should be and do;
> A heavenly light within earth's midnight gloom,
>   A quickening life amidst death's dread decay,
>   A steadfast hand, pointing the upward way,
> A voice of triumph o'er the grave and tomb,
>   E'en when this earth and heaven have passed away.

Old Dr. Samuel Johnson wished to know a poet's companion in times of toil and sorrow. The lyrical Collins handed him the New Testament: "I have but one book, but that book is the best of all."

Alfred de Musset, the French poet, that child of the sunshine and the storm, had a New Testament which his old servant gave to a friend: "I know not what Alfred found in that book, but he always latterly had it under his pillow that he might read it when he would."

A famous Mexican official, whose speech before the Senate was broadcast all over the world, told A. B. De Roos, director of the Latin-American Prayer Fellowship, how he found the truth: "I was out in hiding with my troops in the desert of O. . . . One day the men came back from a foraging trip, and among the spoils they had a little book, which they had found in an abandoned hut. It was a gospel. I read this book every day for four months. There was nothing else to read. My brother had an arithmetic and did problems to keep him from going mad. I found God in that desert through the Gospel."

On the evening of May 26, 735, in a cell at Jarrow on the Tyne, the Venerable Bede, with feeble breath, was dictating the first Anglo-Saxon translation of John's gospel.

"Now, dearest master, there remains only one chapter, but the effort is too great for you."

"Take your pen, write quickly; I know not how soon my Maker will take me."

"Dear master, only one sentence is wanting."

Feebly and painfully that, too, was dictated.

"It is finished," said the scribe.

"It is finished," repeated the saint, and his spirit went to glory as he murmured, "Glory be to the Father and to the Son and to the Holy Ghost!"

PART THREE.

JOHN THE APOSTLE.

HIS EPISTLES.

JOHN THE APOSTLE.   DOMENICHINO.

FIRST EPISTLE.

CHAPTER I.

THE CLEANSING BLOOD.

1 John 1.

I.

THE Word of Life, which was with the Father from eternity, was manifested. The Eternal Life was made known when made man. He is God and man, eternal and historical.

There is no mistake about it — we have heard, we have seen with our eyes, we have gazed upon, and our hands have handled, examined, Him.

This apostolic experience becomes apostolic testimony: "That which we have seen and heard declare we unto you." It is a revelation, not a discovery.

The apostolic purpose of the apostolic testimony is "that ye also may have fellowship with us," the apostles.

"And, truly, our fellowship is with the Father and with His Son Jesus Christ," who made possible the fellowship.

The result of this fellowship is joy — "These things we write to you that your joy may be full."

What joy?

II.

"The blood of Jesus Christ, His Son, cleanseth us from all sin," v. 7.

It has cleansed us at the beginning, when we were justified, and now it keeps on cleansing us as we are being sanctified. Here they are precious words of pardon to give us day by day a holier life.

Cranach's famous altar piece at Weimar is a striking illustration of this verse. In the middle the crucified, to the left the risen Redeemer victorious over His foes; to the right John gives the meaning to Cranach, sprinkled with the blood, and Luther pointing to the open Bible at this verse.

Hedley Vicars, a dashing young captain, picked up a Bible. His eye fell on this verse, and he said, "By the blessing of God I'll have them cleansed away." He became a Christian, and this remained his favorite verse till he led his men at Sebastopol with the words, "This way, men of the 97th!" and he died the death of a hero.

"The saint's preparation for the duties of each day is a fresh application to the blood, in which he bathes his conscience anew each morning

as he rises," wrote Dr. Bonar. So also Robert McCheyne: "I ought to
go to Christ for the forgiveness of each sin. In washing my body, I go
over every spot and wash it out. Should I be less careful in washing
my soul? This is God's way of peace and holiness. It is folly to the
world and the beclouded heart, but is *the way*. I must never think a sin
too small to need immediate application to the blood of Christ."

Bishop Butler was awed at meeting face to face the Judge of the
world. His chaplain spoke to him of the blood of Jesus Christ, which
cleanseth us from all sin. "Ah, that is comfortable," the bishop replied
and peacefully gave up his soul to his Savior.

The Electress Anna of Brandenburg chose for her funeral text: "The
blood of Jesus Christ, His Son, cleanseth us from all sin." Precious words
of pardon to give a peaceful death.

When in 1907 King Oscar of Sweden lay on his death-bed, his queen
repeated these words into his ear; and his last words were, "Thanks be
to Jesus!"

If you cannot live like a king, you can die like a king.

III.

How do we get this forgiveness?

"If we confess our sins, He is faithful and just in order to forgive
us our sins," pardon us, justify us, make us righteous. And He is faithful
and just in order to "cleanse us from all unrighteousness," to sanctify us,
to make us holy. Astounding words!

. He is *faithful;* He promised it to us, and now He owes it to us;
and we hold Him to His promise, and He will keep His promise, He will
keep faith with us. He is reliable, and we will rely on Him in perfect peace.

Not knowing where to turn in his great trouble, the great Reformer
said in his Lutheresque way that he cast his sack before God's feet and
rubbed His ears with His promises until He heard. Oh, for a childlike
and yet robust faith such as Luther's!

He is *just* to forgive us our sins. Just — how so? Christ paid our
debt once, and God cannot collect twice. And so we also rely upon God's
divine justice for the forgiveness of our sins.

A man at Calcutta came to Lal Behouri Sing for baptism. Why?
"Mohammedanism is full of the mercy of God; and while I felt no real
consciousness of guilt as the breaker of God's Law, this satisfied me; but

when I felt my guilt, I felt that it was not with God's mercy, but with His justice that I had first to do. Now, to meet the claims of God's justice, Mohammedanism had made no provision; but this is the very thing that I have found fully accomplished by the atoning sacrifice of Christ on the cross; and therefore Christianity is now the only adequate religion for me, a guilty sinner."

> None but Jesus, none but Jesus,
> Can do helpless sinners good.

On the other hand — "If we say that we have no sin, we deceive ourselves, and the truth is not in us. . . . We make Him a liar, and His Word is not in us," His Gospel is not really living in our hearts.

An old man in Wiltshire was sure of going to heaven. "I am no sinner, not a bit of a sinner am I." "But God says you are a sinner, the same as all men." "God says what He thinks, and I says what I thinks. That is all the difference." "Have you heard of Him who died to save sinners?" "No; and it's no odds to me, for I am no sinner." To-day some say the same thing in about the same words. They make God a liar. They deny the Word of God, they deny the blood of Christ, they deny the work of the Holy Ghost. They wilfully remain in their sins and under God's punishment.

In the heart of his immortal *Divine Comedy,* Dante has set his own confession, telling all who read it that there is but one way to get free from sin — the humiliating way of confession; telling us also that without confession there can be no fellowship with the pure and good.

"I have learned in my long life two rules of prudence. The first is to forgive much, and the second is never to forget," wrote Guizot in an album. Under this Thiers wrote: "A little forgetting would not detract from the sincerity of the forgiveness." Under this Bismarck added: "As for me, I have learned to forget much and to ask to be forgiven much."

IV.

What is the result of the forgiveness?

1. Your iniquities have separated between you and God. When the separating sin has been removed, we have fellowship with the Father and with His Son Jesus Christ.

"God is Light, and in Him is no darkness at all. If we say that we have fellowship with Him and walk in darkness, we lie and do not the truth."

Leonardo da Vinci quarreled with a friend and in hate painted his face for Judas in the "Last Supper." But now, try as he would, he could not make any headway with the Christ and despaired. After a long time the artist forgave and wiped out the face of Judas. The same night he had a vision of Christ and at once put it on the famous canvas where it is seen to-day. If we walk in darkness, we have no fellowship with Him.

God is Light, and if we have fellowship with Him, we must walk in the light as He is in the light. The sun's light kills germs of sickness and gives robust health and vigorous life. The Son's light kills the germs of sin and gives spiritual health and vigor. We are to walk, go onward, forward, upward, in this light.

The sun's light bleaches; the Son's light bleaches us as no fuller can whiten.

God is Light; His eyes are Roentgen rays that go right through us, and we can hide no secret sins. We must walk as in the day, in the light of pitiless publicity. "As He is in the light." "In secret have I said nothing."

Among the heathen, god is made in man's image. The soldier made Mars; the sensualist made Venus; the musician made Apollo, and so on. In Christianity man is made after Christ's image. Christ is holy, "and the blood of Jesus Christ, His Son, cleanseth us from all sin" and day by day makes us more like Christ.

2. "If we walk in the light, as He is in the light, we have fellowship one with another," vv. 7. 3.

"Birds of a feather flock together." "Tell me with whom you go, and I will tell you who you are." If you walk in the light, you will wish to walk with those who walk in the light. "Love the brotherhood."

The Duke of Wellington approached the Lord's Table, when a very poor man knelt by his side. Another whispered to him to step aside until the duke had received the Sacrament. The duke took the hand of the poor man, saying, "Stay; here there is no difference between us, we are both poor sinners and both cleansed by the blood of Jesus."

Lord, in Thy kingdom there shall be
   No aliens from each other,
But even as he loves himself
   Each saint shall love his brother.
One Baptism and one faith have we,
   One Spirit sent to win us,

One Lord, one Father, and one God,
   Above and through and in us.
Never by schism or by sin
   May we that union sever,
Till all, to perfect stature grown,
   Are one with Thee forever.

CHAPTER II.

THE ADVOCATE.

1 John 2.

I.

"HE IS FROM THE BEGINNING."

Vv. 13. 14.

E is the eternal Son of God, who came into this world in the fulness of time when born of the Virgin Mary to become Jesus the Christ. What for? To be

II.

OUR ADVOCATE.

1. "If any one do a sin, we have an Advocate with the Father, Jesus Christ the Righteous," v. 1.

If a prisoner is too poor to retain a lawyer, the State will give him one. In like manner God gives a Lawyer to poor sinners who have no Paraclete, or Advocate, to give legal advice.

What kind of lawyer has God given us? A righteous Lawyer. That is a rare bird, they say. But it is restful to know that our Lawyer is righteous, for one thing. He may, however, be young and without experience. Do not worry. Our Advocate is the eternal Son of God and so knows the Judge very well; He is the Son of Man and so knows His clients very well. Of all lawyers, then, our Lawyer is the ablest and most reliable.

Very well; let the trial begin. The devil's advocate has a mass of evidence, and, worst of all, the damaging testimony of our own conscience clearly proves we have sinned against God.

Just as clear is the Law in the case: "The wages of sin is death." The death penalty is pronounced by the Judge, and the sheriff comes to carry out the death-sentence. Our case is desperate. What now?

2. Now our Advocate turns our Propitiation. As the golden mercy-seat covered the Ten Commandments, so Christ by His perfect obedience covers God's Law and by His precious blood makes a vicarious atonement

[349]

for our sins. He gave His life for our forfeited lives. He paid the fine in our stead, as our Substitute, as our Surety, as our Representative, and thus propitiated, stilled, the wrath of the Judge and satisfied justice.

"Himself the Victim and Himself the Priest." That is Christianity, and there is no other.

What a Lawyer! He serves without pay and in addition pays our fine, our heavy fine, to propitiate, to satisfy, the Judge.

> Jesus paid it all,
>   All the debt I owe;
> And nothing, either great or small,
>   Remains for me to do.
>
> In my place condemned He stood,
> Sealed my pardon with His blood.
>   Alleluia, what a Savior!

With such a Savior and Paraclete we need no Virgin and saints to pray for us.

When Sir Walter Raleigh was unjustly condemned and ferried from Westminster to the Tower, he turned from the cruel earthly king's attorney to his heavenly King's Attorney in these gripping, simple lines: —

> From thence to heaven's bribeless hall,
> Where no corrupted voices brawl,
> No conscience molten into gold,
> No forged accuser bought or sold,
> No cause deferred, no vain-spent journey;
> For Christ is there, the King's Attorney.
>
> And when the grand twelve million jury
> Of our sins with direful fury
> 'Gainst our souls black verdicts give,
> Christ pleads His death, and then we live.
>
> Be Thou my Speaker, taintless Pleader,
> Unblotted Lawyer, true Proceeder!
> Thou giv'st salvation, even for alms,
> Not with a bribèd lawyer's palms.
>
> This, then, is mine eternal plea
> To Him that made heaven, earth, and sea.

If any man do a sin, — and all Christians will sometimes do a sin, — all have an Advocate; and that is the comfort for the best of Christians. The more musical the ear, the more painful a discord; the better a Christian, the more pained he is by an act of sin. That holy primate of Ireland,

Dr. James Ussher, wrote on justification: "But when I came to do so of *sanctification,* that is, of the new creature that God forms by His Spirit in every soul which He doth in truth regenerate, I found so little of it wrought in myself that, apprehending I should write but as a parrot speaketh, by rote and without knowledge, I durst not presume to do so." A few days later his dying prayer was, "God be merciful to me, a sinner."

Even the good works of the Christian are not perfect. Our repentance needs to be repented of, our tears need washing.

3. Still more and still better — "He is the Propitiation for our sins; and not for ours only, but also for the whole world."

What a text for missions! The Savior for the whole world, but the only Savior in the whole world. He is the only Savior because He is the only one in the whole world that died for our sins.

> Other refuge have I none,
> Hangs my helpless soul on Thee.
>
> None but Jesus, none but Jesus,
> Can do helpless sinners good.

Glorious — and serious! Here is a warning: —

"It is the last hour; and as ye have heard that an Antichrist cometh, even now have there come into existence many antichrists; whence we know that it is the last hour. Who is the liar but he that denieth that Jesus is the Christ? This is the Antichrist who denieth the Father and the Son. Every one that denieth the Son hath also not the Father" — is an atheist, as Lavater says. "He that confesseth the Son hath the Father also," vv. 18—23. 26.

In the frescoes of Signorelli we have "The Teaching of Antichrist" — no repulsive figure, but a grand personage in flowing robes and with a noble countenance, which at a distance might easily be taken for the Savior. To him the crowds are eagerly gathering and listening, and it is only when you draw close that you can discover in his harder and cynical expression and from the evil spirit whispering in his ear that it is not Christ.

Something unknown was influencing the orbit of Uranus; the French mathematician Le Verrier said it was an undiscovered planet in a certain place. Dr. Galle of the Berlin Observatory pointed his telescope and found the planet within one degree of the place foretold. What is influencing you for evil? Point your Bible, and you will find Satan.

III.

HOW DO WE GET THIS ADVOCATE?

The darkness is past, and the true light now shineth — in the Gospel. Believe and receive.

Donald Fraser remarks: "It does not occur to John to say that the See of Rome 'was to be occupied in all time coming by a succession of Popes, viceregents of God on earth, and that each of these Popes was to be the supreme and infallible guide of the whole Church.' This is just the place where such a revelation should be made if the thing were true; but it is as clear as possible that the thought of a continuous infallible Papacy never entered into the mind of the Apostle John."

IV.

HOW DO WE KNOW THAT WE HAVE HIM?

"Hereby do we know that we know Him if we lovingly keep His commandments." "Hereby we are continually getting to know by experience that we have experienced and still do experience Him." "If ye know that He is righteous, ye know that every one that doth righteousness is born of Him. He that loveth His brother abideth in the light. He that saith he abideth in Him ought himself so to walk as He walked," vv. 3. 5. 6. 10. 29.

King Wenceslaus of Bohemia one night walked barefooted through the street to a distant church. His servant Redivivus began to faint. The saint told him to step into the place made by the royal feet, and the servant was helped. Our King goes before and breaks the crusted snow and then bids us follow Him in the path He eased for us.

On the other hand, "He that saith, I know Him, and keepeth not His commandments, is a liar, and the truth is not in him. He that saith he is in the light and hateth his brother walketh in darkness and knoweth not whither he goeth, because that darkness hath blinded his eyes," vv. 4. 9. 11.

"They fancy that they are going to rest and glory and yet go to hell," comments Luther. John Bugenhagen's motto was: "If you know Christ well, it is enough, even if you know nothing else; if you do not know Christ, it is nothing, even if you know all else."

"Love not the world, neither the things that are in the world. If any man love the world, the love of the Father is not in him. For all that is in the world, the lust of the flesh and the lust of the eyes and the pride of life," — the trinity of world, — "is not of the Father, but is of the world. And the world passeth away and the lust thereof; but he that doeth the will of God abideth forever," vv. 15—17.

This cursed antitrinity lured Adam and Eve in Paradise.

1. The lust of the flesh — "the fruit was good for food."

2. The lust of the eyes — it was "pleasant to the eyes."

3. The pride of life — "and to be desired to make one wise."

The same cursed antitrinity tempted Christ.

1. The lust of the flesh — "Command that these stones be made bread."

2. The lust of the eyes — "Cast Thyself down from the pinnacle of the Temple to make a scene and sensation."

3. The pride of life — "All the kingdoms of the world and the glory of them will I give Thee."

But Christ conquered by "It is written." So are we to conquer.

The Apostle John outlived twelve Roman emperors: Augustus, Tiberius, Caligula, Claudius, Nero, Galba, Otho, Vitellius, Vespasian, Titus, Domitian, and Nerva. He certainly saw that "the world passeth away" like a pageant on a stage.

Plutarch says King Pyrrhus would conquer the world. Cineas asked him, "And then?"

"Then we will sit down and enjoy ourselves."

"Sir, may we not do it now? Have you not already a kingdom of your own? And he that cannot enjoy himself with a kingdom cannot with the world."

V.

HOW DO WE REMAIN WITH GOD?

"Ye, let that which ye have heard from the beginning abide in you. If in you abides that which ye have heard from the beginning, ye also shall abide in the Son and in the Father," vv. 24. 27. 28.

The Gospel has brought us to God, and if we remain in the Gospel, we remain with God. The Gospel is the means of grace, the channel through which we get grace. "Whoso keepeth His Word, in him verily is the love of God perfected; hereby know we that we are in Him," v. 5.

VI.
WHAT IS THE END OF REMAINING WITH GOD?

"This is the promise that He hath promised us — eternal life," v. 25.

VII.
THE CONCLUSION.

"And now abide in Him that, when He shall be manifested, we may have confidence and not be ashamed away from Him at His coming," v. 28.

When, shortly before his death, the saintly Oettinger was praised for his great wisdom, he replied with a smile: "Yes, I have learned many things; but the most precious knowledge I learned as a child is Luther's Small Catechism, which comprises everything I desire to keep and carry away with me to the seeing face to face." Yes, with that in our hearts, we shall not be shamed away from His face when we shall see Him face to face.

CHAPTER III

THE MANIFESTED SON.

1 John 3.

I.

THE Son of God was manifested, vv. 5. 8, made known as the Son of Man, when born of the Virgin Mary in a stable at Bethlehem.

II.

"For this purpose the Son of God was manifested, to take away our sins" and "that He might destroy the works of the devil," vv. 5. 8.

III.

"Every one that committeth sin, committeth also lawlessness. And sin is lawlessness," v. 4.

"He that committeth sin is of the devil, because the devil sinneth from the beginning," v. 8.

IV.

"Hereby perceive we the love, because He laid down His life for us" — in our stead, as our Substitute, the Just for the unjust, v. 16.

This is the Gospel, and when we believe this Gospel, we are born again, not of corruptible seed, but of incorruptible, by the Word of God, which liveth and abideth forever, 1 Pet. 1, 23—25. Born of God, we are the children of God.

V.

"Behold what manner of love the Father hath bestowed upon us that we should be called the children of God; and we are." V. 1.

Bartholomaeus Ziegenbalg set a young Hindu to translate Luther's Small Catechism. When he came to the words "that we should be called the children of God," he balked. " 'Children of God,' that is too much, too high. Let me rather put it 'that we should be allowed to kiss His feet.' " Can you blame him? John himself, the Apostle of Love, stops to call our attention to this heavenly love. Behold! A wonder! What manner of love — boundless and endless! What manner of love given to us — sinful rebels! What manner of love God hath bestowed upon us

children of the devil in order that we should be called children of God —
and such we are! Glory! Behold! Look and look again and again;
look long and look intently; get the habit of looking. Let your eyes
drink in the miracle of God's wondrous love. Behold! Sink on your
knees, worship, adore. Why worry if the world does not know us? It
does not know the children because it does not know the Father.

When God lovingly calls you "My child," then you trustfully call
Him "my Father." You are not worthy? Certainly not! Who said so?
But that is not the question. The question is, Did God give His love
to you? God gave it, Christ earned it, the Holy Spirit makes it your
own through the Gospel. Take it, and welcome to it.

Do not steal a child from God. Do not be obstinate and make yourself an orphan, a prodigal with the swine, and fill a felon's grave in potter's
field. Correggio stood entranced before a fine painting and then cried,
"Thank God, I, too, am a painter!" We look with wondering eyes at the
wonderful love of God and joyfully cry out, "Thank God, we, too, are
children of God!"

VI.

"This is His commandment, That we should believe on the name of
His Son Jesus Christ and love one another, as He gave us commandment.
He laid down His life for us, and we ought to lay down our lives for the
brethren. And every man that hath this hope in Him halloweth himself,
even as He is holy. He that doeth righteousness is righteous, even as He
is righteous," vv. 23. 16. 3. 7.

What foreign country has not a multitude of graves filled with missionaries who laid down their lives for the brethren? Luther was willing
to lay down his life when he went to Worms in 1521 and when in 1527
he stayed in Wittenberg and nursed those stricken with the plague. Tacitus
said the Christians were as inflexible in their faith as they were ready to
show mercy. God give us more such Christians!

Some courtiers said to the emperor: "You will gain nothing by persecuting Bishop Chrysostom of Constantinople; for in exile he would find
a home with his God. You deprive the poor, not him, of property. He
kisses his chains, death opens heaven to him. There is only one way to
make him unhappy: force him to sin; he fears nothing in the world
but sin."

VII.

"In this the children of God are manifest and the children of the devil," v. 10. John, the Apostle of Love, knows only two classes of men, only two — the children of God and the children of the devil.

Here are the children of the devil: "Whoso hateth his brother is a murderer; and ye know that no murderer hath eternal life abiding in him. But whoso hath this world's good and seeth his brother have need and shutteth up his heart from him, how dwelleth the love of God in him?" Vv. 4. 8. 10. 15. 17.

Here are the children of God: "Let us not love in word, neither in tongue, but in deed and in truth. And he that keepeth His commandments dwelleth in Him and He in him. And whatsoever we ask we receive of Him, because we keep His commandments and do those things that are pleasing in His sight," vv. 11. 12. 18. 24. 22.

Do you belong to the children of the devil? "He that loveth not his brother abideth in death," v. 14.

Do you belong to the children of God? "We know that we have passed from death to life because we love the brethren," vv. 14. 19.

VIII.

"Beloved, now are we the children of God, and it doth not yet appear what we shall be; but we know that, when He shall appear, we shall be like Him; for we shall see Him as He is," v. 2.

Too wonderful for words! One theologian said these glowing words of glorious promise strained his faith more than anything else in the Bible. We say with Lucy Larcom: —

> What yet we shall be none can tell.
> Now are we His, and all is well.

Even in this life "we all, with unveiled face beholding as in a mirror the glory of the Lord, are transformed into the same image from glory to glory," 2 Cor. 3, 18.

Even in this world the face of a Christian may grow Christlike. Jenny Lind, the Swedish Lutheran Nightingale, took a last look at a dead friend and said: "It was not her *own* look that was in her face. It was the look of Another that had passed into hers. It was the shadow of Christ that had come upon her. She had seen Christ."

Prof. Henry B. Smith says Dr. Thomas H. Skinner "became more and more a living epistle, a Gospel of God's grace, known and read of all men. He grew day by day toward the measure of the stature of a perfect man in Christ Jesus."

Luther says a Christian is not in the being, but in the becoming. Yes, but in that life we shall have become. We shall be fully "conformed to the image of His Son that He might be the First-born among many brethren," Rom. 8, 29.

In that day our Savior shall fashion anew the body of our humiliation that it may be conformed to the body of His glory, according to the working whereby He is able to subject all things unto Himself," Phil.3, 21.

The day which others dread as the death-day of time we hail as the birthday of eternity. "We shall be like Him!"

We say with good old Richard Baxter: —

> My knowledge of that life is small,
>   The eye of faith is dim;
> But 'tis enough that Christ knows all
>   And I shall be like Him.

CHAPTER IV.

GOD'S GREAT GIFT.

1 John 4.

I.

THE GREAT FACT.

OD is Love," vv. 8. 16. This is the sublimest sentence and simplest summary of the whole Bible, the greatest sentence in all the world, in all the universe. Love loves to show its love by gifts of love, and herein is manifested the love of God that sent us

II.

THE GREAT GIFT,

wrapped in swaddling-clothes and lying in a manger. In this wondrous wise the great God sent His Son, the Only-begotten, into the world, vv. 9, 14, for

III.

THE GREAT PURPOSE

that we might live through Him, to be the Savior of the world, vv. 9. 14.

IV.

THE GREAT METHOD.

God sent His Son to be the Propitiation for our sins, v. 10.

God is Love, but holy love. Our God has principles and has character. He cannot weakly sigh over our sins or even wickedly wink at our sins. Because of sins cometh the wrath of God over the children of disobedience. Eph. 2, 3; 5, 16; Rom. 1, 18.

And yet God hath not appointed us to wrath, but saved us from the wrath to come by Christ, who stilled the wrath of God that we might live through Him, v. 9.

[359]

V.

THE GREAT EFFECT.

1. LOVE OF GOD.

"Herein is love, not that we loved God, but that He loved us. Now we love Him because He first loved us," vv. 10. 19.

And we declare our love with Francis Xavier: —

> I love Thee, O my God, and still
> I ever will love Thee,
> Solely because my God Thou art,
> Who first hast lovèd me.

2. LOVE OF MAN.

"This commandment have we from Him, that he who loveth God love his brother also. As He is, so are we in this world," vv. 21. 17.

Christ is represented by His Christians. What kind of representative are you? Do you represent Him, or do you misrepresent Him?

"Beloved, if God so loved us, we ought also to love one another.

"Beloved, let us love one another; for love is of God; and every one that loveth is born of God and knoweth God. If we love one another, God dwelleth in us, and His love is perfected in us.

"If a man say, I love God, and hateth his brother, he is a liar; for he that loveth not his brother whom he hath seen, how can he love God, whom he hath not seen?" Vv. 11. 7. 12. 20.

Just in passing, note the Holy Trinity. The Father loved us and gave us His Son. The Son reveals the love of the Father. From our love to one another we know God has given us of His Spirit, vv. 13—16.

William James, America's great philosopher, said that, after all our philosophy and science had reached their limits, the simple, human, personal interests in other people were the chief things that were worth living for. And Dr. Will Durant, the student of philosophy, says the only real love is "absolute devotion, desire to give full service to another." They only feebly echo what the Bible said long ago.

Let us pray with Charles D. Meigs: —

OTHERS.

Lord, help me live from day to day	Help me in all the work I do
In such a self-forgetful way	To ever be sincere and true
That even when I kneel to pray,	And know that all I'd do for You
My prayer shall be for — *others*.	Must needs be done for — *others*.

Let self be crucified and slain
And buried deep; and all in vain
May efforts be to rise again
Unless to live for — *others.*

And when my work on earth is done
And my new work in heaven's begun,
May I forget the crown I've won,
While thinking still of — *others.*

Others, Lord; yes, others,
Let this my motto be;
Help me to live for others
That I may live like Thee.

3. BOLDNESS AT THE JUDGMENT.

"There is no fear in love, but perfect love casteth out fear; because fear hath torment. He that feareth is not made perfect in love. Herein is our love made perfect that we may have boldness in the Day of Judgment," vv. 18. 17.

Jesus, Thy blood and righteousness
My beauty are, my glorious dress;
Midst flaming worlds, in these arrayed,
With joy shall I lift up my head.

Bold shall I stand in that great Day,
For who aught to my charge shall lay?
Fully through these absolved I am
From sin and fear, from guilt and shame.

VI.

THE GREAT CONFESSION.

We have known and believed the love that God hath to us and confess that Jesus Christ is the Son of God and is come in the flesh. We have seen and do testify that the Father sent the Son to be the Savior of the world. Vv. 16. 15. 14.

And every spirit that confesses this is "of God," begotten of God, a child of God, and God dwelleth in him and he in God; and he that knoweth God heareth us. Vv. 2. 15. 6.

On the other hand, He that is not of God heareth not us. Hereby know ye the spirit of truth, and the spirit of error, the spirit of Antichrist.

"Beloved, believe not every spirit, but try the spirits whether they are of God; because many false prophets are gone out into the world," vv. 3. 6. 1.

In view of the many antichrists gone forth into the world we Christians must do our very utmost to make known the Christmas-message of the true Christ, the Son of God come into the flesh, the Savior of the world.

The dying Professor Elmslie said over and over again, "God is Love, God is Love; I will go out and tell this to all the word. They do not know it."

Will you tell this — *before* you die?

CHAPTER V.

THE COMING OF THE SON.

1 John 5.

I.

"THE Son of God is come," v. 20. He came when He was born of the Virgin Mary and became the Son of Man, our Brother in the flesh, flesh of our flesh and bone of our bone.

II.

The Son of God is He that came by water and blood. He came by water when He was baptized; He came by blood when He shed it for the remission of sins on the cross.

He is ever coming with the water in Holy Baptism, the washing of regeneration and the renewing of the Holy Ghost. In the Lord's Supper He is ever coming with the blood shed for the remission of sins and which we drink in remembrance of Him.

"And it is the Spirit that beareth witness, because the Spirit is the Truth; the Gospel words are spirit and truth," vv. 6. 8. John 6, 63; 17, 17; 1 Thess. 2, 13.

There are three who bear witness, the Spirit in the Gospel and the water of Holy Baptism and the blood of the Lord's Supper; and all three are at one in bearing witness that Jesus is the Son of God and the Savior of the world.

III.

"Whosoever believeth that Jesus is the Christ is born of God," v. 1.

"He that believeth not God hath made Him a liar, because he hath not believed in the testimony which God hath given concerning His Son," v. 10.

IV.

All that is born of God — the joy of having been born in Zion! Milton says: —

> Both they who sing and they who dance
> With sacred song are there;
> In thee fresh brooks and soft streams glance,
> And all my fountains clear. (Ps. 87.)

"All that is born of God conquers the world; and this is the conquest which hath conquered the world: the faith which is ours. Who is he that conquers the world if not he that believeth that Jesus is the Son of God?" Vv. 4. 5.

"We know that we are of God, and the whole world lieth in the Wicked One. We know that whosoever is born of God sinneth not; but he that is begotten of God keepeth himself — from sin — and that Wicked One toucheth him not. We are in Him that is true, in His Son Jesus Christ," vv. 18—20.

V.

"Every one that loveth God, that begot him, will also love the other one that is begotten of God," v. 1.

He is God's child as well as myself, and I will love God's child for God's sake if not for his own sake. If I cannot love him directly, I will love him via God.

"By this we know that we love the children of God, when we love God and keep His commandments. For this is the love of God, that we keep His commandments, and His commandments are not grievous," vv. 1—3.

VI.

"This is the confidence that we have in Him, that, if we ask anything according to His will, He heareth us. And if we know that He hear us whatsoever we ask, we know that we have the petitions that we desired of Him," vv. 14. 15.

As the Roman ediles had their doors open always to all requests, so God's ears are always open to all true prayers. If at times it seem not so, Augustine says God regards our *well* rather than our *will;* He hears our intentions more than our expressions; He hears the unspoken prayer of the heart more than the spoken prayer of the lips.

Quaint old Quarles tells us: —

The masterpiece of knowledge is to know
But what is good from what is good in show.

Our all-wise Father has that masterpiece of knowledge, and we are content.

VII.

"We know that the Son of God is come and hath given us a sense that we know the True One; and we are in the True One, in His Son Jesus Christ," v. 20.

VIII.

"Jesus Christ is the real God," v. 20. Without Christ men have no God and are without hope, Eph. 2, 12. All other gods are idols, and an idol is nothing, 1 Cor. 8, 2. Make every personal effort to guard yourselves against idols, v. 21. Hold fast the true revelation of the real God as revealed in Jesus Christ, His Son, our Savior.

IX.

"Jesus Christ is the eternal Life," v. 20.

"God gave us eternal life, and this life is in His Son. He that hath the Son" — by a living faith — "hath the life; and he that hath not the Son of God hath not the life," vv. 10—12.

X.

"These things have I written unto you that ye may believe on the name of the Son of God, that ye may know that ye have eternal life," v. 13.

APOSTOLIC PRAISE, JOY, AND WARNING.

I.

THE AUTHOR.

THE author calls himself "the Elder." John was an elder in age and by office. Papias calls elders those who had personally known the Savior, and John was now the last living elder and he was *the* elder, of greatest influence in Asia Minor.

II.

THE RECEIVER

of the letter is "the elect lady." And that is all we are told, and so that is all we know.

III.

THE GREETING

is most tender: "Grace be with you, mercy, peace, from God the Father and from the Lord Jesus Christ, the Son of the Father, in truth and love."

IV.

THE CONTENTS.

1. APOSTOLIC PRAISE OF FEMALE PIETY.

The elect lady was an outstanding Christian — "whom I love in the truth, and not I only, but also all that have known the truth, for the truth's sake, which dwelleth in us and shall be with us forever."

Christian love is reasonable; it is for the sake of the truth. One gave a very high estimate of Luther and added: "This estimate does not spring from love, but the love from the estimate."

The aged apostle writes this private, personal letter to "the elect lady," whom he honored as a wife and a mother.

John had been brought up by his pious mother Salome, and he had taken into his own house the mother of our Lord and cared for her from the crucifixion till her death. He had the greatest respect for wifehood and motherhood. In all his writings there is not the least hint of the superior holiness of the unmarried state. That heathenish and unscriptural notion crept into the Church at a later and unhealthier age.

The finest flower of Christian civilization is the home, where woman is the queen and her children her jewels. The home is her sphere and home-making her career. Her best walk is her domestic walk in truth and in love; "and this is love, that we walk after His commandments. This is the commandment, that, as ye have heard from the beginning, ye should walk in it."

The Apostle of Love teaches practical common sense, no romantic nonsense.

2. APOSTOLIC JOY OVER YOUNG CHRISTIANS.

"Eureka, I have found it!" joyously cried Archimedes, when he at last had solved the great crown problem. "Eureka, I have found it!" joyously cried the Apostle John — "I rejoiced greatly that I found some of thy children walking in truth, as we have received a commandment from the Father."

To find something in science is great, no doubt; to find a holy life is unspeakably greater. How much greater the joy of John than the joy of Archimedes!

It seems some of the children of "the elect lady" had left home and found work in the great city of Ephesus. And though they lived in a very wicked city, they lived a Christian life, as they had been trained in a Christian family. When in Ephesus, they did not do as did the Ephesians.

Alas! how many a pastor's heart is saddened at the sight of young Christians coming from the country into the big city and falling away from Christ into the underworld!

The sturdy Christian life of these young people greatly rejoiced the heart of the aged Apostle of Love, and he told of his joy. His body was old, but his heart was young. Out of the fulness of the heart the mouth speaketh. What an example for us! Are we sympathetic with our young people? Do we encourage them? Do we show proper interest in them?

John wrote the good news to the anxious absent mother and of course greatly rejoiced the heart of that "elect lady." What greater joy for fond Christian parents than the knowledge that their children are upstanding and active Christians in a crooked and perverse city?

3. APOSTOLIC WARNING AGAINST ANTICHRIST.

"Jesus Christ coming in the flesh" is the great truth of Christianity, and with it all other Christian truths are united.

Whosoever confesseth not this truth is the deceiver and the Antichrist.

We can have no church-fellowship with him; in fact, we must oppose him with might and main.

Every one who transgresseth, goes beyond Bible-teaching and enters into unauthorized and misguiding speculations condemned in 1 Tim. 6, 4; 2 Tim. 2, 14. 16, and abideth not in the doctrine of Christ, hath not God. "He that abideth in the doctrine of Christ, he hath both the Father and the Son."

"Many deceivers are gone forth into the world, who confess not Jesus Christ coming in the flesh."

They are like wandering planets, designing men, foisting their pernicious propaganda upon the people and turning them away from Christ; especially silly women, "womanlings" Paul severely terms them in 2 Tim. 3, 6. Their insolence and greed were outrageous, 2 Cor. 11, 26.

"If there come any unto you and bring not this doctrine," — that Christ is true God and true man, — "receive him not into your house, neither greet him; for he that greeteth him is partaker of his evil deeds."

Yes, truth is intolerant of lies. The more we love Christ, the more we hate Antichrist.

What does that forbid?

1. That forbids unionism, church-fellowship with Unitarians, Jews, Mohammedans, Christian Scientists, Christless lodges, as we see it on Memorial Days, Thanksgiving Days, at dedications of churches, lodge temples, and on other occasions.

2. That forbids syncretism — sinking of doctrinal differences, as we have it in the community churches and the community Christmas-tree.

3. That forbids intimate sociability and hospitality. Keep your social calendar and visiting list up to date, up to the Bible. Roosevelt would not banquet with Senator Lorimer. Would you go to a dinner party with people having contagious diseases? Denying Christ is a much more deadly disease than any in the isolation hospital.

Our Government refuses to admit undesirables and deports them when found. Can the Church be less careful of her well-being?

What does that *not* forbid?

1. That does not forbid liberty in religion. Luther condemned the burning of John Hus — "It is against the Holy Ghost to burn heretics."

2. That does not forbid charity in religion. Love, do not hate; teach and preach, do not persecute. We send missionaries to all people without Christ. Luther protected his own opponents against his own government.

3. That does not forbid being a Good Samaritan. No matter who it is that is hurt, rush him to the emergency hospital.

4. That does not forbid cooperation in business, professional, civil, and patriotic matters.

4. WARNING.

"Look to yourselves that we lose not those things which we have wrought."

Beware of indifference and disobedience; thereby you will lose Christ and salvation.

5. EXHORTATION.

"Look to yourselves . . . that we receive a full reward" — in heaven.

THIRD EPISTLE.

The Third Epistle of John is also a private, personal letter; it gives

THREE PEN PORTRAITS.

I.

GAIUS.

THE name was so common that in Roman law it was used like our John Doe and Richard Roe.

Who he was we are not told, but he was "the well-beloved Gaius." And why was he well beloved? "Whom I love in the truth" — for his true faith and his sterling Christian character. To be loved by the Apostle of Love — what a distinction!

Follows a most uncommon prayer: "Beloved, I pray that in all things thou mayest prosper and be in health, even as thy soul prospereth" — makes progress.

Usually we have to pray the soul of our friend might prosper as well as his health and business. Gaius was a man of sterling Christian character, and he was growing in the grace of Christ.

You are growing — in what direction?

How did John know the soul of Gaius prospered? "The brethren came and testified of the truth that is in thee, even as thou walkest in the truth." The right faith begets the right life.

How did that affect the faithful pastor? "I rejoiced greatly. . . . I have no greater joy than to hear that my children walk in the truth."

That little sentence is a self-portrait of John himself, of the heart of the faithful pastor for his converts and members.

How did Gaius walk in the truth? "Beloved, thou doest as a work of faith whatsoever thou doest to the brethren and to strangers; who have borne witness of thy charity before the Church; whom if thou bring forward on their journey worthily of God, thou shalt do well."

In other words, Gaius was a real helper to the preachers traveling about to spread the Gospel. He did not ask what others were doing or not doing; he did his Christian duty "worthily of God."

In Gaius, the robust brother, Truth had a gentle twin sister, Love. Gaius was a credit to God, not a discredit. He walked "worthily of God." What praise! Do you deserve that praise?

Why did these preachers need help? "Because that for His name's sake they went forth, taking nothing of the Gentiles."

Preaching for His name's sake, they were poor — poor, but self-respecting — they would not lower themselves to beg from the heathen. Paul, too, would rather die than be dependent on others. Rom. 9, 12—18.

Gaius was a self-respecting and Christ-respecting Christian, and he saw to it that preachers of Christ did not depend on rejecters of Christ.

Churches are not to beg from outsiders.

What was the reward of Gaius? "We therefore ought to receive such hospitably that we might be fellow-workers for the truth."

You cannot preach, but by supporting the preacher you are a fellow-helper to the truth. You cannot go to India, but by sending a missionary, you become a partner in God's own work.

Want anything more?

II.

DIOTREPHES.

"I wrote somewhat to the church; but Diotrephes, who loveth to have the preeminence among them, receiveth us not, . . . prating against us with wicked words; and not content therewith, neither doth he himself receive the preaching brethren hospitably and forcibly hindereth them that would do so and casteth them out of the church."

A sad sight. Church-members violently opposed Christ, a church-member violently opposed the apostle of Christ. He was a proud, haughty, cruel, domineering man. Such characters have always crept into the Church and made trouble in the Church by defying the Lord of the Church.

There is a perpetual Diotrephes in the Pope at Rome, who, like Diotrephes, loves to have the preeminence, though Christ in all things is to have the preeminence, Col. 1, 18. We sometimes find such a Diotrephes in a congregation, a bossy man, who wants to rule the church contrary to the rule of Christ, the Lord of the Church.

That cannot go on for all time. "Wherefore, if I come, I will bring to remembrance the works which he doeth."

The simple recital will be a censure. Here is a broad hint of visitation and discipline. If the ambitious and domineering tyrant will not reform, he must be ousted. It is not a pleasant thing to do, but it is demanded by the welfare of the church.

"Beloved, imitate not evil, but good. He that doeth good is of God; but he that doeth evil hath not seen God."

III.

DEMETRIUS.

We are not told who Demetrius was, but he was a good man. And his goodness could not be hid, he was known as a good man. "He hath a good report of all and of the truth itself; yea, and we also bear witness; and ye know that our witness is true."

John says it with flowers — before Gaius and Demetrius are dead. When do we use flowers?

To be known of all as "a good man" — is there greater greatness than goodness?

Tennyson says: —

> Kind hearts are more than coronets
> And simple faith than Norman blood.

Barnabas, too, was "a good man," Acts 11, 24.

That truest greatness is within reach of all, of each and every one of us. Would you be entirely great?

APPENDIX.

A CHORUS OF PRAISE.

Luther says: "This is the unique, tender, genuine, chief Gospel. . . . Should a tyrant succeed in destroying the Holy Scriptures and only a single copy of the Epistle to the Romans and the Gospel of John escape him, Christianity would be saved."

Meyer, the ablest grammatical exegete of the age, by a lifelong study of the Word of God rose from a rationalistic to an almost orthodox standpoint and endorses Luther's eulogy and speaks of "the wonderful gospel of John, with its fulness of grace, truth, peace, light, and life."

Adam of St. Victor: —

> John, the eagle's feature having,
> Earth on love's twain pinions leaving,
> Soars aloft, God's truth perceiving,
> In light's purer atmosphere.

Clement of Alexandria calls John's the "spiritual gospel." Jerome judges: "John excels in the depth of divine mysteries." Origen thinks: "Those only can understand it who lean on the bosom of Jesus and there imbibe the spirit of John, just as he imbibed the spirit of Christ." Augustine holds: "John has lifted higher and far more sublimely than the other three his proclamation, and in lifting it up, he has wished our hearts also to be lifted up."

Chrysostom: "John has pervaded and embraced the whole world; he has filled it with his cry, not by the greatness of the sound, but by a tongue moved by divine grace. And what is wonderful is that this great cry is not harsh, not destitute of sweetness, but sweeter and more charming, endowed with more power to attract than all the harmony of music; and besides all these, it is most holy and awe-inspiring, filled with such secrets, conveying such good things, that those who receive and guard it with diligence and earnestness are no longer men, no more abide upon earth; they have placed themselves above the things of time; they are partakers of the state of angels and thus dwell upon earth as if it were heaven."

Lessing calls John's gospel "the most important portion of the New Testament." Julius Grill holds it "a literary masterpiece." Herder thinks "John wrote his gospel with a pen dropped from an angel's wing."

[375]

Ernesti esteems it "the heart of Christ." Schleiermacher finds "eternal, childlike Christmas joys pervade John's soul."

Tholuck says: "This gospel speaks a language to which no parallel whatever is to be found in the whole compass of literature; such childlike simplicity, with such contemplative profundity; such life and such deep rest; such sadness and such serenity; and, above all, such a breadth of love, an eternal life which has already dawned, a life which rests in God, which has overcome the disunion between the human and the divine."

J. P. Lange: "Since Irenaeus it [John's gospel] has remained for the sons of the apostolic spirit the crown of the apostolic gospels; . . . the diamond among the gospels which is most fully penetrated by the light of life and which reflects the glory of the Godhead in flesh and blood even in the crown of thorns."

Adolf Saphir writes: "There is a simplicity which is the result of full and profound knowledge, of varied experience and conflict; a simplicity which is the indication of abundance and depth, which is the result of meditation, prayerfulness, and a humble walk with God. They who are fathers in the Church, who, like the Apostle John, lean on the bosom of Jesus, who behold the glory of the Only-begotten and in singleness of heart rest in His love, reach a lofty and calm mountain height, and they express their knowledge and experience with great simplicity and brevity. . . . To reach this simplicity is the object of the Christian individual and of the Christian Church."

Schenkel: "Without this gospel the unfathomable depth, the inaccessible height, of the character of the Savior of the world would be wanting to us, and His boundless influence, renewing all humanity, would forever remain a mystery."

Matthias Claudius: "Above all do I like to read the gospel of John. There is something truly wonderful in it: twilight and night; and athwart flashes the vivid lightning. A soft evening sky and behind the sky, in bodily form, the large full moon. Something so sad, so sublime, so full of presage, that one can never weary of it. Every time I read John, it seems as if I could see him before me leaning on the bosom of his Master at the Last Supper, — as if his angel were standing by my side with a lamp in his hand and, when I come to particular passages, would clasp me in his arms and whisper a word in my ear. There is a great deal that I do not understand when I read; but I often feel as if John's meaning were floating before me at a distance, even when my eye lights on a dark place, I have nevertheless a presentiment of a grand and glorious sense that I shall some day understand.   On this account I grasp eagerly at every new exposition of John's gospel.   But, alas! the most of them only ruffle the evening clouds, and the bright moon behind them is left in peace."

Philip Schaff: "The gospel of John is the most original, the most important, the most influential book in all literature. . . .   It is simple as a child, and sublime as a seraph, gentle as a lamb, and bold as an eagle, deep as the sea, and high as the heavens."

President Timothy Dwight of Yale: "We learn from it that the richest life of the richest soul perchance the world has ever known came to its earthly perfection through its following of Jesus as the incarnate Son of God."

Donald Fraser: "We must read this gospel, while with joy, also with deep reverence; for heaven lies about us, and a cloud of glory hangs about the page"; and Ellicott says wisely: "If the heart studies the Christ as portrayed in this writing, it will need no other proof of His divinity."

William Wordsworth traced his religion to gratitude for God's mercies. "I meditate upon the Scriptures, especially the gospel of St. John; and my creed rises up of itself with the ease of an exhalation, yet a fabric of adamant."

Canon Liddon: "The most conspicuous written attestation to the Godhead of Him whose claims upon mankind can hardly be surveyed without passion, whether it be the passion of adoring love or the passion of vehement and determined enmity."

A. T. Pierson: "It touches the heart of Christ.   If Matthew corresponds to the Court of Israel, Mark to the Court of the Priests, and Luke to the Court of the Gentiles, John leads us past the veil into the Holy of Holies.   Here is the innermost Temple, filled with the glory of God."

Farrar: "The first three evangelists give us diverse aspects of one glorious landscape.   St. John pours over that landscape a flood of heavenly sunshine, which seems to transfigure its very character, though every feature of the landscape remains the same."

Bishop Westcott: "No writing combines greater simplicity with more profound depths."

W. T. Davidson: "The fourth gospel is unique among the books of the New Testament. In its combination of minute historical detail with lofty spiritual teaching, in its testimony to the person and work of the Lord Jesus Christ, and in the preparation it makes for the foundations of Christian doctrine it stands alone. Its influence upon the thought and life of the Christian Church has been proportionately deep and far-reaching. It is no disparagement of other inspired Scriptures to say that no other book of the Bible has left a mark at the same time upon the profoundest Christian thinkers and upon simple-minded believers at large."

James Drummond: "Whether we regard the sublimity of its thought, the width and spirituality of its conception of religion, the depth of its moral insight, or the tragic pathos of its story, we cannot but feel that we have before us the work of a master mind. And when we remember how it has molded the faith and touched the heart and calmed the sorrows of generations of men, we must approach it with no ordinary reverence and with a desire to penetrate its inmost meaning and become more thoroughly imbued with its kindling power."

Armitage Robinson: "We would not willingly give up for any other form of narrative a gospel which reveals to us what the Christ grew to be in the mind of one who leaned upon His bosom in youth, had cherished a perpetual recollection of Him throughout long years of toil and suffering for His name, and at the close wrote as in his Master's very presence his testimony of what his Master had been and forever should be — the Light and the Life of men."

Eckermann disputed the authenticity of the fourth gospel in its present form in 1796; in 1807 he recalled his criticism.

In 1820 Bretschneider published what Weiss called an "epoch-making book" against the genuineness of John's gospel. His objections were answered by Luecke, Tholuck, Olshausen, and Crome. Bretschneider withdrew his objections and declared he was satisfied that the authenticity of the gospel was fully established.

Bauer and his Tuebingen School renewed the attack. There is no longer a Tuebingen School.

Harnack recalled his former opinion and declared the fourth gospel the work of an eye-witness.

Strauss likened it to the seamless coat of the Savior — do not rend it.

www.ingramcontent.com/pod-product-compliance
Lightning Source LLC
Chambersburg PA
CBHW050402110426
42812CB00006BA/1776